RADFORD UNIVERSITY
MEN'S SOCCER
The First 50 Years: 1975 – 2024

On the Cover:

The view from Radford University's Patrick D. Cupp Memorial Stadium overlooking Lillard Field, with the New River and the Blue Ridge Mountains beyond. A passing shower had just moved down the valley.
By the way, the rainbow is real!

Special thanks to:

Dr. Jamal Haddad MD, for his unique contribution to very special recipients of this book.

Neil Gillespie, for his personal dedication and extensive involvement in the editing and professional presentation of this book.

William R. Iandolo, for his computer prowess and ongoing administrative and financial support of Radford University.

John T. White, for his supplemental research and ongoing dedication to the coaching and administration of the Radford University Men's Soccer program.

John Ravnik, Todd Howes, Tom Lillard, Don Staley, Spencer Smith, Marc Reeves, Chris Barrett, and **Michael Ashley** for their personal submissions.

Rick Rogers and **Judy Crowder**, the first SID and the first administrative assistant to **Chuck Taylor**, respectively, for their work at the beginning of men's soccer.

Corporate Sponsors of the Radford University Men's Soccer Program over the years, including, among others, Puma, Nike, BSN Sports, Adidas, Under Armour, ESPN, ESPN+, and Eleven-West.

The Writers, Editors, and Photographers of the Radford University yearbook, The *Beehive,* and the student newspaper, The *Tartan.*

The Writers, Editors, Photographers, and Graphic Artists of the Radford University Sports Information and Publications department, and Alumni Affairs.

The Librarians at Radford University's McConnell Library for access to Special Collections and research support, especially **Jennifer Resor-Whicker**.

The media presentations and records created and maintained by the **Big South Conference**.

The **Athletic Directors** of Radford University, **Chuck Taylor**, **Greig Denny**, and **Robert Lineburg**, for their unwavering support and promotion of men's soccer.

The **Presidents** and **Administrators** of Radford University.

THANK YOU!

PROLOGUE

"This is the definitive history of the first 50 years of the overachieving soccer Highlanders of Radford University. It's a story of great people, including *All-America* players and legendary coaches, on an amazing journey from a 1970's sports start-up to a Division I dynamo. In the bucolic and beloved Blue Ridge Mountains of Virginia, the big wins, tough heartbreaks, and marvelous moments are all still part of the Radford University men's soccer championship DNA."
– Michael Ashley

When men's soccer first started at Radford College as a club in 1973, the school was not affiliated for competition with any nationally-recognized sports organization, such as the **National Association of Intercollegiate Athletics (NAIA)** or the **National Collegiate Athletic Association (NCAA)**. Upon being recognized as a varsity sport in 1975, however, Radford men's soccer was accepted as a full participant in the **Virginia Intercollegiate Soccer Association (VISA)**.

From its formation in 1960, the VISA was apparently unique in the country because all schools in the state, no matter what their affiliation or their undergraduate enrollment (commonly referred to as Division I, Division II or Division III), competed for a State Championship. This changed in 1979 when the Division I schools in Virginia conferred and then all withdrew from the VISA. In the same year, newly-authorized Radford University was accepted into the NAIA, but this did not affect the University's participation in the VISA. In the NAIA, Radford competed as part of "District 19."

In 1983, Radford became a founding member of the **Big South Conference**, which was accepted into the NCAA as a full participant in Division I competition beginning in 1984. As a result, Radford withdrew from the VISA and the men's soccer team has competed in the Big South ever since. When men's soccer was implemented at Radford, it immediately became Radford's major, fall, outdoor varsity sport. Radford does not compete in American football.

RADFORD UNIVERSITY MEN'S SOCCER
The First 50 Years: 1975 – 2024

TABLE OF CONTENTS

RADFORD UNIVERSITY MEN'S SOCCER
The First 50 Years: 1975 – 2024

Introduction

The **Radford University Men's Varsity Soccer team** is an intercollegiate sports team of Radford University, a public, state-supported, institution of higher education located in Radford, Virginia. The team is a Division I member of the Big South Conference of the National Collegiate Athletic Association (NCAA). The team was founded in 1974 as a club team, but as the result of the combined efforts of student-activist **Tom Lillard**, University President **Dr. Donald N. Dedmon**, and Athletic Director **Dr. Charles (Chuck) Taylor**, the team would start a varsity, intercollegiate schedule in 1975. President Dedmon would further be instrumental in the creation of the Big South Conference a number of years later. Radford University and its men's soccer team would become charter members of the Big South in 1983.

From its conceptualization between 1972 and 1974, through its formalization in 1975, to its 50th intercollegiate season in 2024, the Radford University Men's Varsity Soccer program has experienced most of the developments imaginable over an extended period of time.

- **The timeline that follows summarizes this history**, including highlights of nine different coaches, ten championships, three *All-Americas*, Olympians, national rankings, NCAA Tournament appearances, a wonderful soccer stadium, and a serious rivalry with a next-door neighbor.
- **The extended narrative that follows details the amazing history of Radford's Men's Soccer program.** This narrative includes personal insights, season and game summaries, many major accomplishments, photos, and *something to do with a big rock pulled from the nearby river!* None of this would have been possible without all of the contributions by a large group of players and very special people who were committed to the program to ensure its success.
- **The Appendices** include additional content that expands upon and highlights several aspects of RU Men's Soccer history.
- **Do you want to know how you can "MAKE A DIFFERENCE" in the lives and education of dozens of RU students each year and for years to come?** *Make a generous donation to RU Men's Soccer!* See Appendix 10 for details.

SUMMARY TIMELINE
RU Men's Soccer 50th-Year Highlights

The 1970's 1972-79				
		1972	**Dr. Donald Dedmon** appointed President of Radford College	
		1973	**Dr. Charles Taylor** appointed first Athletics Director	
		1973	Club Soccer team recognized for extramural intercollegiate competition. Coached by **Ivo (John) Ravnik**	
		1974	**Tom Lillard** matriculates to Radford College	
		1974	**Moffett Field** lined for soccer. Club team engages in home and away scrimmages, exhibitions and games representing Radford College	
		1974	Dr. Dedmon, Chuck Taylor, and Tom Lillard promote Club team as ready to move up	
		1975	Club team recognized for varsity intercollegiate competition. **Ivo (John) Ravnik appointed first coach**	
		1975	First varsity win	
		1976	**Peter Howes appointed second coach**	
		1976	Team wins first school soccer trophy ever	
		1976	First win over Virginia Tech	
	1977 to 1979	1977	**John Harves appointed third coach**	
		1977	First winning season	
		1978	First unique emblem specific to Radford soccer introduced	
		1978	13-game undefeated streak. First double-digit wins. First "scholarship" recruits	
		1978	First mention of Radford in *Sports Illustrated*	
		1978	Radford College becomes Radford University	
		1979	First recognition in regional rankings	
		1979	First post-season play	

The 1980's 1980-89		1980	Tom Lillard appointed fourth coach	
	1980 to 1985	1980	First post-season title achieved, NAIA District 19 Champion	🏆
		1981	Virginia Intercollegiate Soccer Association (VISA) Champion	🏆
		1981	Tom Lillard named VISA Coach of the Year	
		1982	Dedmon Field inaugurated	
		1982	Bill Gerber arrives at Radford	
		1982	The team plays the University of Virginia for the first time	
		1983	Bill Gerber becomes Radford Men's Soccer first All America ever	🇺🇸
		1983	The Radford University Board of Visitors approves moving to Division I status	
		1983	The Big South Conference is formed. Radford moves to the NCAA Division I	
		1984	Big South Conference play starts. This includes a regular season and a post-season tournament	
		1984	Team reaches Big South tournament semifinals	
		1984	Bill Gerber again nominated for All America status	
		1985	Undefeated in Big South regular season	
		1985	Team reaches Big South tournament finals	
	1986 to 1993	1986	Don Staley becomes the fifth head coach	
		1987	Big South Regular Season Champion	🏆
		1988	Dante Washington arrives at Radford	
		1988	The "New River Rock," for competition between Radford and Virginia Tech, is introduced. Virginia Tech takes it home	
		1988	Big South Regular Season Champion	🏆
		1988	Big South Tournament Champion	🏆
		1988	Most games ever played in one season, 24	
		1988	Dante Washington leads the nation in scoring	
		1989	Radford claims "The New River Rock" for the first time	

The 1990's 1990-99				
		1990	Radford sets a new school record for wins with 15	
		1990	**Dante Washington** again leads the nation in scoring	
		1991	Big South Regular Season **Champion**	
		1991	**Don Staley** named Big South Coach of the Year	
		1991	**Dante Washington** named Radford's first-ever Division I consensus First-Team **All America** and Commonwealth of Virginia Player of the Year	
		1991	Dante Washington plays with the United States National Team	
		1992	Dante Washington closes out his career with Radford and Big South all-time scoring records	
		1992	Dante Washington plays on the United States Olympic Team	
	1994 to 2009	**1994**	**Spencer Smith becomes Radford's sixth head coach**	
		1994	**Spencer Smith** named Big South Coach of the Year	
		1995	**Ian Spooner** ranks third in the nation in points	
		1996 to 2005	Dante Washington plays professionally in Major League Soccer	
		1996	**Bill Gerber** inducted into **Radford University Athletics Hall of Fame**	
		1997	Start of a four-year winning streak against Virginia Tech	
		1997	**Dante Washington** inducted into **Radford University Athletics Hall of Fame**	
		1998	Big South Regular Season **Champion**	
		1998	Big South Tournament **Champion**	
		1998	**Spencer Smith** named Big South Coach of the Year	
		1999	Big South Tournament **Champion**	
		1999	First-ever **NCAA** Tournament appearance	

The 2000's 2000-09		2000	Big South Tournament **Champion**	
		2000	Second **NCAA** Tournament appearance	
		2000	**John White** inducted into **Radford University Athletics Hall of Fame**	
		2001	"The New River Rock" is unilaterally retired by Virginia Tech	
		2002	**T.J. Rolfing** takes over third place in all-time goals, after Dante Washington and Ian Spooner	
		2003	**Patrick D. Cupp Memorial Stadium** dedicated	
		2005	Spencer Smith goes over the 100-win mark at Radford	
		2008	The National Soccer Coaches Association of America recognized Radford for the second straight year as one of its 2008 Team Academic Award winners, an honor given to programs with a team grade point average of 3.0 or better. Among men's programs, Radford was one of just two Big South institutions, one of 35 NCAA Division I teams, and one of 106 four-year colleges across the country, to earn the distinction in 2008	
		2009	"*I Played Soccer at Radford University*" Facebook page debuts	
		2009	The John Harves Radford University Men's Soccer Fund is **established by Will Iandolo**. *Please DONATE to support RU Men's Soccer* . *"How do I donate?"* **See Appendix 10 for details.**	Make a difference! PLEASE DONATE NOW. *Thank you!*
		2009	Dante Washington's Jersey Number 9 was permanently retired	
The 2010's 2010-19	2010 to 2016	2010	**Marc "Reevo" Reeves named Radford's seventh head coach**	
		2010	First time ever undefeated at home	
		2011	First "Polar Plunge," raising money for the Special Olympics Virginia (SOVA)	
		2012	The Radford University #9 Soccer Scarf debuts, honoring Dante Washington	
		2012	**Ian Spooner** inducted into **Radford University Athletics Hall of Fame**	

...The 2010's 2010-19	**2013**	Ryan Taylor signs a professional contract with the Richmond Kickers
	2014	Hit #20 national ranking
	2014	Big South Regular Season **Champion**
	2014	**Marc Reeves** named Big South Coach of the Year
	2014	**Tom Lillard** inducted into **Radford University Athletics Hall of Fame**
	2015	Big South Regular Season **Champion**
	2015	Third **NCAA** Tournament appearance (At-Large Bid)
	2016	Radford appeared in the Top-25 National Rankings five times, on one occasion going four weeks in a row, and reached a peak at Number 18 in the country
	2016	Big South Regular Season **Champion**
	2016	Big South Tournament **Champion**
	2016	Fourth **NCAA** Tournament appearance
	2016	**Marc Reeves** named Big South Coach of the Year
	2016	**Jo Vetle Rimstad** named **All America**
	2017	Jo Vetle Rimstad selected 43rd in MLS Superdraft
	2017	**Nick Mayhew** becomes Radford men's soccer second Olympian
2017 to 2019	**2017**	**Bryheem Hancock named eighth head coach**
	2017	Eighth best scoring record in the country
	2017	Radford defeats the University of Virginia for the first time
	2017	**Don Staley** inducted into **Radford University Athletics Hall of Fame**

...The 2010's 2010-19		2018	Dante Washington inducted into the Maryland Soccer Hall of Fame
		2019	The Highlanders qualify for the Big South Championships for the 25th consecutive season, the longest streak in conference history
		2019	Nick Mayhew named 2019 U. S. Soccer Player of the Year with a Disability by the United States Soccer Federation
		2019	Jeff Majewski inducted into **Radford University Athletics Hall of Fame**
The 2020's 2020-24	2020 to Present	2020	**Chris Barrett named ninth head coach**
		2021	Nick Mayhew sets a Paralympics world record in the 200-meters
		2021	Freshman Hansy Velasquez was selected for the Under-20 Puerto Rico National team for upcoming friendlies and CONCACAF qualifiers
		2022	Coach Barrett carried the largest roster in school history, offering an opportunity to up to 50 student-athletes to showcase their talents
		2023	After a break of nine years, Virginia Tech finally agreed to play Radford again. Upon resuming in 2022, Radford promptly tied Tech, 0-0, and then defeated them, 3-2, in 2023
		2024	The field at Patrick D. Cupp Memorial Stadium is named **"Lillard Field"** in honor of Tom Lillard
		2024	**<u>Radford University celebrates the 50th Season of the Men's Varsity Soccer Program</u>**

The Beginning

Tom Lillard played serious soccer both as a youth and as a student at Yorktown High School in Arlington, Virginia. Upon graduation from Yorktown in 1974, he chose to attend then-named Radford College, knowing full well that the school did not have a varsity men's soccer team, but that he still wanted to keep playing. At the time, Radford College was undergoing significant change. Formerly, it had been an all-women's school, known particularly for its education and nursing curricula. Unfortunately, enrollment had been falling at Radford due to major expansion at nearby Virginia Tech, which had dropped a military requirement for men in 1964 and then actively started recruiting women and significantly increasing its student capacity.

1972 Dr. Donald Dedmon

When President **Dr. Donald N. Dedmon** arrived at Radford in 1972, one of his first improvements was to make the institution co-educational. Another was to expand and improve the entire scope of the school's mission and instructional offerings, ultimately achieving University status. As part of the transformation, he included upgrading Radford's athletic programs, adding men's sports, and expanding the number of offerings for both women and men. Dr. Dedmon was intimately familiar with helping schools in need. He had come from the presidency of Marshall University where he had guided its recovery from a horrific plane crash on November 14, 1970. The crash killed 37 members of the varsity football team, eight coaches, and 25 school boosters. [Dedmon's heroic actions to help the school recover from this tragedy were unfortunately not given the appropriate recognition he deserved in the movie, "*We Are Marshall*."]

To the mix of Lillard and Dedmon, came the third party to the beginning of varsity men's soccer at Radford University, **Chuck Taylor**. The first-ever Athletics Director in school history, Taylor made an everlasting mark on the "Hustling Highlanders." After first arriving at the school as a professor, Taylor served as athletics director from 1974 to 1996, leading Radford on a remarkable journey from a six-sport, unaffiliated, small-college program to NCAA Division I. Today, the Highlanders sponsor 16 varsity sports and have proudly played at the Division I level since 1984. During his tenure, Radford Athletics was nationally recognized as a leader in opportunities for women and minorities, as well as

1973 Chuck Taylor

in graduation rates for student-athletes. This is a legacy that continues to this day. In competition, seven different programs achieved national rankings in his time guiding the Highlanders.

The scene and the set had been created, and the three main actors came together. Tom Lillard arrived with the intent of playing on a men's varsity soccer team and Dr.

Dedmon and Chuck Taylor were ready to oblige to create one. All three men were gregarious and outgoing. Even at 18-years old, Lillard had no problem approaching and meeting repeatedly with senior administrators to make men's varsity soccer a reality. Dedmon encouraged success as part of his larger plan, and Taylor was always ready and willing to help anyone advance athletics. All that was needed were players and a coach. Fortunately, a club team was already in place.

The Club Team (1974)

Right at the beginning of school in the fall of 1974, Lillard joined the drumbeat of what would ultimately become the core of the first varsity team. In 1973, a group of guys had previously coalesced, first in front of Muse dorm and McConnell Library, and then on Radford College's central student courtyard, "Moffett Field," just to kick around because of their love of soccer. They were then recognized as a formal extramural club team and played other clubs and college junior varsity squads. It took well into the fall, but Moffett Field (sometimes called Moffett Lawn when not used for sports) was lined for soccer and would become home turf. Lillard knew that this was the group that was needed for varsity, intercollegiate, competition and Lillard promoted their readiness to Dedmon and Taylor. A graduate student, **Ivo (John) Ravnik**, had been the club coach (assisted by **Bob Ola**) and the team had demonstrated through scrimmages, exhibitions, and full games – both at home and away – that they could perform. Coach Ravnik, who had left his native Yugoslavia as a teenager, played soccer in high school in America and later at San Francisco State University.

1974 Club Team

Coach Ravnik recalls how it all began: "I was born in Europe on the borderland of Slovenia and Italy, but the area ended up under Italian control. So, my parents decided to emigrate to California where they knew some friends near San Francisco. I was then about 13 years old and had played some soccer in our town youth leagues. I began teaching Political Science courses, then under the History Department, at Radford College in 1972. Readers in the audience may recall that the College had recently changed to a co-ed program and young men began to then attend the college in large numbers. They obviously needed some sports outlets and one of them was soccer. Walking through the campus, I noticed a group of young men playing a game of soccer. Being young then, I joined them. During our discussion afterwards, they impressed me that they would like to form a regular college team.

Very soon this need reached President Dedmon and he was most receptive. He called Mr. Taylor, head of the Sports Department. He ordered all the equipment needed for some 15 players thus far, and the boys designed their own uniform! I was sent off for a week at the US Soccer Federation coaching camp somewhere in Delaware. Fortunately, I did qualify for a C License – not bad for an amateur! We then played some of the neighboring colleges, which were already well established. We did not do well, but we did get better and learned how to play more as a unified team. A couple of years into the soccer program, I was lucky to have Peter Howes, a good, British footballer, join the program and he did an excellent job with all of the many details needed. He was especially well organized with a practice system that would push the boys into some real teamwork. So, thanks Peter Howes."

Following his success with the club program, Chuck Taylor asked Coach Ravnik if he would be willing to stay on as the first varsity coach, and Ravnik agreed.

The First Two Varsity Teams (1975 – 1976)

Coach John Ravnik willingly took on the challenge of starting a varsity team, along with another graduate student, **Peter Howes**, as his assistant. Home base was a couple of closets in Peter's Hall, which was already showing its age. At least the goals that had been purchased for the club were brand new.

1975

Coach John Ravnik

Coach Ravnik has the distinction of getting **the first varsity win in school history in 1975**. The win was against Averett College, 5-1, on Homecoming Weekend, Saturday, October 25, 1975. After being down 1-0 at halftime, goals were scored by **Scott Bailey** (2), **Jeff Hoare** (2), and **Tom Lillard.**

The first men's varsity soccer team at Radford would go on to win three games, with the additional wins coming over Lynchburg Baptist and Luther Rice, ending its season with a record of 3-9 (.250). The first varsity game with Virginia Tech would be significant this season, if only because it established an on-again/off-again relationship with a logical rival, given that the two institutions are only 15-miles apart. The game was a wild affair with the Hokies winning 6-3. A notable arrival to join the first team was **Randy Metzger** who would become a four-year starter at midfield and a team captain. Lillard and **Mike Hillegas** would establish the first scoring and assist records.

Fall 1975 – The First Radford University Men's Varsity Soccer Team

1st Row: Jack Carpenter, Dave Coleman, Scott Bailey, Jim Olsen, German Ruiz, Mike Hillegas, Jeff Hoare, Randy Metzger, Rick Perry, Gary Pechtimaldjian, Bob Sahagun
2nd Row: Asst. Coach Peter Howes, Dan Seyler, Billy Easton, Preston Trible, Neal Aker, Steve Schulte, Tom Lillard, Tim Ryan, Rick Rector, Mgr. Mary Lee Cline, Brian Nace, Coach John Ravnik

The first teams inherited the Radford College school colors of Gray and Purple. The school newspaper even reflected this color scheme, going by the name, "*The Grapurchat*." Both would change in 1978 when the newly-authorized Radford University adopted the Scottish Highlander theme of a multi-colored plaid. From the many available options in the plaid, the primary team colors became red and white. The newspaper changed its name to the "*The Tartan*."

Coach Ravnik moved on and the 1976 team would be coached by **Peter Howes.**

1976

Peter Howes was born in Enfield, an outer borough of London, England, where he played soccer as a youth. His family emigrated to Canada in 1966 and he worked at a number of U.S. military bases as a contractor with the Marconi Company. It was at one of these bases in southern Maryland where he met his future wife. They married shortly thereafter and moved to Christiansburg, VA, where they lived while Howes attended Virginia Tech for both his BS in Computer Science and then an MBA. Howes played soccer at Tech as an undergraduate and continued to play in local competitions as an adult after graduation. Although Howes had been an experienced soccer player, his first love seemed to be running. And so, the **1976** team ran and ran, from Moffett Field to a local car dealership, *Harvey's Chevrolet*, and back again, about 3 miles round-trip, almost every day. By

Coach Peter Howes

running some unexpecting opponents ragged, Radford accomplished another three-win season, finishing 3-10-1 (.250). One of these wins, however, was a huge upset of, and **the very first win against Virginia Tech, 4-2**, on Wednesday, October 6, 1976, at Radford. This team also had the distinction of capturing the **first soccer trophy ever for Radford by finishing second in the King College (TN) Invitational Tournament**.

Former club stalwarts in the Virginia Tech win included **Tom Lillard**, **Neal Aker**, **Brian Nace**, **Preston Trible**, **Steve Schulte**, and **Mike Hillegas**. Notable new arrivals included **Charlie Laslie** and **Jamal Haddad**. After being down 1-0 at halftime, **Scott Bailey** would score first for the Highlanders with an assist from Haddad. Haddad would score the next two goals, one received from a corner kick and the other off a penalty kick. Bailey would end the scoring with another assist from Haddad. Goalkeeper **Tim Ryan** made 10 saves. Laslie would go on to earn state honors every single year for four years at his center-back position. Haddad would become a consistent goal scorer and eventually have the unique distinction of later having a son, **Noah Haddad**, play for Radford.

1976 - Neal Aker and Tom Lillard Present Radford's First-Ever Soccer Trophy to Dr. Dedmon

At the end of the 1976 season, Coach Howes announced that he was moving on.

It was time for Lillard to once again take action. Lillard had played for, and with, a coach in Arlington named **John Harves**. Lillard's friend and neighbor, **John White**, had played for Harves from U-15 to U-18. In talking with White, Lillard knew that Harves had announced that he was leaving White's youth team to return to Virginia Tech to get his MBA. Harves was slated to again become the Assistant Coach at Tech, where he had played as an undergraduate from 1970 to 1973 and was previously the assistant coach in 1974.

Lillard, together with White, showed up at Harves's house unannounced in the early summer of 1977. Lillard made a pitch that Radford needed a coach and that he wanted Harves to take the job. Harves demurred because he felt a strong connection with Coach **Jerry Cheynet** at Tech and wanted to again coach for his alma mater. Shortly thereafter, Cheynet would inform Harves that, as hard as he had tried, there would not be any money allotted for an assistant soccer coach at Tech. Harves told Cheynet about the meeting with Lillard and Cheynet responded, "As much as I would still like to have you, why would you want to be an Assistant Coach here when you can be the Head Coach over there?"

1977 Tom Lillard vs. Virginia Tech

Unbeknownst to Lillard, upon hearing that there was no funding at Tech, Harves had also interviewed at the University of Richmond to be the Head Soccer Coach there. When Harves learned of all of the demands that Richmond was attaching to their position, including teaching and an inflexible class schedule, although he was offered the job Harves turned it down. After speaking again with Lillard, and then interviewing with Chuck Taylor, **John Harves** accepted the head coaching position at Radford. Lillard had been a team Captain and player for the club team and the first two varsity years. He would play for Harves for his final season and then become the assistant coach.

John Harves Era (1977 – 1979)

3 Seasons

Overall Record: 29-16-4 (.633)

- 1977 8-7-0
  First Winning Record

- 1978 10-3-3
  Longest Unbeaten Streak - 13 games

- 1979 11-6-1
  First Post-Season Appearance
  NAIA District 19 Finalist

Coach John Harves

Assistant Coaches: Tom Lillard, Will Iandolo, Reg Ridgely

John Harves [här-vəs] grew up in Arlington, Virginia, where he played organized soccer for the first time at Yorktown High School. He founded a member club of the Arlington Soccer Association (ASA) and started coaching youth soccer before graduation. His first youth team was composed of both boys and girls ranging in age from 6- to 15-years old. During the summers and for three years after graduation from college, Coach Harves managed and played for the Arlington Americans "open" team (semi-pro) and was a founder of the Capital Soccer League of Washington, DC. In addition, he officiated for the Metropolitan Washington Soccer Referees Association and earned a United States Soccer Federation national coaching license. Also, during this time, Coach Harves founded and directed both the Arlington Soccer Association's youth referee program and their youth coaching instructional school. He is an inductee of the Arlington Soccer Hall of Fame.

1977

At Radford in the Fall of **1977**, the very first question a team member asked Coach Harves was, "Will we be running to *Harvey's Chevrolet*?" Harves responded, "No, and anyway I don't even know where that is." The technical work then started with a fury. After only six days of practice, Coach Harves and the Radford Men's Soccer Team won their opener, defeating Hampden-Sydney 2-1. (Harves would later be told by another college coach that this win "sent ripples" through the state.) The team would go on to have **Radford's first winning season, finishing 8-7**. Notable arrivals would include **Alfredo Duran**, **Tim Mann**, **John Smith** (now Smith-Sreen), and **Cesar Collantes**. Duran and Mann would earn state honors at midfield and Smith would be a standout at left back. Collantes would set the next single-game scoring record, previously held by Lillard, with four goals. **Neal Aker**, having played mostly in the field in earlier seasons, was solid, durable, and reliable in goal.

1977 - Lillard Scoring

Two of the wins were most notable. The first of these was the final game of the season, against Roanoke College. The team entered the game with a record of 7-7 and the first winning season on the line. **Jamal Haddad** scored first and then **Alfredo Duran** scored a spectacular goal from midfield, lofting the ball over the goalkeeper and under the crossbar (well before David Beckham made the shot famous in 1996). Roanoke tallied its lone goal just before halftime. With the score staying at 2-1, the second half was a furious affair with Radford trying to get the icing goal and Roanoke trying to tie. **Randy Metzger** and **Preston Trible**, in particular, worked tirelessly to keep the ball in the Roanoke end. At the final whistle, all of the Radford players were so exhausted that no one seemed able to appreciate what they had just accomplished.

The players had no idea, but the seed of that first winning season had been planted before the very first game. Shortly after the season started, Chuck Taylor called Coach Harves into his office and said that he was getting repeated phone calls from the Athletic Director at the University of Richmond, insisting that Radford had a commitment for a game at Richmond. Taylor informed Harves that Radford could not find a contract for such a game and that Richmond couldn't produce a copy of one either. For financial reasons, Taylor was inclined to say, "No," but indicated that the date was open and then asked Harves, "Is it a 'W'?" Harves, as a result of knowing the conditions that the coach at Richmond was operating under, replied "Yes." Radford would end up going to Richmond and winning 3-1. Years later, Harves would tell Taylor that, "It was the only game in my entire life that I ever guaranteed. I was so nervous I couldn't wait for it to be over and I never guaranteed another game again in my life."

Players of the 1977 squad gave the very first youth soccer clinic to the Radford City Parks and Recreation Department.

In 1978, even though he had one year of eligibility remaining, because his knees had given out, Tom Lillard became the Assistant Coach to John Harves. Together, they instituted the first "Soccer Support Team," consisting entirely of co-eds, who graciously volunteered their time at home games and acted as ball-persons, timekeepers, and scorekeepers.

Coach Harves designed and introduced the first soccer-specific emblem prior to the 1978 season, which incorporated the Radford logo in use at the time.

1978 Arrow and Soccer Ball Logo

1978

In **1978**, Harves knew that he was returning a core of solid players capable of performing at a college varsity level and he needed more, so the first serious recruiting effort began. Lillard and Harves combined to convince goalkeeper **John White** and central striker **Will Iandolo**, who was friends with White and had also played for Harves, to come to Radford. Both were touted as being Radford's first "scholarship" soccer players when all the school could actually afford was a small, one-time, tuition credit to each. White was a first-rate goalkeeper and Iandolo was a true goal-scorer, also having been first-team Virginia high school All-State.

Will Iandolo

Exceptional starting center-midfielder **Alfredo Duran** announced that his brother, **Edwin Duran**, was coming and that, "He's better than I am." (This would be the first pair of brothers to ever play for Radford soccer at the same time.) Out of the blue, **Dennis Gunson**, another Virginia high school first-team All-State striker, just showed up. In addition to Iandolo and White, the first recruiting class at Radford included **Rob Ercolano**, **John Chomeau**, and **Garnet Smith**. The team finished 10-3-3, losing their first two games and their last one, with **an undefeated streak of 13 straight games** in the middle, a record that would last for decades. White started a shut-out streak and Gunson was the leading scorer. Coach Harves had dreams of going to the Virginia Intercollegiate Soccer Association (VISA) championship game, but the losses were all in-state.

The VISA was a unique organization and the first league in which Radford men's soccer participated. Its unique nature stemmed from the fact that it involved all colleges and universities in the Commonwealth of Virginia, at all levels – Division I, Division II, and Division III – competing on an equal footing, no matter what their affiliation. As such, it was believed to be the only organization in the country known to

have a structure that created a true state champion among all schools of higher education.

At the end of each season, the VISA – in addition to determining the Champion – announced the Coach of the Year, the Player of the Year, and Division All-Stars. Every year that Radford played in the VISA, the Highlanders were represented by at least one athlete designated as a State All-Star who then participated in the VISA All-Star game.

Jamal Haddad -- VISA All-Star Game

In 1978, the men's soccer team also achieved **Radford Athletics' first mention in "*Sports Illustrated.*"** Unfortunately, it was because, with a victory over the Highlanders, the coach at Lynchburg College was the first men's soccer coach in the country to ever go over 300 wins.

1979

In **1979**, **Tom Lillard** would again be the Assistant Coach to **John Harves**, together with transfer student **Reg Ridgely**, and, joining recruit **Wayne Bentley**, another surprise player, **Randy Jones**, just showed up. Radford also joined the National Association of Intercollegiate Athletics (NAIA) that year. Together, they would combine for a record of 11-6-1. The team set a continuous scoring mark that lasts until this day. This team also achieved the distinction of going to the **first post-season play ever** enjoyed by the Radford University Men's Soccer program, ending as the NAIA District 19 finalist. **Charlie Laslie**, **John Smith** and **Dennis Gunson** would earn first-team District 19 honors, with **John White** and **Tim Mann** earning honorable mentions. During the season, Harves was also the President of the VISA. (Harves had been elected as the Vice President, but the Division I schools had conferred secretly during the summer and agreed to all drop out, implying that the risk of losing to Division II or Division III schools was detrimental to their rankings. Until this point, the VISA, founded in 1960, had been composed of all colleges and universities in the state with soccer programs. Since the VISA President was from a Division I school, he resigned and Harves advanced to the position.)

1979 – Will Iandolo

In 1979, **Will Iandolo** would be the team's leading scorer, followed closely by Gunson. Unfortunately, before the conclusion of the season, a catastrophic knee injury would end Iandolo's playing days. Iandolo would go on to become an assistant coach to Lillard and later the women's team coach for two years. With the women, Iandolo would coach **Radford's first All-America ever – in any sport – in Helen Negrey** in 1982, and win the State Championship in 1983. As a freshman, Jones would break into the lineup in mid-season and go on to become a starter for the next three years. Further, he would also eventually become the women's team coach. Senior **Jamal Haddad** established the new all-time scoring record.

During 1979, a new athletics and convocation center was being designed and the exterior contained provisions for a new soccer field. When the designers met with Harves, they said that their problems with space were limited to inside the building and that he had "all of the space he needed on the outside" for the soccer field. Ultimately, this would mean the end of playing at Moffett Field. Moffett was at best "mid-sized," but its location right in the center of campus, surrounded by dorms and Southern Magnolias, attracted large crowds to home games. The students were very knowledgeable and attendance swelled for Homecoming and the contests with Virginia Tech. Because it was used for multiple events, the grass was virtually non-existent by the end of each season, and players had to pick up rocks due to poor fill dirt.

1979 would also mark the **first time that Radford men's soccer ever appeared in collegiate rankings**, coming in at Number 14 in the Mid-Atlantic Region in October, ahead of the University of Maryland and Virginia Tech. Prior to the start of the 1979 season, Harves postponed his graduate studies. As a result, Coach Harves became the first dedicated, full-time coach in the history of the Radford University Men's Soccer program, even though it was still for a minimal stipend. Harves had been recently married and, at the end of the 1979 season confided to Lillard that, unfortunately, he had to leave "to go back to Arlington, be with my wife, and get a real job."

1979 (L-R) John White, Tom Lillard, Coach Harves after loss to Lynchburg

And now to try to address the Gorilla in the State at that time: The University of Virginia. Even though he had physically left, Harves was still responsible for putting together the 1980 schedule. He called Charlottesville to try to obtain a match with the Cavaliers. He was blown off by an assistant with, "Oh, that will never happen." (This would subsequently change in 1982 when Tom Lillard was able to reach an agreement with UVa Coach **Bruce Arena**.)

Subsequently, in 2009, Coach Harves was honored with the establishment of the John Harves Radford University Men's Soccer Fund. **This permanent endowment was created by Will Iandolo, and the initial funding came from Iandolo and other former teammates who had played for Harves.** This is a standing capital fund. Only the earnings from the fund are available for scholarships or operations. _Anyone may contribute by check or by credit card online to the Radford University Foundation, Inc. Please be sure to indicate that the contribution is for the "John Harves Men's Soccer Fund." Please contribute to this fund! Thank you!_

GIVE A GIFT THAT KEEPS ON GIVING:

PLEASE SUPPORT THE RADFORD MEN'S SOCCER PROGRAM

by making a generous donation to the

JOHN HARVES RADFORD UNIVERSITY MEN'S SOCCER FUND

Credit card contributions may be made on-line: Visit **https://connect.radford.edu/together-give** Using the "Other (please specify)" selection, designate your gift to the "John Harves Soccer Fund"

Fund: Other (please specify)

Other (please specify): John Harves Soccer Fund

To donate by check, please mail your check to:
Radford University Foundation, Inc.
PO Box 6893
Radford, VA 24142

1001

Your name
Street address
City, State ZIP

Date: _____

PAY TO THE ORDER OF ___Radford University Foundation, Inc.___

_____ DOLLARS

MEMO John Harves Soccer Fund

1234567

EDITOR'S NOTE: This permanent endowment fund was established by Will Iandolo in 2009, in honor of John Harves' groundbreaking, tireless, and enthusiastic contributions to RU's soccer program. The initial funding came from Iandolo and other former teammates who had played for Harves. Every donation goes into the endowment's capital fund. (Of course, neither Will nor John receive a penny from these funds.) To ensure the ongoing viability of the fund, only the *earnings* are available for use in the men's soccer program. RU Men's Soccer and *especially the students/players* appreciate your financial support!

Editor's P.S.: This book is another of the countless significant examples of John's substantial and indefatigable contributions to RU soccer and to the many people who have been a part of this program. You could not imagine -- or maybe you can! -- the many months and the many, many hundreds of hours he has tirelessly worked to bring this project to completion. To truly give a gift that keeps on giving, please consider making a generous contribution to this fund, to help change the lives of dozens of these student-athletes each year for many years to come. If you can, make it an annual event!

At the end of the 1979 season, there was never any question about who would be the next coach. AD Taylor asked Harves to provide a simple letter of recommendation for his files, no other candidates were considered, and **Tom Lillard** would start the sixth season of the Radford University Men's Varsity Soccer program as its fourth Head Coach.

Tom Lillard Era (1980 - 1985)

6 Seasons

Overall Record: 47-51-7 (.481) - Big South: 7-3-0 (.700)

- 1980 8-4-3
    NAIA District 19 Champion
    NAIA Area 7 Finalist

- 1981 8-7-2
    Virginia Intercollegiate Soccer
      Association (VISA) State Champion
    NAIA District 19 Finalist
    VISA Coach of the Year

- 1982 4-12-0

- 1983 7-9-0

- 1984 10-10-0; Big South: 2-2-0
    Big South Tournament Semifinals

- 1985 10-9-2; Big South: 5-1-0
    Big South Tournament Finalist

Coach Tom Lillard

Assistant Coaches: Will Iandolo, Edwin Duran, Randy Jones, Don Staley

1980

After serving as the Radford University Men's Soccer assistant coach for two years, **Tom Lillard** was selected as the Head Coach for the **1980** season. **Will Iandolo** became his assistant coach. In the regular season, the team achieved a statement win over James Madison University. **The team took Radford's first post-season title ever by winning the NAIA District 19 championship** over Rutgers-Camden, 1-0. From the beginning of the match, Radford dominated play with ball control and several scoring threats. Then, with an assist from **Alfredo Duran**, **Ron Carter** put the ball into the upper-right corner of the goal with just under six-minutes remaining in the first half. Radford outshot Rutgers-Camden, 29-7, and never allowed a serious scoring threat throughout the game. **John White** recorded his third shutout of the season in goal. Unfortunately, the team then lost in the NAIA Area 7 title game to Dowling College, 1-0, missing the national tournament by the one game. The Dowling game involved travelling to New York during exam week. The team also missed going to the VISA Championship by one game. **Edwin Duran**, Alfredo Duran, John White, **Randy Jones** and Ron Carter were named to the VISA All-West team.

1980 – Coach Lillard Raises the NAIA District 19 Championship Plaque

1981

In **1981**, Lillard would guide the team to first place in the Western Conference of the Virginia Intercollegiate Soccer Association, defeating Lynchburg, 3-0, in the semi-finals, and then **win the VISA Championship, Radford's first major title ever**, defeating Averett College in the final, 2-1, in triple overtime. Sophomore **Jim McIntire** would score the game-winning goal with seconds to spare. With 25-minutes remaining in the first half, **Ron Carter** broke a scoreless tie with a fabulous shot from the right side of the goal. Averett did not fold, however, and the Cougar's *All-America* candidate, Pekka Kaartinen from Helsinki, Finland, broke in on Radford goalie **John White**. The play was such that White was left with no choice but to bring down Kaartinen, who then took the ensuing penalty kick and scored with 12-minutes left in regulation. Although the Highlanders dominated the overtimes, they couldn't buy any luck, seeing three shots clang off the posts before McIntire's heroics. Fullbacks **Kevin DuPont** and **Edwin Duran** contained the Averett forwards for goalkeeper John White during all three overtimes. (The team had previously lost to Averett in the regular season.) As a result of this success, Lillard would be named the VISA Coach of the Year in 1981. Further, the team again advanced in the NAIA District 19 tournament, having beaten Spring Garden, 2-1, but lost in the district title game to Rutgers-Camden, 2-0. Against Spring Garden, **Greg Gilmore** had the first goal with an assist from **Ron Carter**, and **Bruce Williams** scored the winner. In a regular-season game against Mount Saint Mary's, **Randy Jones** took over the all-time scoring record for a season with 10.

Dogpile After Winning 1981 VISA State Championship

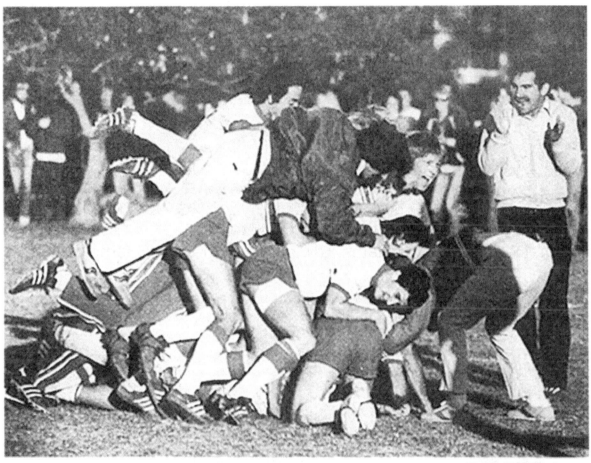

Photo by Neil McNeely

WHERE DID HE GO? Sophomore Jim McIntire is on the bottom of this mass of happy Highlanders. McIntire's long-range boot in the third sudden death overtime gave Radford their first state soccer championship. McIntire, number 9 for the Highlanders, scored the game-winner with nine seconds to play in that third and deciding overtime.

VISA = Virginia Intercollegiate Soccer Association.
For additional information about the VISA, see the Prologue at the beginning of this book.

Dr. Dedmon congratulates Edwin Duran on VISA Championship

1981 - Coach Tom Lillard at one of the last games at Moffett Field

Lillard would also be pivotal in the formation of the Radford University Women's Soccer program in 1981, serving in a dual capacity as both the women's first head coach and head coach of the men during the same year.

JOHN WHITE

John White

Instrumental to the championship successes in 1980 and 1981 was the play of goalkeeper **John White**. One of the most decorated athletes in the early years of men's athletics at RU, White still holds numerous records. He was a four-year starter and a three-time Virginia Intercollegiate Soccer Association all-star from 1978-81, and he still holds records for saves in a season (138 in 1979) and saves in a career (475). His four shutouts and 1.19 goals against average (GAA) in 1981 paced the Highlanders to the Division II and III (VISA) State Championship. In 1979, the Arlington native posted a record six shutouts, including four in a row, on his way to a 0.941 GAA and NAIA All-District honors. His career 1.23 GAA still ranks among Radford University's best ever.

John White was inducted into the Radford University Athletics Hall of Fame in 2000.

1981 John White

THE DEDMON CENTER and a NEW HOME FIELD

The Dedmon Center opened in 1981 and the soccer team played on the "upper Dedmon Center field" or just "Dedmon Field" for the first time in the fall of 1982. The new soccer field, ultimately to be enclosed with fencing and a bleacher capacity for over 3,000 spectators, was still mid-sized. The designers didn't understand the need for a maximum-sized field and were constrained by an access road on one sideline and a railroad right-of-way on the other. The field was well-graded, but it took a while for the grass to take. When it rained, mud would become a challenge. It eventually was seeded with a mix of fescue and Bermuda grass, and was considered to be "cozy." It was a substantial improvement over Moffett Field, because of its access to the Dedmon Center facilities, but it was a real hike from the center of campus for the students. It would ultimately become an excellent practice field.

The Dedmon Center itself features a 5,000-seat multi-purpose arena with a main basketball floor and a secondary volleyball arena for intercollegiate competition and four recreational courts for basketball or volleyball. The complex also includes an eight-lane, Olympic-sized pool with a diving well. Further, it opened with the school's first serious team locker rooms and administrative offices. As originally constructed, it had only the tenth air-supported roof built in the United States.

After more than 20 years, the Dedmon Center was in need of renovation. The original air-supported fabric roof was removed in April 2008 and replaced with a fabric roof supported by steel trusses. It reopened on January 21, 2009, with a new lighting system, sound system, and a new basketball floor. Upgrades were made that featured a 1/6-mile indoor jogging track, five racquetball courts, a weight-training room with Nautilus and Universal equipment, spacious locker rooms, several team rooms, showers and steam-rooms. Outside, in addition to the soccer field, several adjoining facilities were upgraded for intramural soccer, football and softball, and intercollegiate fields and courts for baseball, softball, field hockey and tennis.

In 1982, Lillard started the men's soccer program's transition to NCAA Division I, which occurred in 1983. The Big South Conference was certified in 1983 and Radford joined in its full competitions in 1984. A recognized Division I conference of the NCAA, including men's soccer, a number of institutions have come and gone in the Big South. The current membership includes Charleston Southern University, Gardner-Webb University, High Point University, Longwood University, Presbyterian College, Radford University, the University of North Carolina at Asheville, the University of South Carolina Upstate, and Winthrop University.

There was a brief downturn in 1982, but Lillard had struck gold in the recruitment of **Bill Gerber**. **<u>Gerber would become Radford's first men's soccer *All-America* selection, earning the honor in 1983.</u>**

BILL GERBER

Bill Gerber

Gerber was Radford's first men's soccer All-America selection, earning the honor in 1983. A four-year starter on defense and as a midfielder, he went on to play professionally with the Washington Diplomats of the American Soccer League. Gerber had 16 goals and 14 assists for the Highlanders from 1982-85, while playing primarily on defense. A second team Division II *All-America* in 1983, the Annandale, Va., native earned a selection on the Division I All-Region team in 1984, and was named to the first Big South All-Conference squad in 1985.

Bill Gerber was inducted into the Radford University Athletics Hall of Fame in 1996.

1985 Bill Gerber

1982

Radford played a challenging schedule in **1982**, losing two games to top-ten teams, the University of Virginia and George Mason University. This was the first meeting ever with the Virginia Cavaliers, brought about by some "Lillard-scheduling magic" with a personal call to Bruce Arena (which was helped along by the VISA Championship from the year before). The season was tough and frustrating for the players and the coaches, with many close games and matches that went the wrong way in overtime. In addition, there were numerous injuries that had to be absorbed. The team had graduated a large number of seniors from the previous year but finished strong, with Radford again upsetting Virginia Tech.

The Highlanders were led by senior midfielder **Randy Jones**, who was named to the **NSCAA**'s * second team All-South squad. Jones scored seven goals this season, extending his all-time scoring record to 27 goals. **John Chomeau** also finished his senior year. **Brian Bruce** and **Brian Czerlinsky** shared duties in goal. Czerlinsky suffered a horrible scare, getting kneed in the back of the head in one game, suffering a blackout-concussion, and even having a brief seizure. He would be tended to by superior RU training staff and amazingly be declared fit to play a number of days thereafter. The season ended with an overall record of 4-12.

1982 Randy Jones

---

* NOTE Re.: **NSCAA** -- The *National Soccer Coaches Association of America (NSCAA),* founded in 1941 and mentioned numerous times throughout this book, changed the organization's name in 2017 to *United Soccer Coaches.*

1983

In **1983**, although the men's soccer team didn't produce a winning season, statistically they outshot all of their opponents except George Mason, West Virginia Wesleyan, and UVa. Tri-captains **Jim McIntire**, **Greg McCarthy** and **Brian Udy** led their team to a 7-9 record. After an impressive debut against Charleston and Eastern Mennonite, the men fell 2-1 to Roanoke College, followed by a disheartening weekend tournament against nationally-ranked Division I George Mason and Division II West Virginia Wesleyan. **Bill Gerber** was recognized for the all-tournament team.

In front of a boisterous crowd, the men sought revenge in a tournament Homecoming Weekend as they nipped Marshall University, 3-2. Unfortunately, their second game handed them a disappointing loss to Randolph-Macon, 2-1. During Parents' Weekend, a road trip was taken to the Va. Tech tournament where an offside trap cost the Highlanders a 2-1 overtime defeat. RU then beat Wilkes College, 7-0. Top honor of the tourney went to **Stephen White** for best offensive player while Gerber and **Willie Kee** were named to the all-tournament team.

1983 Brian Udy

Brian Udy then scored the only goal in a 1-0 victory over UDC. Next came a crushing loss to Shenandoah, 1-0. An exciting game followed with Washington & Lee, when RU took an early lead as Kee took advantage of the goalie with a one-on-one shot. W&L scored twice in the second half. Even so, **Joe Montagne**, with a mere 1:39 minutes left, saw an opening and put one off the keeper to the left. Two, 10-minute, overtime periods enabled McIntire to deposit the ball precisely in the goal and RU won, 3-2. The Highlanders rounded out the season bowing to nationally ranked UVa. Ball possession was observed repeatedly, but scoring opportunities were scarce.

1984

The Radford University Board of Visitors approved moving to Division I status in the Fall of 1983. With the entry into NCAA Division I and the Big South Conference, Radford soccer bid goodbye to the VISA.

In **1984**, Lillard took the team to the Big South Tournament semifinals. Lillard guided Radford University to a 5-1 Big South finish and its first tournament appearance. In the fall, RU's soccer team experienced its first season as a participant in the Division I athletic circuit. The exciting season began on September 8, when they defeated the University of Richmond, 3-2. Other wins for Coach Tom Lillard and his men included triumphs at the College of Charleston tournament where the Highlanders hustled to win 2-0 over Charleston and then 4-1 over Baptist College. **Anoput Phimmasone** had shown promise the previous season as a walk-on, but a severe knee injury ended his career.

Unfortunately, losses to James Madison, Campbell, and UNC occurred in the George Mason tournament. Later, despite losing 5-0 to the University of Virginia, it was the first time that the Cavaliers had played at Dedmon Field and Bruce Arena was the one who volunteered to come to Radford. Coach Lillard mentioned that it was quite an accomplishment to get Virginia to come to Radford given their stature. When the teams met, Virginia was ranked seventh in the country. RU held UVa to just one goal in the first half, but struggled in the second.

1984 Eric Sigurdson

The three captains of the team were **Greg McCarthy**, **Bill Gerber** and **Brian Udy**. McCarthy was the only senior and Lillard said he would be a great loss. Junior Gerber was a Division II *All-America* selection and also a leader who would be relied on in the future. Udy was also a junior who, together with sophomore **Stephen White**, was critical to the success of the team.

In the early 1980s, Radford University youth summer soccer camps started. Many players from both the men's and women's teams become counselors.

Coach Lillard and Randy Jones with campers

Greg McCarthy
By Chad Osborne

STITCH!

That's what Greg McCarthy's '85 teammates called him soon after he started his first soccer game at Radford University. It was a nickname painfully earned. "We were playing in West Virginia — at Marshall, I think — I was going to head the ball, and a guy on the other team brought his foot up too high, and he kicked me in the face. I had to go to the hospital, and I got about eight stitches right here," he recalled, laughing and running his finger across his upper lip. "I looked like I had a mustache."

Greg McCarthy

McCarthy missed the game's second half, but he didn't miss another minute of soccer during his remaining four years at the University. "Except for that first game, I never had an injury," he said. "I was healthy the whole time, and I was the team captain for my sophomore, junior and senior years." When McCarthy was a high school senior living near Baltimore, Maryland, he wrote down everything he was looking for in a college. He wanted to play sports and earn a valuable degree in business. Research led him and a friend on a road trip to visit Radford University.

"I fell in love with it for obvious reasons," McCarthy said of Radford. "I met Tom Lillard [1979 graduate and current associate vice president for University Advancement], who was the soccer coach and responsible for bringing me to campus. I met some students, and I knew this was where I wanted to be."

Over the next four years, McCarthy learned many valuable life lessons at Radford, like time management. "I played almost year-round," he said, "with just a little time off in the winter." He played on the soccer and lacrosse teams and played indoor soccer in between. "We were quite successful at indoor soccer," McCarthy recalled. "I remember winning tournaments at William & Mary, the University of Virginia and George Washington, against some really big Division I schools."

Working well with people is another skill that sports often teach, McCarthy noted, recalling road trips in which multiple teammates often shared beds in hotel rooms. "It was four sweaty guys to a room," he joked. "We doubled down on beds, removing mattresses to have someone sleep on the floor and someone else sleep on the box springs." Managing those situations and serving three years as the soccer team's captain — starting at age 17 — gave McCarthy the equivalent of an advanced degree in leadership. "I learned a lot about leading," he said, "and that now translates into my business life." For the past five years, McCarthy has served as president and CEO of Key Solutions, Inc., a consulting company in Chantilly, Virginia, that "works with contractors to win government contracts," he explained. His brother started Key Solutions in 1983, and McCarthy joined the company 17 years ago. In April 2020, he purchased it.

"I've learned the business from the ground floor and have helped advance the company to where it is today, and I'm proud of our reputation," in the Washington, D.C., area, he said. "We have a staff of almost 50 people, a talented group from diverse backgrounds and skill sets, qualities I learned to value at Radford." McCarthy's father worked in sales, and "he always encouraged me to follow that track," he said. "There was no sales degree at Radford, so I majored in marketing, and it was a really good base for me. I learned marketing, but also accounting and finance, and I earned a great amount of knowledge about the business world. "I'm grateful for the education I received at Radford," McCarthy continued. "It was the right spot for me."

Today, McCarthy relishes the opportunity to stay connected as a donor and volunteer with Radford University — stitching together "time and treasure," he said — to give back to the University that prepared him to be the person and business owner he is today. McCarthy gives his time to the Radford University Athletic Foundation Board of Directors. "I love to help those student-athletes, like me, who may have been overlooked, but are growing into leadership roles," the former soccer captain said. He also serves on the Davis College of Business and Economics Advisory Board. "Radford University is a great destination for my time and money because of what it did for me and the way I've seen the University grow and the quality of students it is attracting," McCarthy explained. "If I can help one student get closer to a business school degree, I feel I've helped in a small way."

1985

Finishing undefeated in the Big South Conference with a record of 4-0 in **1985**, the men's soccer team headed into post-season play in first place. The team won a first-round playoff match against Augusta College. As a result, RU advanced to the Big South Championship game against Campbell University. **Scott Washburn** scored the only goal for RU in a 3-1 loss.

The team was led by record-setting midfielder junior **Stephen White** who scored 14 goals, breaking the previous team record of 12. The Highlanders finished with an overall record of 10-9-2. The team's biggest victories were against conference rival and defending champion Campbell University at RU. The game was very physical with many penalties. Struggling after losses to Old Dominion University and powerful George Mason, the team had a very important battle. Led by White, the team was victorious in front a large and exuberant crowd at Dedmon Center field, defeating Campbell, 2-1. The team also visited the University of Virginia in Charlottesville again, losing 5-0 at Klockner Stadium.

Coming off a three-game winning streak, the team faced James Madison at RU in front of the largest crowd at Dedmon this season. The team played a strong game with great enthusiasm. They were victorious over the Dukes, 2-0, as RU goalie **Justin Bryant** turned away numerous chances.

Defensively, the team was led by backs **Kevin Taylor**, **Joe Montagne** and *All-America* nominee of 1984 **Billy Gerber**. The team allowed only 36 goals in 21 games, with nine coming from two soccer powers in the nation, George Mason University and the University of Virginia. Goalkeeper Bryant played

1985 Bert Diesel

most of the season but backup keepers **Jeff Brown** and **Fran Henry**, playing a combined total of 670 minutes, allowed only eight goals.

Offensively, seniors **Bert Diesel**, **Brian Udy,** and Gerber helped to build strength and power for the team. The Highlanders were assisted in scoring by freshmen **Alan Valencia** and **Scott Washburn**.

TOM LILLARD

Coach Tom Lillard

Beginning in 1986, Lillard moved on to serve Radford Athletics in various administrative roles, including as Executive Director of the Highlander Club, Director of Athletics Development, and Associate Athletics Director for External Affairs. He was instrumental in the completion of the Dedmon Center complex, the design and construction of Cupp Stadium, and the creation of the Radford University Athletics Hall of Fame. He was an ongoing benefactor of the Men's Soccer program and a member of coach recruitment and selection committees. Later, he would serve in the Radford University Foundation as the manager of major gifts. He would finish his career as the Associate Vice President for University Advancement.

Tom Lillard was inducted into the Radford University Athletics Hall of Fame in 2014.

1977 Tom Lillard vs. Virginia Tech

Tom Lillard demonstrates all coaches' job stress

Tom Lillard was the single person who provided substantial, ongoing, continuity for the Radford University Men's Soccer Program from the Club team in 1974 to its Varsity 50th Season in 2024. Tom's wife, Kathy Leonard Lillard supported him during his entire career and was well known and helpful to all of his players and friends.

Kathy and Tom Lillard

Don Staley came to Radford as a men's assistant to Tom Lillard in 1984 and was hired as Lillard's replacement in 1986.

Don Staley Era (1986 – 1993)

8 Seasons

Overall Record: 85-65-17 (.560) - Big South: 37-16-2 (.691)

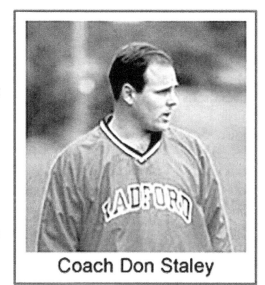

Coach Don Staley

- 1986 9-9-1; Big South: 6-3-0
  Big South Tournament Semifinals

- 1987 9-7-3; Big South: 5-1-0
  Big South Regular Season Champion
  Big South Tournament Semifinals

- 1988 12-7-5; Big South: 5-1-0
  Big South Regular Season Champion
  Big South Tournament Champion

- 1989 13-6-3; Big South: 4-2-0
  Big South Tournament Semifinals

- 1990 15-8-0; Big South: 4-2-0
  Big South Tournament Quarterfinals

- 1991 15-4-2; Big South: 6-0-0
  Big South Regular Season Champion
  Big South Tournament Semifinals
  Big South Coach of the Year

- 1992 8-11-0; Big South: 4-3-0
  Big South Tournament Quarterfinals

- 1993 4-13-3; Big South: 3-4-2

Assistant Coaches: Billy Gerber, Joe Wyskoski, Matt Kinney, Kenny Dale, Phillip Neiland, Jonathan Lindsey, Keith Eck, Steve Arkon, Teddy Wilson, Dustin Fonder

Coach Staley: "When I reflect on my time at Radford University as the Men's & Women's Soccer coach (1985-1993), these are the things I remember most:

The incredible view coming down the hill on Tyler Avenue, seeing the campus for the first time. Head Coach Tom Lillard taking a chance on a young HS/Club coach from Va Beach. Dr. Chuck Taylor who, like Tommy, *was* Radford University Athletics. The "WordMan" **Mike Ashley**, getting hip checked into the brick wall at Peters Hall during my introduction to the women's team; taking over the men's team and quickly challenging the soccer powers in the state with comments like: "I'm putting Bruce Arena and all the other big boys on notice, I'm the Billy Martin of Southwest Virginia Soccer, look out here comes a bull in a China Shop."

This was to a team that had beaten RU 7-0 or 9-0 the year before, so what did I have to lose. We lost the match in the closing minutes to UVA 1-0, so began the beginning of, as the WordMan would say, "the Carnival barker." I remember playing annually one of the toughest schedules in the country on both sides, with players who were passed over by the top programs. At the risk of leaving out names, let's just say I was incredibly fortunate to have been left with great talent from Tommy Lillard, Randy Jones and Will Iandolo, then was able to continue the progression of building two powerhouses in southwest Virginia.

Mike Ashley

On the men's side I remember UVA, the "King" Bruce Arena, Jerry Cheynet and the tough Va. Tech squads, the "Fight", the rematch at Lane Stadium, the battle of the New River Rock, the always tough Campbell University, and our pals from Coastal Carolina. While on the women's side, it was national powerhouse UNC and also the "King" Anson Dorrance, George Mason, and basically anyone in the top 25 willing to play us, of course, seldom at our place. I remember winning the WAGS tournament, and the Big South men's championship. I remember long van rides and double headers with both teams. I remember trips to Pittsburgh, Penn State, Cincinnati, Boca Raton, Western KY and Huntington, WVA twice, and so many others.

I remember the incredible crowds we had at The Dedmon Center (thanks DJ Shock) and the love the community had for our players. I remember Dante Washington playing on the Olympic and National teams and being one of RU's best ambassadors and the only member of the Olympic team not to take the waiver to sit out classes; that semester he received a 4.0 for a full class load.

However, what I remember most was the two men who gave me an opportunity of a lifetime to not only get my degree (while coaching both programs) but allow me to launch my career. For the record, Tom Lillard was a much better technical coach, tactician, and better all-around athlete, than this young coach and, although I was much too confident to admit it then, what I learned under his tutelage I carried throughout my 25-year college coaching career! I may have won 323 games during my career, but had TL stayed in the coaching ranks, he surely would have surpassed me!

Honestly, I think my strengths for both programs were recruiting, in-game management, having outstanding goalkeepers, talented/highly intelligent center-mids, some of the fastest/tenacious frontrunners in the country and we were one of the toughest games on anyone's schedule and teams hated to play the Highlanders for many of those reasons. Yet at the end of the day, why we were so successful were the players who put on the Radford University jersey!

As for Dr. Chuck Taylor, who had to be not only the best dressed AD in all of college athletics, but he also was long on patience with his young coach. Lastly, I'll let the players tell the stories since this not so young coach's memory isn't what it uses to be anymore, but what I'll say is this… When I look back at my 25-year coaching career at Radford University and The University of Alabama, what will always stand out are the people and the players I was so very fortunate to get to coach and work with during those periods."

[*Ashley Note* – Coach Staley apparently forgot the time he yellow-carded the fans at UNCG…]

In **1986**, in **Don Staley's** first season as head coach with the men, the team finished with a 9-9-1 record, 6-3 in the conference, and made it to the Big South tournament semi-finals. Highlights of the regular season included wins over Coastal Carolina, 1-0, and Charleston Southern, 2-1. The win over Coastal may have been the most impressive of the season. Playing before a boisterous Dedmon Center crowd, the Highlanders knocked off the Big South's top-ranked squad. Highlander netminders **Justin Bryant** and **Fran Henry** teamed to record the shutout and earned conference co-player of the week honors. They combined to stop nine Coastal shots and effectively shut down the Chanticleer's scoring leaders. **Brian Eagon** scored the game's lone goal when he recovered a loose ball and fired a shot past the Coastal goalie 57-seconds into the second half. The defense did the rest. In the first round of the Big

South tournament, the Highlanders again defeated Charleston Southern, 2-1, but, in the second round, Coastal Carolina turned the tables from the regular season and won, 5-2.

One of the most notable games of the 1986 season was actually a loss to the University of Virginia, 0-1, at Radford on September 24, where Virginia Coach Bruce Arena would engage in a bit of dubious gamesmanship. Later, although Arena would continue to schedule the Highlanders in the future, he was so unnerved by this result that he refused to play RU again anywhere but in Charlottesville.

1986 Brian Eagon

Homecoming weekend saw an 11-0 rout of Armstrong State. **Pete Bouker** completed a hat trick within 14-minutes of the start of the game. A 6-0 halftime lead came about with solo goals by **Eric Sigurdson**, **Stephen White** and **Willie Shepherd**. Second half goals were scored by **Mike Pfeiffer**, **Alan Valencia**, **Mike Dopp**, **Kevin Taylor** and White.

RU's Own "Deflategate"

Mike Ashley, 02/19/2015: "The Belichick (NFL, New England Patriots) deflated balls controversy reminded me of a 1986 soccer game at RU when Bruce Arena did the same thing at halftime of a game when the Highs had the wind in the second half. Refs wouldn't do anything. They, too, had deflated… well, you get the idea."

1987

Since they lost fifteen players off last year's squad, **1987** was expected to be a rebuilding year, but the Highlanders pulled off a winning record and first place in the Big South regular season. The men faced one of their toughest seasons ever as they played teams such as UVa, Old Dominion, Loyola, and NC State. But with RU's balanced attack, they proved to be worthy opponents for these nationally-ranked teams. Head Coach Don Staley said, "The toughness of the schedule helped mature the younger players, seeing as RU started seven to eight freshmen each game." Unfortunately, the men lost to ODU and Loyola in the first two matches of the season, but these games helped the freshmen, including **Doug Majewski**, see what it was like to play at the Division I level. RU took their record to 2-4-1 but then began to tear through the rest of their schedule. They had lost big to UVa, but the Cavaliers were loaded with players who would go on to represent the United States in national competition and become household names. These included Coach Bruce Arena, Curt Onalfo, John Harkes, Tony Meola, and Jeff Agoos. The team would roll on to shut out two nationally-ranked teams that year, James Madison and Coastal Carolina. The men benefitted from the field play of **Bruce Griggs** and the goalkeeping of **Mike DeSarno**. The Highlanders ended the season at 9-7-2 after defeating Coastal Carolina, the number-one team in the Big South, 4-1.

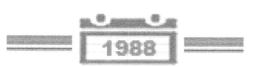

1988

1988 saw the arrival of **Dante Washington** and the scoring binge began. It was also notable for the biggest "Mud Bowl Game," played in horrendous rain that turned the Dedmon field into a huge quagmire. The season was also the first appearance of "The New River Rock," won by Virginia Tech. *Big South*: "As a freshman for Radford in 1988, **Dante Washington** immediately burst onto the Big South soccer scene with his amazing talent. He led the Highlanders to the **Big South Regular Season and Tournament Championships** that season with a school-record 27 goals scored and 22 assists for a Big South single-season record 76 points – a Conference record that still stands

Dante Washington - 1988

today. The All-Conference selection also **led the nation in scoring in 1988**. In that first season, he scored six goals in a game and dished out four assists in another."

The 1988 team also played the most games in a season with 24, finishing at 12-7-5.

1988 – Teddy Wilson

November 3, 1988 Tartan: The RU men's soccer team racked up a tie and three wins last week to end their season on a high note. The Highlanders started the four-game week with a meeting against William and Mary. W&M had been ranked 11th in the national poll earlier in the year. "We had the opportunity to beat them," said coach Don Staley. "We missed a couple of shots that could have given us the win." The Highlanders tied the Williamsburg school 1-1. "Everyone gave an all-out effort," said **Brian Eagon**. "We really applied a lot of pressure." Eagon had the only goal for the Highlanders. On Saturday, the men began a three-day, three-game stretch when they faced UNC-Asheville. The Highlanders did not have too much trouble with them as they took a 4-0 win. **Bruce Griggs**, **Dave Cossaboon**, **Dante Washington** and **Teddy Wilson** scored for the Highlanders. The men will face UNC-Asheville in the first round of the Big South Tournament this week, so the win really boosted them up. Lenoir-Rhyne was the next victim for the Highlanders. RU dropped them, 6-1. The bright spot in the game was national scoring leader Dante Washington. He blasted three in to earn the hat trick on the day. Another strong point for the Highlanders was the play of the bench. "The bench really showed some strong play," said Eagon. RU hosted state rival VMI to round out the week and the regular season. The Highlanders won, 4-1. **Paul Adams** found the promised land twice in the game. Washington and Cossaboon added one apiece. Going into the tournament, the Highlanders feel that they are peaking. "We are playing well. Everyone's attitude is up. We are going to come back with the conference trophy," said Eagon. **Jeff Brown** took care of business in goal.

In the Big South Tournament, Radford defeated UNC-Asheville, 2-0, in the semi-final, and Charleston Southern, 3-1, in the final. **Steve Arkon**, Dave Cossaboon, Brian Eagon, **Doug Majewski**, **Jeff Majewski** and Dante Washington all set the school record for most games in a season by playing in all 24 contests.

THE NEW RIVER ROCK

Michael Ashley: "To drum up even more attention in what was another great rivalry, Staley and Virginia Tech coach Jerry Cheynet fished a huge rock out of the New River and made it a prize for the winner of the annual game. It worked. We got more newspaper and TV coverage, and the game was always played in front of large crowds. Admittedly the bench-clearing fight in 1990 didn't hurt but "The New River Rock" became a thing. Although I feared for Staley's life one year we won and he tried to heft it above his head for the cameras. I thought he was going to crush his own skull.

Whichever school won "The Rock" got to take it "home" for a year to display and paint the school logo and score on it. We turned that over to our talented graphics folks in the Public Information Office. We and the Virginia Tech SID office would crank things up with a news release before the next meeting in the fall highlighting the rivalry.

My competitive nature kicked in one year when Tech sent out a release with some facts on The Rock -- where it was fished out and how much it weighed. These releases are lost in files somewhere back in a storage at RU, next to Indiana Jones' Ark of the Covenant.

So, when we won The Rock back, I --okay, a couple of our students-- took it over to our geology department to my undergrad geology professor, **Dr. Robert Whisonant**. We had them analyze it. I can't remember what period the rock came from (*Staleyenzoic*, I think), but I was able to include a couple of paragraphs with a much more technical analysis and yes, every paper ran it and credited Radford University.

None of these details mattered in the long run. Dante & Co. were so much fun to watch play that attendance at the old Dedmon Center upper field was never an issue. It was a raucous atmosphere and fans rarely went home disappointed. In addition to his Hall of Fame coaching career, Staley was quite the showman and recruiter."

1989

The **1989** fall season for RU men's soccer was full of surprises. In the second game, sophomore sensation **Dante Washington** broke his ankle and was out for the rest of the year. (He would be granted a "red-shirt" option.) Senior **Magnus Ramquist** said, "Replacing the number one scorer in the nation was impossible, but the team did all right." He dismissed any intra-team competition between himself and Washington, who were the two leading scorers in the nation the previous year. The Highlanders went on to beat Virginia Tech, 1-0, to take the "New River Rock" for the first time. Ramquist recalled, "It was a great feeling to beat Tech. It was probably one of the biggest wins of the season." The attitude the team shared was that they could have done better, considering their power and past performance. Ramquist said, "I know we could have done so well. We were so close to a breakthrough. We had bad luck with a lot of rain and close games." Ramquist was more optimistic about future seasons, although the native of Eskilstuna, Sweden, had finished out his Radford career. Ramquist retired after scoring a total of 40 goals.

Whitney Keiller versus Old Dominion, 1989

Although the fire power of the injured Dante Washington was missed, a lot of the difference was made up by Ramquist, **Whitney Keiller**, **John Barry** and **Jeff Majewski**. Jeff had joined his brother **Doug Majewski** the year before.

The team pulled together to end up with a third-place finish in the Big South and a final record of 13-6-3. Even with such a successful record, Head Coach Don Staley summed up the 1989 season by saying, "We'll always look back and wonder 'what if' about this season. That's not a position we wanted to be in, and it's one I'm sure the team won't allow to happen next year."

Coach Don Staley with the Team and "The New River Rock," 1989

1990

In **1990**, Radford got a huge lift with the return of **Dante Washington**. After breaking his ankle, he came back in his third year, second year of eligibility, **to again lead the nation in scoring for the second time**. He finished the year with 23 goals and 18 assists.

1990 Dante Washington (#9)

RU goalkeeper **Frederic Rondeau** registered ten shutouts, a school record. One of those shutouts was a 1-0 victory at Howard. **Whitney Keiller** scored the only goal in the 63rd minute for the Highlanders. Howard was ranked in the top-twenty at the time.

The team set a school record for wins, finishing 15-8, that also included an upset win on the road over Maryland, 2-1, with Washington scoring both goals, but the season had opened with defending national champion Virginia. The Highlanders scored first but fell 3-1. Radford went on a five-game winning streak following an overtime loss to Penn State. **Jeff Majewski** would have a hat trick in a 3-0 win over Campbell, the first victory ever for RU at Buies Creek. The biggest controversy of the year happened when the Highlanders traveled down Prices Fork Road to take on Virginia Tech. The game was rough, to say the least, as ten yellow cards were given out in the first half. A bench-clearing brawl broke out between both teams at halftime and the game was called off. The game was cancelled with VT leading 2-1. VT wanted revenge and both schools promoted a replacement grudge match.

Radford was prematurely knocked out of the Big South Tournament when Davidson beat the Highlanders 2-1 at the Dedmon Center. Jeff Majewski, Dante Washington and **Doug Majewski** would all be named to the Big South all-conference team.

The season ended on a winning note, however, when, after a month of indecision, the game against Virginia Tech was rescheduled – to start from scratch – on a cold, windy November night in Blacksburg. Radford soundly defeated the Hokies, 2-0, estimated to be in front of over 5,000 fans, a record attendance for a Tech soccer game at the time. Because of the size of the crowd, the game was held in the Virginia Tech football stadium. It was further recorded at that time as the largest-attended college soccer game in the state of Virginia's history. The victory let RU retain possession of the New River Rock. The senior class, including Columbia, Md., natives **Sean Peay** and **Doug Majewski**, **Teddy Wilson** of Manassas, Va., and **Steve Arkon** of Randolph, N.J., finished their careers with a 49-28-11 mark, the best four-year record in school history. Together with **Dante Washington**, the five would remain lifelong friends.

Steve Arkon, 06/19/2024 – "Teddy and I went on to create the Teddy & Steve Pre-Game Show, a men's and women's team favorite. As assistant coaches for the Fall after graduation, my job was to video practices and games and then review them with the team. Teddy was more of a technical, on-field coach. I was working on a minor in communications and had an interest in taking things to the next level. I needed a side kick, a straight guy – it was Teddy. We would travel the east coast interviewing referees, opponent's coaches, TV/Newspaper reporters, school administrators, and general workers of whatever school we visited. It was a combination of Howard Stern and David Letterman where we would poke fun at our own, while having fun with our guest. We would script our content, have no rehearsals, and then Teddy would drop the best one-liners off script. He was a classic. The pre-game shows were a favorite for our long tour-bus rides home before we aired the matches for the team to see. Teddy had a warm wit and charm unlike any other."

(L-R) Dante Washington, Teddy Wilson, Sean Peay, Steve Arkon

The *Roanoke Times*: "One of the most memorable moments of Staley's career was Radford's fight-marred match with Virginia Tech in 1990. Since then, the Radford-Tech match has drawn large crowds and garnered increased media attention. Before the 1991 Tech match, Staley made derogatory comments about Tech players, students, and even football players, in an interview with Radford's student newspaper. Insiders knew Staley was simply trying to stir up interest in the match, but athletic officials were steamed and Staley later apologized. A then-record crowd [at Radford] of 4,000 fans turned out for the match. "The bark was worse than the bite," Staley said. "I guess I was the Billy Martin of southwest Virginia soccer. That was my style. There was a rhyme and a reason to everything I did. We gave some people some thrills over the last nine years."

1991

1991 saw a Big South Conference regular season championship as a result of an undefeated 6-0 run. The final overall result of 15-4-2 tied a school record for wins and set a new RU winning percentage of .762. The team ranked as high as fifth in the region. Unfortunately, a 1-0 loss to Campbell in the Big South tournament cost the team a berth in the NCAA playoffs. **Dante Washington** finished with 16 goals and 14 assists, for 46 points, en-route to becoming Player of the Year in both the state and the Big South. **Dante Washington was then named Radford's first-ever Division I consensus First-Team *All-America*.**

1991 Dante Washington

Senior **Jeff Majewski** closed out a sparkling career as the team's Most Valuable Player, compiling 35 goals and 23 assists in four seasons. Freshman **Ian Spooner** played beyond his years as he tallied 16 goals and six assists. His efforts left him tied for third in scoring in the region and 14th in the nation. His teammates voted him co-offensive MVP alongside Washington. The defense may have yet been the backbone of the Highlanders, however, led by junior **John Barry**, who received the team's defensive MVP honors. Barry was covered by junior goalkeeper **Frederic Rondeau** who allowed just 19 goals and had five shutouts. Backup goalkeeper **Chris Barrett** also had two shutouts.

Two of the most celebrated players of the Staley era were **Dante Washington** and **Jeff Majewski**.

DANTE WASHINGTON

Big South: "As a freshman for Radford in 1988, **Dante Washington** immediately burst onto the Big South soccer scene with his amazing talent. He led the Highlanders to the Big South Tournament championship that season with a school-record 27 goals scored and 22 assists for a Big South single-season record 76 points – a Conference record that still stands today. The All-Conference selection also led the nation in scoring in 1988. In that first season, he scored six goals in a game and dished out four assists in another.

Dante Washington

Washington missed the 1989 season due to a broken ankle, but came back in 1990 and picked up where he left off as he tallied 23 goals and 18 assists for 64 total points to again lead all of NCAA Division I in scoring. He earned his second All-Conference honor that season and was a National Soccer Coaches Association of America (NSCAA) First-Team All-Region selection.

In 1991, Washington led the Highlanders to a school-best 15-4-2 overall record and the regular-season Big South championship. He was voted Big South Player of the Year after leading the League in scoring for the third time. He tallied 16 goals and 14 assists for 46 points and became the Big South's all-time leading goal scorer and point scorer during that season. He became Radford's first Division I consensus First-Team *All-America* in 1991 and was also the state of Virginia's Player of the Year. Washington also participated on the U.S. Under-23 team in 1991 and became the first African-American to score a goal for the U.S. National Team.

Washington earned more attention in the summer of 1992 when he played for the U.S. Olympic Men's Soccer Team at the Barcelona Olympic Games, where he led the team with six goals in qualifying action. Washington concluded his collegiate career later that fall with his fourth All-Conference honor. He posted 13 goals and 11 assists in his senior season to finish his brilliant career with 82 goals scored, 66 assists and 230 total points – all Radford and Big South Conference records. His 82 goals scored still rank second all-time in NCAA history. Washington is one of 22 college players to be part of the 40-40 club, having both 40 goals and 40 assists in their college career.

Washington earned a double major in history and political science while at Radford, earning Adidas Scholar Athlete *All-America* honors in 1992.

He moved onto the professional circuit and later joined Major League Soccer in 1996 as a member of the Columbus Crew during their inaugural season. He played three games for the Crew before moving onto the Dallas Burn later that season. He spent just over three years in Dallas and helped the Burn reach the playoffs every season with the squad. In 1997, he was named an MLS All-Star and scored a goal in the All-Star Game. He finished 1997 with 12 goals and six assists, and tallied two playoff scores as well. In all, Washington scored 24 goals during his time in Dallas.

Washington re-joined the Crew in 2000 and earned his second All-Star distinction that year. He scored a career-high 15 goals in addition to nine assists for Columbus, and notched a goal and an assist in the 2000 All-Star Game. Washington and the Crew made the playoffs in 2001, 2002 and 2004 before he moved onto Real Salt Lake in 2005. He played nine games for Real Salt Lake in what would be his final MLS season. Washington spent nine seasons in MLS and scored 57 goals and had 31 assists in 189 career regular-season and playoff games. He still ranks as the Crew's fifth all-time leading goal scorer with 28.

Following his playing career, Washington later worked as a broadcaster for the Crew. In July 2007, Washington joined the MLS front office as a regional ambassador for Region I (Mid-Atlantic/Northeast), which consists of 13 states, including MLS markets Washington, D.C., New York and New England. He is responsible for league and soccer development in Region I, which includes relationship building with youth clubs and tournaments, player development efforts sponsored by the league, and fan building with MLS and its respective clubs."

Dante Washington was inducted into the Radford University Athletics Hall of Fame in 1997.

1992 – Dante Washington

JEFF MAJEWSKI

Jeff Majewski

"Distinguished by four years in a Highlander uniform and four years as a First Team Big South All-Conference member, **Jeff Majewski** ('92) is one of 23 players in the Big South to earn all-conference accolades four times in a career, earning the distinction each season from 1988 to 1991. Majewski also earned All-Big South Tournament honors three times in his career (1988, 1990, 1991) and was the conference's player of the week on multiple occasions. Throughout his stint as a Highlander, Majewski brought home two Big South Regular Season Championships (1988,1991) and one Big South Tournament Championship (1988). Majewski tallied 35 goals and 23 assists in his time at Radford, which added up to 93 points – all ranking inside the top five at Radford. The midfielder was also named to the 1990-99 Big South All-Decade Team, which recognized the top players in the conference during the 1990s."

Jeff Majewski was inducted into the Radford University Athletics Hall of Fame in 2019.

Jeff Majewski - 1989

RADFORD UNIVERSITY ATHLETICS
HALL OF FAME

From "Untold Stories of the Press Box" by Michael Ashley:

WASHINGTON SCORED HERE: First, a quote that sums up how things seemed to work for me. **Dante Washington** scored six goals in a game (one of TWO times he did that) and *The Washington Post* called me to ask if we were promoting Dante for the Hermann Award (soccer's top honor). I got quoted in *The Post* for saying, "Hermann Award? Six is a touchdown, we're promoting Dante for the Heisman!"

The Great Names in Soccer: Pelé, Dante, Staley

It's still the early '90s and Don Staley's soccer teams have become some of the most entertaining squads ever at Radford behind **Dante Washington**, **Jeff** and **Doug Majewski** and **Sean Peay** and those are just the guys from Columbia, Md. We had **Ian Spooner**, **Frederic Rondeau**, **Darryl Springer**, **Whitney Keillor**, **Lee Morton** and **John Tierney**, too.

1992

A disappointing **1992** season came to a close with an 8-11 mark for the Radford University soccer team. The season ended one of the greatest eras in Highlander athletics. **Dante Washington** played his last match for the Highlanders and the former Olympic star went out with a flourish. Washington finished the season as Radford's leading scorer with 13 goals and 11 assists. The Columbia, Maryland, native wrapped up his storied career with 82 goals, 66 assists, and 230 total points – all Radford and Big South Conference records, but Washington's heroics this year couldn't save the Highlanders from their first losing season since 1983. Senior **Whitney Keiller** missed nine matches with injury and scored only three of his 25 career goals this season. Sophomore **Ian Spooner**, who had 16 goals as a freshman, scored only six times this year as a painful hamstring pull kept him out of five matches and limited him in others.

1993

Working with youth and inexperience, the team had a successful rebuilding season in **1993**. Staley predicted, "I think you'll see some new stars emerge for us… we've got a chance to build something new." Sophomore **Che Henderson** brought experience among the returning midfielders and strikers. This speedy forward aided the Highlanders in scoring. Freshman **Matt Bennett** helped lead the defense. Junior goalkeeper **Chris Barrett** was one of the team's key returnees. Sophomore **John Tierney**, considered to be one of the top international players who ever attended Radford, was the leading scorer. Freshman **Lee Morton** was a strong midfielder who showed promise for the future. A 2-0 loss to a very strong University of Virginia team, near the end of the season, was actually encouraging. Virginia would go on to win the NCAA National Championship that year, and then take a break from scheduling Radford for the next eight years. The season ended with an overall record of 4-13-3.

Rob Stinnett: "I remember we played them (Virginia) when they were #1 and we got to UVa and had no uniforms! Coach had to ask Bruce (Arena) to borrow their away uniforms."

DON STALEY

Coach Don Staley

Don Staley was hired as the women's coach in 1985, and was given the dual position of coaching both the men's and women's teams in 1986. A rare two-sport coach who helped build both of Radford's men's and women's soccer programs, Staley recorded a combined 182 wins for the Highlanders, posting a 97-64-9 record with the women's team and compiling an 85-65-17 mark with the men. On the men's side, Staley won three Big South regular-season championships, one Big South Tournament Championship, and went 37-16-2 in league play. He led the team to back-to-back program-record 15-win seasons in 1990 and 1991, earning Big South Coach of the Year honors in 1991 with a perfect 6-0 conference record. During his tenure at Radford, Staley coached two *All-Americas*, a men's U.S. Olympic Team member, and a women's Hermann Trophy finalist. Staley is the only hall of fame member to be named Big South Coach of the Year in two different sports. He won the first with the men in 1991 and then with the women in 1993, during his final stint as a Highlander.

Don Staley was inducted into the Radford University Athletics Hall of Fame in 2017.

Don Staley - 1992

At the conclusion of the 1993 season, Staley moved on to become the women's head coach at SEC powerhouse, the University of Alabama. (Staley was quoted as saying, "Not bad for an RU guy.") He would be replaced by **Spencer Smith**.

Spencer Smith Era (1994 – 2009)

16 Seasons

Overall Record: 136-139-30 (.495) - Big South: 56-44-12 (.554)

- 1994 11-7-2; Big South: 6-2-0
  Big South Tournament Quarterfinals
  Big South Coach of the Year

- 1995 11-5-3; Big South: 4-2-1
  Big South Tournament Quarterfinals

- 1996 10-10-1; Big South: 4-3-0
  Big South Tournament Finalist

- 1997 11-8-1; Big South: 4-2-0
  Big South Tournament Semifinals

- 1998 11-4-3; Big South: 5-0-1
  Big South Tournament Semifinals
  Big South Regular Season Champion
  Big South Coach of the Year

Coach Spencer Smith

- 1999 5-11-4; Big South: 2-4-1
  Big South Big South Tournament Champion
  First-ever NCAA Tournament Appearance

- 2000 12-10-0; Big South: 4-3-0
  Big South Tournament Champion
  Second Consecutive NCAA Tournament Appearance

- 2001 4-14-0; Big South: 3-4-0
  Big South Tournament Quarterfinals

- 2002 7-12-1; Big South: 3-3-1
  Big South Tournament Semifinals

71

- 2003 8-9-2; Big South: 2-4-1
  Big South Tournament Quarterfinals

- 2004 7-6-4; Big South: 3-3-1
  Big South Tournament Quarterfinals

- 2005 8-9-0; Big South: 5-2-0
  Big South Tournament Quarterfinals

- 2006 8-6-4; Big South: 4-1-2
  Big South Tournament Quarterfinals

- 2007 11-9-0; Big South: 3-3-0
  Big South Tournament Finalist

- 2008 7-10-2; Big South: 3-4-1
  Big South Tournament Quarterfinals

- 2009 5-9-3; Big South: 1-4-3
  Big South Tournament Semifinals

Assistant Coaches: Keith Eck, Chris Barrett, Jon Freeman, Jonathan Williamson, Richard Shepherd, Eric Ruano, Bill Arthur

"**Spencer Smith** has the most wins of any coach in Radford men's soccer history and was a two-time Big South Conference Coach of the Year. Smith completed 16 seasons at Radford in 2009 and has over 21 years of college coaching experience that also includes time at Lincoln Memorial University and North Carolina Wesleyan. He compiled a 136-139-30 (.495) record at Radford to rank fourth on the Big South Conference all-time coaching list and third among active coaches. His 56 Big South Conference victories rank him fourth on the all-time coaching list. The veteran coach owns a career record of 170-190-44 (.475). He was named Big South Coach of the Year in 1994 and 1998.

Smith has a history of developing players on the field as demonstrated by the number of all-conference performers he has produced at Radford and he has a strong record of producing successful student-athletes in the classroom as well.   Under Smith's guidance, Radford won the 1998 Big South Conference regular season championship and made two appearances in the NCAA Tournament in 1999 and 2000. He has produced 30 All-Big South Conference performers and his 2007 and 2008 Highlander teams were presented the Team Academic Award by the National Soccer Coaches

Association of America. In 2008 Radford was one of only 35 NCAA Division I-programs to earn that recognition for having a team cumulative grade point average of 3.0 or above.

A 1987 graduate of the University of Tennessee, Smith was a four-year starter for the Volunteers, and a captain as a junior and senior. Smith also earned most valuable player honors in 1986. Following college, his professional career took him to Sheffield, England. and included training with Sheffield United F.C., as well as time with the Stannington Village FC. A native of Baltimore, MD, Smith was head coach of the Virginia Olympic Development Program U-18 team from 1994-98. He was also the chairman of the NSCAA South Atlantic Regional Rankings Committee and a member of the NCAA Regional Selection Committee. Smith played at Loch Raven High School in Baltimore, where he was a two-time All-State selection."

Spencer Smith, 3/12/2024: "In February of 1994, I was offered the Head Men's Soccer Coach position. Without the help of my predecessor, **Don Staley**, I would have never had the honor of coaching at RU. Little did I know at that time Radford would change my life. Don was instrumental in me getting an interview. He was able to put me in contact with those who were on the hiring committee. **Tommy Lillard**, **Fred Newhouse** (local banker and friend of RU soccer), **Chuck Taylor**, and **Greig Denny** all served on the committee. As I recall, Chuck and I talked mostly about Tennessee football during my interview. Needless to say, I felt good about my chances of getting the job since Chuck was a huge UT fan. My favorite Chuck story was when he called me during my first year and wanted to go for a ride to get some *Little Debbie's* (his favorite sweet snack). In the car Chuck talked about how the boys needed to pick it up and play harder. After he finished, I politely reminded him we were off to a great start having won 5 consecutive games and that I was pleased with the level the boys were performing. He looked at me and with a slight chuckle said, "I'm not talking about <u>your</u> team, I'm talking about the Vols!"

The '94-95 teams were very good clubs that finished 3rd in the regular season. **Ian Spooner** was POY in the Big South and a very accomplished goal scorer. Spoon could finish from anywhere. He could be a poacher or could score a *golazo* from far out. Many of his goals came from **Eduardo Wissar**. Eduardo (Lima, Peru) was the most skillful player I have ever coached and his ability to play-make as a #10 was superior. **Chris Barrett** led our '94 team in goal. Chris was ahead of his time. He had better foot skills than many of our players and Chris's composure with the ball was second to none. We had complete confidence playing passes back to Chris.

Ian Spooner

In '96 our GK was freshman **Sacha Drouin** (Long Island, NY). Sasha was very imposing in goal. That year we beat UNC 1-0 at Fetzer Field and after the game Elmar Bolowich, UNC coach, came up to me and said, "I think I have the wrong Drouin on my team." Sasha's brother Dimitry was in goal for Carolina. I believe that was the first victory RU had v. an ACC opponent.

The '97 team duplicated the UNC win by defeating them by the same score line 1-0. Again, Sasha was spectacular in goal and for the second straight year the goal scorer was **Kevin Kelly**, a forward from Philadelphia. It also beat #8 NC State at Method Road Stadium 4-1. The Highlanders turned it up in overtime by scoring three goals on the Wolfpack. This team would play for the Big South Championship against UNC-Greensboro who was ranked #1. The Spartans were clearly better but our boys battled hard in a 2-0 defeat.

The '98 team was an incredible array of players. Led by **Troy Washington** (Dumfries, VA), this team defeated #17 Florida International in Miami and took #6 Duke into overtime only to lose on a heartbreaking goal 2-1. The '98ers won the BSC regular season title but suffered a gut wrenching 2-1 loss to South Alabama at Dedmon Center field on a wind-aided, freak goal. This team received votes for national top twenty-five and was ranked as high as #5 in the South Region. Troy was honored as the BSC player of the year.

'99 team was a rebuild but had a group of talented freshmen. **T.J. Rolfing**, from Sioux Falls, S.D. was undeniably one of the hardest working players I have ever coached. His work rate and pace made him a real threat as a freshman. Although the '99 team finished 6th in conference, it put together an incredible three-game run and won the Big South Championship by defeating rival Liberty 4-3 on penalties. This group went on to play top-twenty opponent Furman in the [NCAA] first round and although we lost the match 1-0, much of the game was controlled by the young Highlanders.

T. J. Rolfing

'00 team went on to win the Big South again and RU soccer claimed its first back-to-back titles. Captain **Scott Hance**, from Dallas TX, was stellar as a center-back and voted Big South Scholar Athlete of the year. Again, the Highlanders were led by T.J. Rolfing up top, but the heart of the team was the midfield of **Johnathan Frias** (Miami, FL), **Geraldo Hernandez** (Herndon, VA), **Andre Lewis** (Tampa, FL) and **Mike Adeyemi** (Miami, FL). Unfortunately, the '00 team lost again to a hungry Furman team 2-0 in the NCAA's. During the regular season this Highlander team went on the road and knocked off #3 Duke 3-2. The Highlanders were up 3-0 at half and managed to hold off a charging Duke squad. The win broke Duke's 25-game home unbeaten streak.

'01 team suffered a tough season and got hit with several injuries. This group persevered and made it to the BSC semi-final where it lost to eventual Champion Coastal Carolina 1-0.

'02 team played in one of the most incredible games at Winthrop. The match was to be played at RU but our field was unplayable due to the heavy rain that week. So, the day of the game it was decided we would play at Winthrop in what would be a thrilling but heartbreaking match. The game was played under a thick cloud of fog during a surreal evening. It was a back-and-forth affair, but eventually, Winthrop would prevail 7-6 with the winning goal coming in the 86th minute. These two teams would end up playing in the semi-final of the Big South tournament on the same pitch as earlier and once again the result went in favor of the Eagles 4-3. The winning goal came off a corner kick in overtime.

'03 season produced some quality wins but much of it was a roller coaster of a year. This group seemed to win in streaks or lose in streaks. RU hosted the Big South tournament that year. The first games were played in winds gusting as high as 70-mph. In fact, winds were such a factor that all the goals in the 4 matches were scored with the wind except one. Also, I had never seen this in a match, but the GK of one team ended up catching his own punt. He punted the ball and it went straight up and right back to him. I doubt I'll ever see that again.

'04 season was another solid year but we could not quite break into the top tier of the BSC standings. This team did have some good wins v. Coastal and Furman but were a little snake-bitten in the tournament, losing to Liberty 2-1 on a PK.

'05 team started the year off very well and we were in first in Big South play until we suffered a couple of season-ending injuries to our GK **Omar Zinoveev** and center-back **Paul Caruso**. Down the stretch we couldn't overcome the loss of these two and we ended up losing in the first round of the BSC tournament. What started out as a promising season finished sourly.

'06 season almost mirrored the previous year. Once again, we played well in Big South play only to stumble and lose on PKs to High Point in the first round.

'07 team displayed a great team spirit and produced a fun season. Although the ending was disappointing, the journey with this team was enjoyable. In the semi-final we soundly beat top-seeded Coastal 3-1. It was one of the best performances of any team I coached at RU. That group played an inspired and exciting brand of soccer that day. **James Leith** had a wonder goal. He picked up a ball at midfield and beat three Coastal defenders before slotting it by an on-rushing keeper. Unfortunately, we would not be able to beat Liberty in the final. Going up 1-0 just six minutes into match we looked like we did v. Coastal. Twenty minutes later we missed a golden opportunity to go up 2-0. If we score that *sitter*, I believe we would have won the game. To Liberty's credit they fought back and scored two good goals to beat us and preserve the BSC championship. To this day it is one of the most heartbreaking losses.

'08 and '09 seasons didn't generate a great deal of excitement. '08 group did get a nice result at Clemson with a 1-1 draw and '09 team beat up on Va. Tech at home in front of another great crowd.

On a personal note, I absolutely loved my time at RU. It led me to my wife of 27 years and each of our 3 children were born there. I can't thank all the great people who supported me and the program enough. It will always remain a special place in my heart!"

1994

In **1994**, inheriting a dispirited team from the year before, first-year coach **Spencer Smith** wasted little time in reversing the Highlanders' fortunes, finishing the season at 11-7-2 and second place in the Big South. Radford got off to a fast start under Smith, going undefeated through the first five matches. Senior goalkeeper **Chris Barrett** posted a 1.25 GAA and had seven shutouts in his final season. The shutouts included UMBC, UNCA, Towson State, and Coastal Carolina.

Lee Morton, **Kevin Gealt**, and **Jose Avendano** anchored the defense. Junior midfielder **Eduardo Wissar** led the Big South with 10 assists. Junior striker **Che Henderson** added 13 goals and six assists. Senior striker **Gerald Lakatos** had career bests with six goals and five assists, including the game-winning score against Towson State. Freshmen **Tommy Young** and **Rick Lodge** showed their promise for the future.

1994 – Chris Barrett

Smith was named Big South Coach of the Year and junior **Ian Spooner** Big South Conference Player of the Year. Spooner was also named to the All-South Atlantic Region team with 16 goals and 4 assists. In the Big South tournament, RU was upset by Liberty in the first round. **John Tierney** earned all-tournament honors.

IAN SPOONER

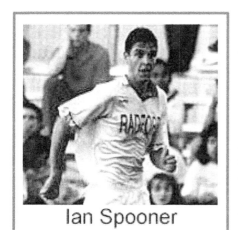

Ian Spooner

One of the most accomplished men's soccer players in Radford and Big South history, **Ian Spooner** is the only two-time Big South Player of the Year in program history. A native of Oxford, England, Spooner ranks second to Hall of Famer Dante Washington on Radford's all-time list in career points (140), points per game (1.89), goals (58), shot attempts (286) and shots per game (3.86), while sitting third in assists with 24. In addition to his career accomplishments, the two-time all-conference performer ranks among Radford's single-season leaders in total points (3rd / 9th), points per game (3rd / 10th) and goals (3rd / T-5th). Spooner is also among the conference's career leaders in goals (4th) and total points (5th), while sitting 10th in single-season goals and total points.

As a freshman in 1991, Spooner led the Highlanders to the Big South Regular Season title before earning all-tournament honors. Spooner enjoyed a six-year professional (1995-2000) career in the United Soccer League (USL). In 1999, he was instrumental in the start of Bridgewater College's women's soccer program when he was named the Eagles' first-ever head coach. Following his two-year stint, he returned to his alma mater as an assistant coach of the Highlanders' women's soccer team, which won a Big South championship in 2002.

Ian Spooner was inducted into the Radford University Athletics Hall of Fame in 2012.

Ian Spooner, 1994 Big South Player of the Year

1995

"A good bunch of lads" is how **John Tierney**, a senior, described the teammates on the **1995** men's soccer team. Radford's team was very multi-cultural, more so than in previous years, giving lots of American students a chance to be introduced to other cultures. Unifying the team and creating new friendships was helped by Coach Smith with unique freshmen orientations, including such things as treasure hunts. The team benefitted from a lack of major injuries and the play of **Ian Spooner**. Spooner, a senior, ranked third in the nation in points. The team finished the season with an overall record of 11-5-3, 4-2-1 in the Big South, and made it to the Big South Tournament quarterfinals. Some team superstitions existed during the year, including the bandanna that **Lee Morton** had to wear and warming up to reggae music. Without elaborating on who it might have been, players also indicated having benefitted from a particular fan who attended games.

John Tierney – 1995

Tierney, from Ireland, represented the vanguard of many international players who would come to Radford over the years. The cultural and societal connections made by these players, in both directions, would prove invaluable to everyone involved. Tierney added, "I would just like to thank previous coach Don Staley, as well as Spencer Smith, for giving Lee, Richard, and me the opportunity to come over here and play."

1995 Che Henderson

1996

Having lost nine seniors last year, four of whom were All-Conference, the **1996** men's soccer team had a difficult time replacing players this season. With only five returning starters, Head Coach Spencer Smith had a young team on his hands, and with that came inexperience. Seniors **Lee Morton** and **Richard Sheppard**, both from England, played well all season. They helped guide the team and were also mentors for their younger teammates. The team finished at 10-10-1, 4-3 in the Big South, and Big South tournament runner-up.

Other key players for the season were sophomore **Sacha Drouin**, a goalkeeper from New York, and freshman **Kevin Kelly**, a forward from Philadelphia. Senior **Chad Long** also performed well on the field. Unfortunately, a serious ankle injury plagued starter **Joe Young** that kept him out for most of the season. Freshman **Kevin Kelly** commented, "The team had a lot of heart and we really stuck together, even though we had a hard time scoring. Next season will be better, though, because we'll have more experience."

1996 was also the year that the "Rowdy Red" mascot would be replaced with "The Highlander."

The Highlander

1997

In **1997**, the men's soccer team finished the regular season with a heartbreaking 3-2 overtime loss to Charleston Southern.   The loss came only three days after the Highlanders won their tenth game of the season, against Campbell University.   Despite playing two men down for two overtime periods, RU defeated the Camels 3-2.   **Troy Washington**'s second goal of the match came at 3:17 of the second overtime period to give the Highlanders the victory. **Kevin Kelly** had won a loose ball ahead of the area and touched a square pass to Washington, who scored on a right footed shot from about 22-yards away.   Despite outshooting Radford, 24-11, the Camels could not get past RU goaltender **Josh Anson**. Washington had scored his first goal with an assist from **Michael Ginsburg**. **Joe Young** had the other.

1997 Nick Butcher

Ironically, RU's season came to an end in the Big South Tournament at the hands of eventual champion Charleston Southern, 2-0. Charleston scored at the 31-minute mark on a penalty kick after a handball call. RU was then forced to play a man down after a red card in the 40th minute. RU had reached the semi-final game against CSU after a 3-2 overtime win over the University of Maryland-Baltimore County. **Kevin Kelly** scored the game-winning goal at the 100:23 mark. RU took the early lead on a goal by **Angel Cardozo**. UMBC then scored twice to go ahead. **Kevin Terne** scored on a penalty kick at 59:04 to send the game to overtime. Kelly and Cardozo were named to the all-tournament team. The 1997 team would defeat Virginia Tech early in the season, 3-2, to win back the "New River Rock" and start what would become a four-year winning streak against the Hokies.

Lisa Worley, "Balancing Act" - 1997: Late study sessions, copying notes, and help from classmates are some things that students do when they miss class. Imagine missing class all the time and having to rely on notes to ace a test. This nightmare to some people is a reality to student athletes.

As one of many travelling sports, men's soccer members had to find different ways to keep up in their classes when they were away. "I usually try to read the book the day before if I'm going to miss a class," senior **Derrick Zimmerman**, starting forward, said. Some team members took tests and did homework ahead of time while others preferred to get notes from classmates when they returned. Sophomore **Kevin Kelly**, starting forward, said, "I get a lot of my studying done on the road. There are not mandatory study halls, but we get our studying done."

Although the team did not travel that far, missing class and returning from trips late took a toll on their professors and work. "Most professors are helpful, but some give you a big hassle if you have to miss class, even if you are an athlete. I think that professors need to be a little bit more understanding of our situation," Kelly said. Zimmerman said that it was harder on younger students. Most members of the team said that they were allowed to make up tests and important papers a couple of days after they returned. "I try to keep focused on what I am doing during the season. I try to take a lighter course load during the season and make it up during second semester," junior **Sacha Drouin**, captain and starting goalie, said.

Before and after trips, soccer members relaxed and prepared. Drouin said that they did not overwhelm themselves and that they had good study habits. "It is usually up to you how much you study and what you do. We have different study habits. Some of us work on the road and some of us wait 'til we get back. It depends on the person," Zimmerman said.

1998

Anchored by five stellar seniors and an excellent group of underclassmen, the **1998** squad finished with an 11-4-3 record and the Big South regular season title. The seniors included **Troy Washington, Jason Gvozdas, Michael Ginsburg, Sacha Drouin**, and **Angel Cardozo**. The team defeated Virginia Tech in an early away match, 2-1, to retain the "New River Rock" for the second year. In the Big South post-season tournament, the team lost in the semi-finals to the University of South Alabama, 2-1. Both teams struggled to score for over 75-minutes and then all three goals dropped. South Alabama scored first in the 77th and Radford returned the favor in the 82nd. **Bill Castillo** played a ball from midfield down

1998 Jason Gvozdas

the left side to **Troy Washington**. Washington beat his defender at the end line, then fed a perfect pass to the foot of **Nick Butcher**, who scored the tying goal. It looked like the game was going into overtime, but South Alabama scored just two minutes later and that goal proved to be the winner. Coach Smith was honored as Big South Coach of the Year.

1999

After an extremely difficult regular season of 2-10-4, which did include a 4-1 win over Virginia Tech to retain the "New River Rock" for the third straight year, the **1999** post-season ended in spectacular fashion.

1999 Team with The New River Rock

The Radford University men's soccer team won the 1999 Big South Conference tournament championship by defeating Liberty. The game was scoreless at the end of regulation and four overtime periods. Radford then prevailed, 4-3, on penalty kicks. With this championship, ***for the first time in school history, the 1999 Radford University Men's Soccer Team gained automatic entry to the NCAA Division I***

national tournament. In the first round, the team would bow out, losing to #6 Furman, 1-0, but the history had been made and the showing was most admirable.

Scott Hance scored the game-winning goal and sixth-seeded Radford stunned top-seeded Liberty, 4-3 in penalty kicks, to claim the 1999 Big South Men's Soccer Tournament crown hosted by Coastal Carolina. With the win, the Highlanders advanced to their first-ever NCAA Tournament, where they took on Southern Conference Champion Furman, in a play-in game. The match with Liberty, which was played at Coastal Carolina Soccer Stadium, officially ended in a 0-0 tie after 150 minutes, 90-minutes of regulation and four, 15-minute, overtime periods. Radford's **Jonathan Frias** opened the shootout by putting the ball into the bottom-left corner. Liberty then tied. Following **Ryan Caton's** goal to the top-right corner for Radford, Liberty then hit the frame, giving the Highlanders a 2-1 advantage with three kicks remaining for both teams.

T.J. Rolfing and Liberty exchanged goals before the Highlander's **Chris Waltz's** attempt sailed high. Liberty then tied the kicks, 3-3, in the bottom of the fourth round. Hance's goal into the bottom-right corner proved to be the difference-maker as Liberty then hit the left post in the fifth and final round before sudden-death PKs, giving the Highlanders the win. The 150 minutes of play was just as even as the shootout as Liberty finished with a 14-13 edge in shots. Both teams had many chances to score, but the goalkeepers turned in solid performances. Radford's **Greg Anderson**, who made five saves, was named the tournament's Most Valuable Player. Radford's 1999 team was the lowest seed to ever win a Big South Conference Tournament in any sport up to this point.

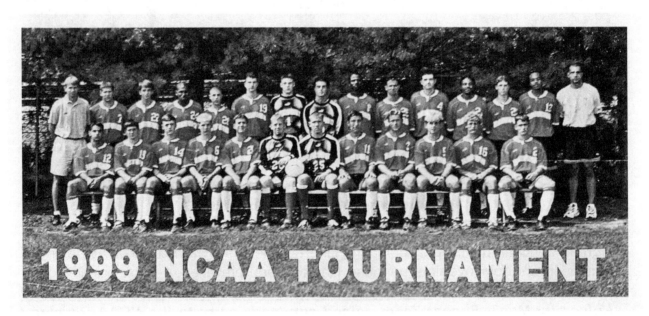

2000

The Radford men's soccer team succeeded in winning their second straight Big South Conference Tournament Championship in **2000**. They beat Elon in the final, 2-0. As a result, **the 2000 *Radford University Men's Soccer Team returned to the NCAA tournament for the second year in a row***. The young team, with only three seniors, proved to their critics that they had the dedication to win this title. "It felt good to win the crown this year, because a lot of our opponents thought we shouldn't have won last year," said senior and team captain **Scott Hance**. Winning this title meant a great deal to this team, as part of true resilience. The team had gone into overtime eight times, with six of those games ending in victories. Senior **Jonathan Frias**, the other team captain, was named the Big South Tournament MVP. Both Hance and Frias were named to the all-tournament team, as well as junior **Ryan Caton**, and sophomores **Geraldo Hernandez**, **T.J. Rolfing** and **Mike von Essen**. Unfortunately, the team would again bow out in the first-round the NCAA's, losing again to Furman, this time 2-0, and finish the season at 12-10-0.

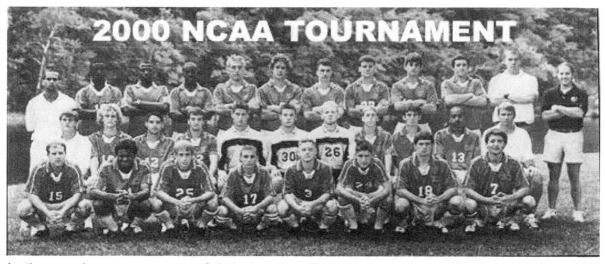

In the regular season, one of the wins was October 4 when the team upset #5-ranked Duke, 3-2, snapping a 25-game home regular season win streak for the Blue Devils. Another was a 2-0 victory over Virginia Tech in early September, allowing the team to capture the "New River Rock" for the fourth year in a row. Against Elon, Radford scored the game's first goal in the 9th minute when **Jonathan Hooker** played a ball into the middle of the box to **T.J. Rolfing**, who settled the pass and blasted a shot past the Elon goalkeeper from about 10 yards out. The Highlanders extended their advantage prior to intermission when **Jonathan Frias** headed home a **Mike Von Essen** corner kick with just over 10-minutes to play in the opening frame. Elon, which attempted six of its seven shots in the second half, failed to put a shot on frame as Radford's **Andrew**

Essey recorded his second shutout of the season without having to make a save. The Highlanders finished with a 16-6 advantage in shots and a 6-3 margin in corner kicks.

2001

A difficult season in **2001**, concluding with an overall record of 4-14-0, which included a lot of close games, was capped by a frustrating 1-0 loss to Coastal Carolina in the quarterfinals of the Big South tournament. The season featured an interesting pair of back-to-back games against Elon and Alabama A&M. "RU was victorious over Elon with a score of 1-0 to remain undefeated in the Big South Conference. The Highlanders were not as lucky as they were the day before, as a tough Alabama A&M team defeated RU, 3-0. RU celebrated homecoming Saturday sneaking by a BSC-winless Elon team. Conference leader goal scorer **T.J. Rolfing** notched his sixth goal of the season with only 24-seconds left in the first half. Goalkeeper **Andrew Essey** made one save and gained his second shutout of the season. Twenty hours later, RU came out to the Dedmon Center Stadium to face Alabama A&M in very sloppy weather." Essey played the first half and freshman **Harper Thornson** played the second half in goal. "They were very quick," freshman defender **Adam Pahl** commented, "probably the fastest we've seen all year." A loss to Liberty, 2-1, late in the season sent Radford into the Big South tournament as the fifth seed. Junior captain **Jon Fosu** scored the lone goal.

Senior **Ryan Caton** summarized his years at RU, stating, "The word pride reflects the type of person you are. Pride is knowing that whatever you did, you gave it your best and you did it for others." He also stated that he gained a considerable amount of experience in friendships, opportunities, challenges, rewards, and failures. Caton says that this will allow him "to grow as an individual and develop the type of work ethics and foundation." Caton said his most memorable moment was from his freshman year. "We were playing at home in our last conference game of the regular season. We were undefeated

2001 Ryan Caton

going into the game against Coastal Carolina and if we won, we would get a first-round bye in the conference tournament. I hadn't played the entire game and I came in there with thirty minutes left in the game and scored the tying and winning goals. It was the first time I really contributed to the team's success with results and it gave me a lot of confidence from then on." Caton gives this advice if you plan on trying out for soccer or any other sports: "First do it because you love it. Because if you want to become a great player then you need to be able to sacrifice and put in the effort aside from practices and games. You can only do that if your heart is truly in it."

2002

Despite a number of losses during the regular season, the **2002** team ended up with a 3-3-1 record in the Big South and a 4-3 quarter-final win against UNC-Asheville in the Big South Tournament. This propelled them to a tough semi-final loss to number-one-ranked Winthrop, 4-3, in overtime. In the regular season, the team defeated Virginia Tech and Tech's new head coach, 2-0. The season ended with a disappointing overall record of 7-12-1. In the middle, a six-game losing streak started to show promise with two, one-goal drops. The first of these was to Liberty University, 2-1, with the lone goal being scored by **Chris Waltz**. Radford's **Harper Thorsen** was a stalwart in goal. The second was to Birmingham Southern, 4-3. RU's **Mike Von Essen** led the Highlander offensive attack with two goals, the first coming from 20-yards out at the 16:22 mark and the second following at 24:35. The Highlanders went into halftime with a 2-1 lead and, just 13 seconds after the break, took it to 3-1. **T.J. Rolfing** picked off a BSC pass and set up **Jonathan Hooker** for his first goal of the season. Unfortunately, this game was followed by a 7-6 barn-burner, losing to Winthrop. **T.J. Rolfing**, **Erick Sokolik**, **Chris Waltz**, **Andres Hernandez**, **Mike Von Essen**, and **Jonathan Hooker** were all involved in the offensive action but needed even more goals. The losing streak mercifully came to an end with a 3-0 win over High Point.

This was followed by a win in the last game of the regular season, over UNC-Asheville, 3-1, that moved the Highlanders to fourth place and the Bulldogs to fifth in the Big South. **T.J. Rolfing**, **Chris Waltz** and **Mike Winstead** scored for Radford. Rolfing's goal marked his 15th of the year and his 41st all-time. The goal moved him up to sole possession of third place in career goals for RU. The top two leaders remained Dante Washington (82) and Ian Spooner (58). "T.J. is the epitome of a true student-athlete," Coach Spencer Smith said. "He's been a great example of our soccer program. I really couldn't be happier for him." Radford promptly turned around and had to face UNC-Asheville again in the Big South tournament, and avoided a revenge scenario. In the semi, Rolfing scored first on a Sokolik assist in the 11th minute. The Eagles tied the game in the 25th minute and went ahead right after halftime. Rolfing would score again in the 66th minute and senior **Geraldo Hernandez** scored off a rebound to put the Highlanders ahead, 3-2, in the 74th. Winthrop tied the game three minutes later and got the winner in OT.

From 1995 to 2002, Radford would defeat Virginia Tech six times over the eight-year span, including four-straight, from 1997 to 2000. So, **what became of The New River Rock?** After Coach Jerry Cheynet was replaced at Tech following the 2001 season, and RU won again in 2002, it seems that the Hokie's new coach conveniently opted to ignore the whole rock thing. Rumor has it that he considered it to be silly. One wag suggested that The Rock may be in someone's garden or that it was returned to the river. Anyway, a formal request was made to Tech in 2024 to see if they could find the erstwhile stone and, if they did, to return it to Radford University to be updated and permanently retired to a place of honor and respect. (And, anyway, Radford had won again in 2023...)

2003

2003 saw the Highlanders finish with a final, overall record of 8-9-2, 2-4-1 in the Big South. This included statement wins over NC State, 1-0, Virginia Tech, 5-1, George Washington University, 4-2, and Delaware, 2-1. In the last game of the regular season, Radford met Birmingham-Southern and tied 3-3 in overtime on a Sunday at home. Ironically, in the Big South Tournament quarterfinals, Birmingham-Southern had to return to Radford the following Thursday. The Panthers should have been exhausted, but wound up winning, 2-1. This would be the last game for senior goalkeeper **Andrew Essey**. The team would see the arrival of **Omar Zinoveev**, originally from Uruguay, who transferred from Virginia Intermont where he had been an NAIA honorable mention for each of his two years there as a goalkeeper. In addition, **Patrick Colas**, originally from France, arrived as a freshman forward, having scored eight goals with two assists in 15 games in his last season with the Stade Rennes FC club.

2003 Andrew Essey

PATRICK D. CUPP MEMORIAL STADIUM

The Patrick D. Cupp Memorial Stadium changed soccer forever at Radford University. Dedicated on August 27, 2003, Cupp Stadium has a seating capacity for 5,000 spectators and is the largest soccer facility in the Big South Conference. In addition to a full-sized soccer field, the complex includes four large locker rooms, an on-site athletic training room, and a dedicated laundry room that highlight the amenities for student-athletes and teams. It also includes a large, fully functional press box with dedicated storage and restrooms, standard phone lines, and wireless and hard-wired internet connections to serve all possible media needs. In addition, the press box houses the stadium's leading-edge scoreboard controls and sound system.

"Without question, Patrick D. Cupp Stadium is the finest soccer stadium in the Big South Conference and one of the top venues in the nation. It has all the amenities and it's an excellent place to get the full soccer experience whether you are a player or a fan." – Rich Posipanko, Head Soccer Coach, Winthrop University

The addition of Cupp Stadium created a soccer complex that rivals any college or university in the Commonwealth of Virginia. Because the addition of Cupp Stadium allowed the men to use the Dedmon field for practices, the new game field and facilities created a complex that competes with any of those in the country. The field surface is a Bermuda blend, natural grass field. A state-of-the-art drainage system was added to assist in keeping the field in top shape year-round. The stadium and its facilities are so inviting that the Virginia High School League regularly holds championships there.

The Patrick D. Cupp Memorial Stadium was a gift of Patrick "Pat" Cupp and his wife Sandra "Sandy" Cupp. Pat Cupp (1940 – 2000) was a native of southwest Virginia and, after getting his start with his father, built houses in Blacksburg and then moved on to real estate management and development. Sandy Cupp was equally involved in real estate and property management. Together, they were long-time donors to Radford University, both for athletics and business education.

Pat and Sandy Cupp

2004

The highlight of the **2004** season came in October as the RU men's soccer team enjoyed a significant four-game winning streak. The Highlanders proceeded to defeat Coastal Carolina, 2-1; High Point, 1-0; Winthrop, 2-1; and George Mason, 2-1. **Patrick Colas** of Rennes, France, scored in the 50th minute to lift host Radford over High Point. The lone goal of the game came when the Highlanders' **Andres Hernandez** served a pass into the box to Colas, who fired a shot into the back of the net. High Point had two particularly challenging one-on-one situations in the first half where RU goalkeeper **Omar Zinoveev** came out and made big saves. RU freshman **David Stannard** was named the Big South player of the week after scoring two unassisted, game-winning goals against both Winthrop and Mason. The team remained undefeated over five games with a 1-1 tie against Appalachian State. The streak would come to an end with a prescient 1-0 loss to Liberty University. The wins over Coastal, High Point, and

2004 Omar Zinoveev

Winthrop were all in the Big South and helped propel the team to the quarter-finals of the Big South Tournament at the end of the season. In Birmingham, Alabama, they would be ousted by a 2-1 loss to Liberty. **Jon Smith** scored the only goal for the Highlanders. The season ended with an overall record of 7-6-4, 3-3-1 in the Big South. Colas, Stannard, and Zinoveev were all honored before the game with Liberty. Colas received the Big South 2004 Men's Soccer Scholar Athlete of the year award. Stannard was named to the All-Freshman team and Zinoveev was named First Team All-Conference.

2005 saw a strong start, with wins over Mount St. Mary's, 1-0, and High Point, 2-0. This was followed by a gap of three losses in four games. Then came the highlight of the season with five-straight wins. These included excellent offensive and defensive efforts all-around, with victories over Elon, 1-0; VMI, 4-0; Coastal Carolina, 2-1; UNC-Asheville, 3-1; and, Birmingham-Southern, 2-1. Although positioned well in the Big South, hopes were dashed when RU lost the next five games in a row. The team then bowed out in the first game of the tournament, losing to VMI, 2-1. The season ended with an overall record of 8-9, 5-2 in the Big South. **Patrick Colas** finished the season as the points leader with 6 goals and 2 assists. **Ramon Negron** had a hat trick against High Point and 2 assists against VMI. **Omar Zinoveev** led the team in saves. Zinoveev, **Armando Romero** and **Taylor Rowe** were Big South First Team All-Conference. **Coach Spencer Smith went over the 100-win mark at Radford during this season**.

The Tartan, 11/16/2005: Despite seeing his Highlander soccer team lose in the first round of the Big south playoffs to VMI… it has been an overwhelmingly positive season for RU senior goalkeeper Omar Zinoveev. Zinoveev collected four shutouts on the season, two of which came on an impressive streak the Highs put on in mid-season when RU dispatched five straight Big South rivals. "I love playing soccer for Radford," said Zinoveev. "To be able to go study then play a sport, a competitive sport, it's what I like. I can't really imagine myself in school without playing a sport." The 5-foot, 10-inch Zinoveev not only represents a keeper on the field, he also represents his birth country, Uruguay.

"It's really good because I like soccer a lot and what's better than getting your scholarship here and playing soccer," said Zinoveev. "I'm really happy I came here especially at Radford because I like Radford a lot, I like the team and the coaches and the school in general." "I also think Americans have really good goalkeepers," Zinoveev added. "I brought something new here and also learned something from them here. Everywhere you go you've got something to learn." Head Coach Spencer Smith couldn't compliment his keeper more this season. "He understands the game at a higher level than most college players. It's great to have him on the team," Smith noted after a 3-1 victory over UNC-Asheville where the RU defense allowed a late goal to spoil what could have been a sixth shoutout for the Uruguay native.

2005 – Devon Cooley

"I played some of the field in the past and that's why I can see some things that some other keepers might not see," Zinoveev added. "Even when I'm back there, I still try to help my team by trying to get my offense going. A lot of other keepers just play back and play defense." The Highs' five-game winning streak over conference rivals Elon, VMI, Coastal Carolina, UNC-Asheville and Birmingham Southern was part of the first 4-0 in-conference start for Radford since 1998. The contest against VMI was perhaps the most impressive when the Highs won 4-0 while attempting 15 shots and holding the Keydets to seven shots, most of which came late in the second half when RU dropped back to play defense and run out the clock.

Zinoveev selected a different team as the Highs' best opponent, however. "Birmingham Southern was the best because we had never beat them and lost the year before twice and we killed them," said Zinoveev. "They finished first in the conference but we killed them and that shows we were really good this season." As for his plans beyond Radford, Zinoveev likely won't be seen on the soccer field. "I've got a couple of job offerings after Radford, and I'll miss soccer a lot."

2006

The **2006** campaign saw a roller-coaster ride of alternating wins, losses, and ties, ending with a very promising regular-season victory over High Point, 4-0. This propelled the team to the number-three seed going into the Big South Tournament, facing the number-sixth seed... High Point. Both games were at Radford, but High Point was better prepared the second time around. The Highlanders scored first, roughly midway through the first half, on a goal by **Davorin Husadzinovic**. High Point scored with approximately 15-minutes remaining to tie the game, 1-1, which held to the end of regulation. RU goalkeeper **Zach Roszel** stayed clean for the half and the game remained tied at the end of triple-overtime. The game then went to penalty kicks, with High Point advancing, 3-2. The regular season featured statement wins over Jacksonville, 2-1 in overtime, Coastal Carolina, 5-2, and the University of Charleston, 2-0. The season ended with an overall record of 8-6-4.

In mid-October, goalkeeper **Zach Roszel** posted two shutouts, 0-0 against Longwood, and 2-0 over the University of Charleston. At that point Roszel, a sophomore, had four shutouts on the year, tying last year's team total. "I have to give credit to the defense more than anything," Roszel said. "Everyone is coming up big on defense." The RU keeper only faced four shots in the match against UC, but came up with three big saves to keep the Golden Eagles from making a comeback. Juniors **Jeremy Delpino** and **Davorin Husadzinovic** scored for the Highlanders with **Devan Cooley** getting the assist on Delpino's goal. Radford was also pleased to see the return of **Ramon "Kike" Negron** in the UC game. He saw action in a limited role for the first time after suffering a knee injury three weeks earlier. This game was followed by a 1-1 in-conference tie with Big-South-leading

2006 - Paul Caruso

Winthrop. The Highlander goal was scored by Delpino on an attempted pass to Negron but, instead, the ball curved into the net. Radford ended the regular season with the 4-0 victory over High Point. Negron scored twice while Husadzinovic and freshman **Justin Zimmer** had a goal apiece. Together with Roszel, **Jonathan Smith** and **Taylor Rowe**, both seniors, lead a stout defense.

2007

The Radford men's team always enjoyed and benefitted from the home-team advantage forged at Cupp. **2007** would be no exception with a final record of 6-1 at home during the season. The season started with mixed results, going 3 and 5 during the first eight games. The following seven games would change the math, however, with the Highlanders knocking out four straight wins, then two more, sandwiching a 2-1 loss to Winthrop away. A 1-0 loss to Coastal ended the regular season but set the tone for the Big South tournament. In the quarter-final round, the team advanced by defeating VMI, 2-0. In the semifinal, they had their rematch with Coastal and beat them convincingly, 3-1. Unfortunately, in the final, Liberty won, 2-1, in an extremely hard-fought battle, leaving RU as the runner-up.

2007 Davorin Husadzinovic

The regular season, however, included a statement win over North Carolina State University. *October 17, 2007 Tartan*: The Highs were ready to score against the Wolfpack on Saturday, Oct. 6. They found the net a mere 45 seconds into the game. RU senior **Davorin Husadzinovic** received the ball from fellow senior **Tyler Leveski** and then rocketed it past the Wolfpack's goalkeeper, giving RU a quick lead. The defense held the Wolfpack at bay; NC State couldn't find the net until the 70th minute when they finally sneaked past RU's defense. They had a few more chances to score but couldn't find the net again. Near the end of the game, NC State had a free kick of which the RU defense was able to take control. RU senior **Franklin Ehimbi** sent the ball to Husadzinovic, who once again scored for the Highs, giving RU the victory, 2-1. NC State managed to lead the game in shots, 14-12. RU junior goalkeeper **Zach Roszel** recorded five saves. The victory over the Wolfpack signifies Head Coach Spencer Smith's sixth win over a different ACC team. The game was also the Highs' second win in a row, coming off their victory against California State-Bakersfield.

Radford made it three in a row with a victory over UNC-Asheville. In the 26th minute, RU freshman **James Leith** slipped the ball to Husadzinovic who put RU on the board.

Ten minutes later **Brendan Shaffer** passed the ball to **Will Thomsen**, who scored his first goal of the season, resulting in a 2-0 score at halftime that held up for the game.

In the Big South tournament, against VMI **Justin Zimmer** scored the first goal and Husadzinovic had the second. In the semi-final, the Highlanders upset Coastal by first taking a 2-0 lead with goals from freshman **Josh McCrary** and senior Davorin Husadzinovic. The lead held until the 72nd minute as Coastal tried to mount a comeback. The icing goal was then scored by James Leith. In the final, Radford's first appearance in the championship game since 2000, the game started strong for the Highlanders when McCrary scored just seven minutes in. Unfortunately, the team seemed to lose concentration for a brief period late in the second half, allowed two goals, and couldn't score again.

2008

Coach Smith characterized **2008** as a season where his group lacked chemistry. His team finished 7-10-2 overall and 3-4 in Big South action. Radford closed out the season without finding the win column, and scoring just twice, in a six-game span. Key veterans **Brendan Shaffer** and **Justin Zimmer** held forth. Shaffer played every minute of every match as a central defender. Despite having a cast on his left arm the entire season, he helped the defense to a league-best goals-against average. Zimmer scored two goals and assisted on four while also starting and playing in all 19 games. Zimmer was an all-conference second-team selection and a Big South Player of the Week. Big South Freshman of the Year **Iyiola Awosika** began his college career with a bang by scoring six times, but the Highlander's ultimate leading scorer's production dropped off as the season

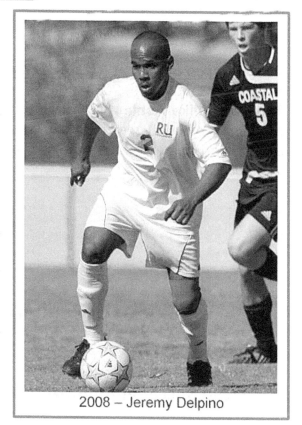

2008 – Jeremy Delpino

progressed. "He was a marked man," Smith said, "and when he was slowed down, we couldn't find the net." The team exited the Big South tournament in the first round.

Highlights included Zimmer's golden goal in the fifth minute of overtime against Appalachian State and a pair of goals by **Jeremy Delpino** to give Radford a 3-1 victory over Presbyterian. This win pushed Radford's school-record home winning streak to 11 games and its Big South home unbeaten string to nine. Another was a 1-1 tie with Clemson which featured an Awosika goal. The National Soccer Coaches Association of America recognized Radford for the second straight year as one of its 2008 Team Academic Award winners, an honor given to programs with a team grade point average of 3.0 or better. Among men's programs, Radford was one of just two Big South institutions, one of 35 NCAA Division I teams, and one of 106 four-year colleges across the country, to earn the distinction in 2008. "This is a great honor for our team," said head coach Spencer Smith. "Our guys continue to show a commitment in the classroom and pride themselves in being quality student-athletes." The 2008 season marked the second straight year and second time overall that Radford has earned the recognition under Smith. In January, 2009, the team earned the Big South Sportsmanship Award for the 2008 season.

The **"*I Played Soccer at Radford University*"** Facebook page was created by **Justin Bryant** on January 19, 2009. It becomes an instant hit with **Cesar Collantes**, **Laura Turk**, and **Mike Ashley**, in particular. Representing both the men's and women's programs, over 60 men's soccer alumni have posted, commented, or otherwise actively participated on the page, including **Kathy Lillard**, on behalf of Tom "I don't do '*Nosebook*'" Lillard.

I Played Soccer at Radford University

Public group · 293 members

2009

In **2009**, with 11 newcomers joining the squad, Smith decided to ask his veterans to become "big brothers" to the underclassmen, "just to help the new guys take care of some of the little things that might be taken for granted." "It's things like getting things moved into a room, getting a bank account set up," he said, "basically just helping these guys get settled in." The season would be a struggle, but the highlight came in a win over Virginia Tech at home in early October. Freshman **James Jordan** put Radford on the board with a rocket from 25-yards out to tie the match at 1-1 in the 55th minute. Junior **James Leith** collected a Tech defender's failed clearance and scored in the 78th minute.   Redshirt sophomore **Aldo Macias**, netted his first career goal off a pass from **Iyiola Awosika** in the 84th to ice the contest. Goalkeeper

Spencer Smith Coaching

Ryan Taylor made a pair of excellent saves at the end to preserve the win.   In September, Senior **Justin Zimmer** scored the 300th goal in program history in a 1-0 win over East Tennessee State University. The Big South tournament saw a wild opening-game win, 4-3, over High Point, but ended with a 2-0 loss to Liberty in the semi-final. The season concluded with an overall record of 5-9-3.

THE JOHN HARVES RADFORD UNIVERSITY MEN'S SOCCER FUND

In October 2009, former coach **John Harves** was honored, on the 30th Anniversary of his final season, with the establishment of the John Harves Radford University Men's Soccer Fund. **This permanent endowment was created by Will Iandolo and the initial funding came from former teammates who had played for Harves**. This is a standing capital fund. Only the earnings from the fund are available for scholarships or operations. *Anyone may donate to the fund at any time, by check or online, to the Radford University Foundation, Inc. Please indicate on the form that the contribution is for the "John Harves Men's Soccer Fund."*

This fund has the potential to help change the lives of dozens of RU student-athletes each year. Here is more detailed information about how you may donate to the RU Men's Soccer Fund:

GIVE A GIFT THAT KEEPS ON GIVING:

PLEASE SUPPORT THE RADFORD MEN'S SOCCER PROGRAM

by making a generous donation to the

JOHN HARVES RADFORD UNIVERSITY MEN'S SOCCER FUND

Credit card contributions may be made on-line: Visit **https://connect.radford.edu/together-give** Using the "Other (please specify)" selection, designate your gift to the "John Harves Soccer Fund"

Fund: Other (please specify) ⌄

Other (please specify): John Harves Soccer Fund

To donate by check, please mail your check to:
Radford University Foundation, Inc.
PO Box 6893
Radford, VA 24142

	1001
Your name Street address City, State ZIP	Date: _____

PAY TO THE ORDER OF __Radford University Foundation, Inc.__

_____ DOLLARS

MEMO __John Harves Soccer Fund__

1234567

> **EDITOR'S NOTE:** This permanent endowment fund was established by Will Iandolo in 2009, in honor of John Harves' groundbreaking, tireless, and enthusiastic contributions to RU's soccer program. The initial funding came from Iandolo and other former teammates who had played for Harves. Every donation goes into the endowment's capital fund. (Of course, neither Will nor John receive a penny from these funds.) To ensure the ongoing viability of the fund, only the *earnings* are available for use in the men's soccer program. RU Men's Soccer and *especially the students/players* appreciate your financial support!
>
> *Editor's P.S.: This book is another of the countless significant examples of John's substantial and indefatigable contributions to RU soccer and to the many people who have been a part of this program. You could not imagine -- or maybe you can! -- the many months and the many, many hundreds of hours he has tirelessly worked to bring this project to completion. To truly give a gift that keeps on giving, please consider making a generous contribution to this fund, to help change the lives of dozens of these student-athletes each year for many years to come. If you can, make it an annual event!*

At the 2009 recognition, the team provided a 3-1 win over Virginia Tech. Former Coach Harves indicated that he really appreciated the win, "In my time as coach, the only team that beat us all three years was Tech. It was really frustrating for me. It seemed like Coach Cheynet had my number."

Radford's Soccer Programs Earn
NSCAA Team Academic Award

RU Media Release, 11/30/2009 – "Radford University's soccer programs were recently recognized by the National Soccer Coaches Association of America (NSCAA) as one of 97 institutions, nationwide, to have **both its men's and women's teams earn the organization's team academic award.** To achieve the honor, a team has to post a cumulative grade point average of 3.0 or higher. <u>**Radford was one of two Big South institutions and the only school in Virginia to have both its men's and women's teams recognized.**</u> All collegiate programs, at all levels, were considered for NSCAA team honors. For the men's program, it was ***the third consecutive season*** that the Highlanders were recognized by the NSCAA, the only team in the Big South to achieve that standard. Radford's team GPA was 3.24, the eighth-highest in all of Division I.

<u>**'This a great accomplishment for our players and program,' men's head coach Spencer Smith said.**</u> **'It is nice to see that we continue to put forth the effort in the classroom. This is an excellent group of young men who have worked hard for this award while displaying the true meaning of student-athlete.'"**

In 2009, **<u>Dante Washington's Jersey Number 9 was permanently retired</u>**. In his honor, the number will never be assigned again.

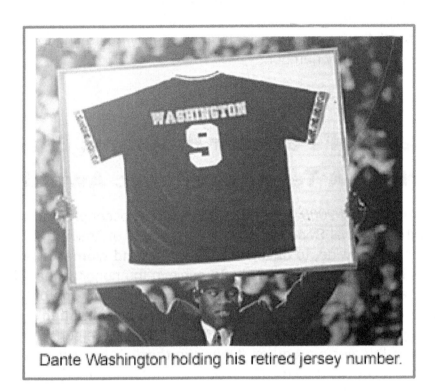

Dante Washington holding his retired jersey number.

At the end of the 2009 season, Coach Smith moved on to become the women's head coach at Winthrop University. A search committee then found **Marc Reeves**.

Marc Reeves Era (2010 – 2016)

7 Seasons

Overall Record: 75-43-20 (.616) - Big South: 42-15-6 (.714)

Coach Marc Reeves

- 2010 7-9-3; Big South: 4-3-1
    Big South Tournament Semifinals

- 2011 9-8-2; Big South: 4-4-1
    Big South Tournament Quarterfinals

- 2012 10-6-4; Big South: 7-2-1
    Big South Tournament Semifinals

- 2013 9-7-4; Big South: 5-3-2
    Big South Tournament Semifinals

- 2014 12-5-3; Big South: 8-1-0
    Big South Regular Season Champion
    Big South Tournament Finalist
    Big South Coach of the Year

- 2015 14-4-2; Big South: 7-1
    Big South Regular Season Champion
    Big South Tournament Semifinals
    NCAA Tournament Appearance (At-Large Bid)

- 2016 14-4-2; Big South: 7-1-0
    Big South Regular Season Champion
    Big South Tournament Champion
    NCAA Tournament Appearance
    Big South Coach of the Year

Assistant Coaches: Maciej Sliwinski, Brian Cronin, Riley Butler, Adam Miller, Mike Handlin, Luis Grande, Scott Bennett, Adam Miller

Radford University named **Marc Reeves,** former associate head men's soccer coach at St. John's, to its head men's soccer coaching position on Monday, March 22, 2010.

Reeves came to Radford after having spent 11 seasons at St. John's, the last four as the program's associate head coach. "I'm unbelievably excited about the opportunity to lead the Radford men's soccer program," Reeves said. "I'd like to thank President [Penelope] Kyle, Robert Lineburg and the members of the search committee. It's a great opportunity, and I can't wait to get to work as soon as possible." Reeves became the seventh head coach in Radford men's soccer history. "We are thrilled to have Marc Reeves as our new head men's soccer coach," Athletic Director Robert Lineburg said. "Marc has a great background, having played a huge role in the tremendous success of St. John's University soccer, one of the premier programs in America. There is no doubt in my mind that with Marc's leadership that the future is extremely bright for Radford University soccer."

The Gillingham Dorset, England, native had been part of an extraordinary run of success at the Queens, N.Y. school. The Red Storm reached the NCAA Tournament Round of 16 in eight of his 11 seasons, including a national championship appearance in 2003, trips to the national semifinals in 2001 and 2008, and four national quarterfinal appearances (2001, 2003, 2004, 2008). In 2009, the Red Storm finished 9-3-9 (6-1-4, Big East), winning the Big East Tournament title on a penalty kick shootout over Notre Dame and getting a NCAA Tournament first-round bye. St. John's was ranked nationally as high as 14th in 2009. Following a 19-3-3 campaign and an NCAA Tournament appearance in 2008, Reeves earned National Soccer Coaches Association of America (NSCAA) East Region Assistant Coach of the Year honors. Reeves was named the National Assistant Coach of the Year by Aflac in 2002, a season after helping guide the Red Storm to the national semifinal game.

As a midfielder with the Red Storm, Reeves was part of the 1998 squad that won the Big East Championship and advanced to the NCAA Elite Eight. St. John's won three Big East tournament championships and racked up at least 10 wins in nine of the 11 seasons during Reeves' tenure. The Red Storm had a No. 1 ranking for five consecutive weeks in 2002 and a No. 2 ranking during the 2005 season. In Reeves' first season as associate head coach in 2006, he helped lead St. John's on an ambassador tour to Vietnam that summer, becoming the first American sports team to visit the country following the Vietnam War. Reeves and the St. John's program took part in cultural experiences and provided volunteer work to impoverished areas while playing four games in Vietnam.

Reeves went on to earn a master's degree in secondary education and began his coaching career in 1999. Prior to arriving at St. John's, Reeves graduated from Brunel University (Middlesex, England) in 1997 with an upper second degree in sports science. Reeves has a USSF A National License and a NSCAA Advanced National Diploma. "I thought that there were a lot similarities between St. John's and Radford in terms of campus size, class size, and a small family-like athletic department, all things that are important to me," Reeves said. "I think the people are the important part. Listening to the search committee, I was very enlightened by their vision for Radford athletics and the men's soccer program."

When Marc Reeves arrived as the new Radford coach in 2010, the first thing he insisted upon was that he be called "**Reevo**."

"Reevo"

2010

In his first season at the helm in the Fall of **2010**, Marc Reeves guided the Highlander men's soccer team to a feat that had never been accomplished in the program's 35-year history. Along with ranking among National leaders in attendance, Reeves' 2010 club posted the first undefeated mark at home in school history. Among those triumphs were three shutouts and a pair of five-goal performances against league competition. Reeves' first season as a collegiate head coach featured significant improvements from previous years. Radford, which advanced to the semifinals of the Big South Tournament, posted two more wins than the year before, its first winning campaign in conference play since 2006, and the most goals scored in eight years.

Individually, four Highlanders, **Ayiola Awosika**, **James Leith**, **Luis Grande**, and **Bernardo Ulmo**, garnered all-conference honors, while Awosika and Leith also earned a spot on the all-state team. Reeves's program also excelled in the classroom, putting together the department's second highest GPA while collecting their fifth-straight NSCAA College Team Academic Award. Although 2010 would finish with an overall record of 7-9-3, it would be the only losing season of the Reeves era. In the Big South semifinal, High Point edged the Highlanders, 1-0, on a goal in the first half. Radford had a pair of good scoring opportunities in the second half. The first was on a free kick from just outside the box by **Mike Handlin**, stopped by an impressive save, and the second was by Ulmo that missed just wide.

In February, 2011, the team participated in its first _Polar Plunge_, garnering credit for community involvement and a little additional notice for bringing soccer balls to the event. The Polar Plunge raised money for the Special Olympics Virginia (SOVA).

Do you believe in Magic?

Maciej ("Magic") Sliwinski

At Radford, Assistant Coach Maciej ("Magic") Sliwinski connects with all aspects of the Radford University men's soccer program, with a special emphasis on recruiting and helping the team in various levels of instruction. Sliwinski, a former two-year assistant alongside Reeves at St. John's, was an assistant at Lafayette before joining the Radford staff in May of 2010. "Maciej is an enthusiastic young coach who I am excited to have on our men's soccer staff," Reeves said. "Maciej brings a variety of experiences, including recruiting, team preparation, camps and alumni communications. He worked under head coach Dr. Dave Masur, the 2008 Big East Coach of the Year, and with Reeves, who was named the NSCAA East Regional College Assistant Coach of the Year.

At Lafayette in 2009, Sliwinski helped the Leopards to a 10-7-2 overall record and a trip to the Patriot League semifinals. While at Lafayette, his duties included goalkeeper training – Sliwinski guided Phillip Nelson to Patriot League Goalie of the Year honors, along with a spot on the All-ECAC First Team and the NSCAA Mid-Atlantic Region Second Team. Sliwinski spent the two seasons prior to his arrival at Lafayette as an assistant at St. John's, where he assisted with multiple aspects of the program preparation. In 2008, the Red Storm earned an at-large bid to the NCAA Tournament and advanced to the national semifinals.

Sliwinski, a native of Poland, enjoyed a four-year playing career at Iona, where he was a two-year captain and was named to the MAAC All-Academic Team in all four of his seasons. He graduated in 2007 with a degree in finance. During his time at Iona, Sliwinski interned with the New York Red Bulls of MLS, with responsibilities in team operations and game preparation. In 2009, Sliwinski earned his master's degree in sports management from St. John's University.

Aldo Macias, October 12, 2012: "Along with the incorporation of Coach Reevo, the Radford team has had a new assistant coach since 2010. His name is Maciej (pronounced "Magic", so we'll just call him Magic for the rest of the blog) Sliwinski. Magic has been another phenomenal asset to the Radford men's soccer team since he first stepped into the Radford locker-room in 2010. He is a native of Poland and he received his college experience as a player at Iona University where he was a two-year captain. His college coaching experience prior to Radford came from being an assistant coach at St. John's and he was also an assistant coach for Lafayette University. If I could describe Magic as a coach with one phrase, I would say that he is a coach that wears his heart on his sleeve during practice and especially during games (just ask the referees during Radford's games). Just like Coach Reevo, Magic has been a great coach for Radford University's men's soccer team."

2011

2011 – Iyiola Awosika

2011, Marc Reeves' second year at the helm of RU Men's Soccer concluded with the program's first winning season in the last four years. An impressive one-third of Radford's regular season opponents (six teams) earned berths in the NCAA Tournament, including Elon (SoCon Champion, 5-1) and Stony Brook (America East Champion, 3-0), which the Highlanders defeated. Under Reeves' guidance, Radford bettered his first year's production by two goals (32) as senior **Iyiola Awosika** and sophomore **Luis Grande** ranked among conference leaders in goals and total points. In addition to his third all-league selection, Awosika finished his standout career ranked among the school's all-time leaders in goals, total points and penalty kicks converted. Fellow senior **Aldo Macias** and Grande joined Awosika on the all-league team earning second-team recognition, while **Dario Redondo** became the third player under Reeves (Grande, and **Bernardo Ulmo** preceded in 2010) voted to the all-freshman team. The Highlanders achieved only the

105

second winning season in ten years with this campaign. Awosika and **Brian Gwanzura** recorded hat tricks during their final season and **Chel Ho Kim Park** ranked 17th nationally in assists. After an eight-year break, Radford would again finally play the University of Virginia, giving them quite a scare, but losing 3-4.

2012

2012 Stephen Hudgens

In **2012**, Radford ran off its most impressive start to a Big South season in school history, remaining unbeaten in its first seven contests (6-0-1), which included a scoreless tie against nationally-ranked High Point. The Highlanders finished the league slate 7-2-1 and earned the No. 2 seed in the league tournament. The season was highlighted by an eight-game unbeaten streak that started with a 2-0 win over Campbell and ended with the tie against High Point. In between was a 1-1 tie with Elon, a 6-1 win over Gardner-Webb, a 3-0 win over Longwood, a 3-1 win over Presbyterian, a 2-0 win over VMI and a 2-1 win against UNC-Asheville.

In the regular season finale, the Highlanders took on the Winthrop Eagles. In arguably their most important match of the season, RU was able to pull off a 2-0 victory that secured a second-place seed in the Big South Conference Tournament. Sophomore **Stephen Hudgens** provided the first goal for the team in the 36th minute for his first collegiate goal. 15-minutes after halftime, freshman defender **Jamie Summers** delivered a long ball down the right side to freshman midfielder **Lucas Diniz**. After having to win the ball between two defenders, Diniz was able to get a shot off which the goalkeeper was able to block, but not secure. Diniz followed-up and put the ball in the net.

In the tournament, Radford defeated Gardner-Webb, 2-0, with **Joe Mayer** scoring one goal and assisting on the other, only to find themselves facing Winthrop again. Unfortunately, the team dropped this one to the Eagles, 1-2, in overtime. Junior midfielder **Bernardo Ulmo** recorded his 11th goal of the season in just the second minute of the game. Winthrop responded 18-minutes later and the deadlock remained through full time. Just three minutes into extra time, the Eagles scored and the differential held to the end. RU finished the season with an overall record of 10-6-4, which included a 1-0 opener over Wake Forest and 4-2 victory over Adelphi to win the "Flash Gordon Motors Invitation" in High Point, NC. The Highs offense was ranked in the top-50 nationally out of 202 teams.

Five members of the team earned All-Big South honors. **Ryan Taylor** and Bernardo Ulmo were named to the first team. **Dario Redondo** earned second team honors, and **Jannik Eckenrode** and **Jamie Summers** picked up all-freshman selections. Taylor and Ulmo were also selected to the NSCAA Division 1 Men's All-South Atlantic region team, with Taylor earning second-team honors and Ulmo appointed to the third team. As a unit, the team was recognized as national scholars for the sixth-straight year.

The *Radford Men's Soccer* official Facebook page kicked off in August 2012. It now has over 1,600 followers (www.facebook.com/RadfordMSOC/). The Radford University *#9 Soccer Scarf* also debuted at this time.

The Radford University #9 Soccer Scarf

2013

Reeves continued to build a highly respected and formidable program in **2013.** The team finished 9-7-4 and set benchmarks in building the program at the same time, including the third year in a row with at least nine wins. The Highlanders pushed to the Big South semifinals and fell to eventual champion and nationally-ranked Coastal Carolina, 3-2. For the seventh straight year, and each of the four under Reeves, the Radford men's soccer team was named an NSCAA National Scholar Award winner. For the second-straight season, RU advanced to the semifinals of the Big South Tournament. The men's soccer team made a late-season push to better its position in the conference standings. After a tight 1-0 setback at No. 8 Coastal Carolina, Radford went 5-1-1 over its next seven contests. Following its thrilling 1-0 triumph in overtime at No. 4 seed Gardner-Webb, the Highlanders challenged top-seeded Coastal Carolina in the semifinals.

The Chanticleers, ranked 22nd in the nation at the time, took Radford's best shot as the Highlanders built a 2-0 lead with 44 minutes to go in the semifinal meeting. Unfortunately, Coastal was able to mount a comeback by tallying three goals during the final 35 minutes to derail Radford's upset bid. **Bernardo Ulmo**, who charted a team-best eight goals, earned All-Big South first team honors. The senior forward ended his career with 23 goals, which were 10th all-time in program history. He was also an all-academic recipient, carrying a 3.4 GPA as a double major in management and finance. Anchoring the Highlanders' backline all season, **Jo Vetle Rimstad** was named to the Big South second team and all-freshman team, while **Matt Janssen** earned honorable mention. Combined, the duo led a Radford defensive unit that yielded only 1.06 goals per game and produced five shutouts.

The Spring saw another *Polar Plunge* and **Ryan Taylor** signed a professional contract with the Richmond Kickers.

2013 Polar Plunge

2014

A strong <u>2014</u> season by the Highlanders earned Reeves 2014 Big South Coach of the Year honors, after Radford posted a 12-5-3 overall record and an 8-1-0 mark in conference play, earning the regular season championship. It was the fourth straight winning season for the Highlanders, which had not been done in nearly 20 years. The Highlanders won seven straight games at one point, which at that time was the longest winning streak in the nation. The team also posted an 11-game unbeaten streak, which is the longest single-season streak as a member of the Big South in school history. Radford earned a national ranking as high as No. 20 during the 2014 campaign. After a three-year break, Radford played eventual NCAA National Champion University of Virginia, losing 0-3. The Highlanders boasted nine players honored by the Big South in the postseason, and **Jo Vetle Rimstad** earned all-region honors. **Aitor Pouseu Blanco** was named VaSID Rookie of the Year for the state of Virginia.

2014 – Aitor Pouseu Blanco

Radford University Men's Soccer Media Release, 12/2/2014: HIGHLANDERS TURN MIX OF EXPERIENCE, YOUTH, AND DEPTH INTO HISTORIC SEASON

"From a team that began the season in August with a number of questions to be answered replacing seven seniors from 2013, to a remarkable campaign in 2014 that turned the season into one of the most historic runs in Radford soccer history, the Highlanders were picked to finish sixth in the Big South, but ended up posting a 12-5-3 record and capturing their fifth Big South regular season title and first since 1998 with an 8-1-0 record. The Highlanders found a mix of experienced veterans, youthful exuberance, and depth at each position to put together a remarkable season and hang another banner at Cupp Stadium. Nine members of the team earned post-season accolades, highlighted by **Stephen Hudgens** being named Big South Men's Soccer Scholar-Athlete of the Year and Capital One First Team Academic *All-America*. Head coach **Marc Reeves** was named Big South Coach of the Year as well.

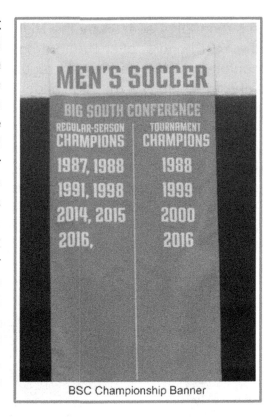
BSC Championship Banner

'I am extremely proud of our group's accomplishments this season,' Reeves said. 'Although our goal was to make the NCAA tournament, I can honestly say we did all we could to maximize our full potential. I am disappointed for our seniors that we came up a fraction short. We played a tough non-conference schedule that featured three teams who were seeded in the top 16 of the NCAA Tournament. Within this, we had some excellent road wins against strong opponents. This fall the Big South had three programs with strong RPIs, and I believe our league has some excellent teams, so for us to be regular season champions is truly rewarding.'

After opening the season with tough one-goal losses at two of those teams to earn NCAA seeds, Clemson and Charlotte, the Highlanders embarked on an 11-game unbeaten streak that included a national-best seven game winning streak. The 11-game unbeaten streak is the longest single-season mark in school history since the Highlanders joined Division I. Radford clinched the Big South title with a 1-0 victory over nationally-ranked Coastal Carolina. It was only the second time in four seasons the Chanticleers had been shut out by a Big South opponent. Radford was ranked as high as No. 20 in the nation at one point and spent the majority of the season regionally ranked by the NSCAA.

Fittingly, **the Highlanders celebrated the 40th year of soccer at Radford in front of nearly 50 returning former players and coaches from throughout the history of the program**. All five men's soccer Radford Athletics Hall of Fame members (**Billy Gerber**, **Tommy Lillard**, **Ian Spooner**, **Dante Washington**, and **John White**) were in attendance to see RU defeat Campbell in overtime. Statistically, Radford led the Big South in goals allowed (17), goals against average (0.82), shots on goal allowed (71), and shutouts per game (0.40). The Highlanders posted eight clean sheets on the season and scored 32 goals on offense. As for the post-season awards, Reeves gave credit to his staff for the Coach of the Year nod, noting it should be a 'Staff of the Year' award, rather than 'Coach.'

'I am very thankful to my assistants Maciej Sliwinski, Riley Butler, and Luis Grande and our immediate support staff for their daily efforts to make our student-athletes have the best opportunity to succeed,' Reeves said. 'Our trainer John Shifflet and his student assistants (Michelle Rawlyk, Dylan Dent, Jacob Zuk) did an incredible job this fall, and I believe a great deal of the groundwork was put in over the previous spring semesters with hard work from our strength and conditioning coaches, Scott Bennett, Tim Ridley, and Michele Huffman.'

Three Highlanders earned first-team All-Big South honors (**Jo Vetle Rimstad**, **Aitor Pouseu Blanco**, and **Krzysztof Nalborski**), and four more earned second-team accolades (Hudgens, **Chel Ho Park Kim**, **Dario Redondo**, and **Fraser Colmer**). **Felix Steinhauser** was named to the Big South All-Freshman team with Pouseu Blanco and Colmer as well. Steinhauser, Pouseu Blanco, and Rimstad earned all-tournament honors from the conference. **Bismark Amofah** was named to the Capital One Academic *All-America*, All-District team with Hudgens. As a team, the Highlanders earned the NSCAA scholar award for team academic performance for the eighth straight season."

Radford University Men's Soccer 40th Season Recognition 2014

2014 also saw the largest presentation of **_The RU #9 Scarf_**, founded by, and in honor of, #9 Dante Washington, at both the home opener and at the 40th Season celebration of the Radford University Men's Soccer Program, held in October. Radford defeated Campbell in the 40th Season contest, 3-2, on a Golden Goal by **Stephen Hudgens**.

In March of 2015, the team once again participated in the *Polar Plunge*.

2015 Polar Plunge

2015

Reeves saw one of his most well-balanced teams in **2015**, as the Highlanders were one of the top offensive threats in the country. Radford led the Big South with 44 goals, ranking in the Top 20 nationally. Meanwhile, Radford's defense was just as impressive, allowing only four goals in Big South play - the lowest recorded in the league. At the end of the season, six players earned All-Big South honors - five named to the first team, a program record. **Daniel O'Keefe** became the first Highlander to be named Big South Defensive Player of the Year, after anchoring the backline of a defense that finished with nine shutouts. **Sivert Daehlie** led the Highlanders and ranked second in the Big South with 13 goals. Daehlie ranked second nationally with seven game winning goals. He finished the season ranked inside the nation's Top-25 in goals, goals per game, points, and points per game. The Highlanders dominated the VaSID awards, sweeping all three major awards with five players earning all-state first team honors. Daehlie claimed the honor of becoming the first player to win both the Player and Rookie of the Year in VaSID All-State history. Furthermore, he was the Highlanders' first-ever player to be named VaSID Player of the Year.

Reeves earned his first career VaSID Coach of the Year award, after putting together a stellar record. The Highlanders finished their Big South schedule with a 7-1-1 record, securing a share of their sixth conference regular-season championship. Overall, the Highlanders finished with a 14-4-2 record and made their third NCAA Tournament appearance in program history. **The Radford University Men's Soccer team received its first NCAA at-large bid in program history on the strength of its No. 20 RPI.**

2015 NCAA Selection Show

In the NCAA first round, Radford dropped a heartbreaking 2-1 match to Charlotte. Charlotte scored first, but the Highlanders leveled the score in the 60th minute off a penalty kick by **Jamie Summers**. **Aitor Pouseu Blanco** kept Radford in the game with clutch saves. The 49ers broke the 1-1 tie with a goal in the 84th minute. RU had two solid chances in the second half with Daehlie's header hitting the crossbar and a Summers free kick curled in from the left side doing the same. The NCAA tournament appearance marked the first appearance by the Highlanders since the 2000 season.

THE RADFORD UNIVERSITY STUDENT OUTDOOR RECREATION COMPLEX

Opening in the Fall of 2015, this 324,000 square foot intramural field expansion brought a new outdoor student athletic facility to an area just four blocks from the main Radford University campus. Features include a 1,350 square-feet restroom/maintenance building, a synthetic turf field with lighting, drainage systems, landscaping, and hardscape improvements such as walkways, a parking lot, and retaining walls. The field dimensions of 162,000 square feet address collegiate and Olympic standards and can be configured to meet all sports' needs. On its face, it is a full-sized soccer, lacrosse, and football field, but can also be broken up into three intramural soccer fields, numerous youth soccer fields, and four flag football fields.

Radford Outdoor Recreation Complex

The men's varsity soccer team has access to the artificial turf field for training in bad weather or in preparation for opponents who play on turf. The team could play a game there, if necessary, but that has not happened other than an exhibition in 2018. In 2023, the team played two games on turf, at Queens College in Charlotte and at VMI. Otherwise, the only team in the Big South that has turf is High Point.

2016

Marc Reeves completed his seventh season at the helm of the Highlanders, leading Radford to greater heights in **2016**. For the second consecutive season, **Radford finished with a 14-4-2 record, while capturing both the Big South Regular Season and the Tournament Championships**. After collecting the third straight regular season title, Radford ended its 16-year absence as kings of the Big South, winning its first tournament championship since 2000 with a 1-0 decision over sixth seeded

2016 NCAA Selection Show

Longwood, **punching its ticket to the NCAA Tournament for the second consecutive season**, Radford dropped a 2-1 decision to former Big South foe Coastal

Carolina. Trailing 2-0 at halftime, Radford fought back, limiting the Chanticleers to only one shot in the second half. On October 17, Radford tied the University of Virginia in Charlottesville, 1-1, after regulation and double overtime.

In 2016, Radford appeared in the Top-25 National Rankings five times, on one occasion going four weeks in a row, and reached a peak at Number 18 in the country.

Under Reeve's tutelage, Radford put together one of its best defensive seasons in program history. The Highlanders led the Big South with 10 shutouts, yielding only 13 goals total and two in league play. Radford ranked ninth nationally with a 0.63 goals-against average and 13th with a 0.50 shutout percentage. Finishing with a 0.824 save percentage to rank 10th nationally as a team, **Aitor Pouseu Blanco** ranked 13th nationally in the individual category. Pouseu Blanco also ranked 10th in the country with a 0.611 goals-against average. Reeves was rewarded with his second Big South Coach of the Year honor as eight Highlanders earned All Big South honors. Radford's defensive backline of **Jo Vetle Rimstad**, **Fraser Colmer**, and **Amofah Bismark** joined Pouseu Blanco on the first team. The trio also joined Pouseu Blanco on the All-Tournament team as Pouseu Blanco earned MVP honors.

Reevo's Last Senior Night 2016 – Garland Smith (17), Zack Turk (25), Gabriel Amba (16), Coach Reeves, Bismark Amofah (6), Jo Vetle Rimstad (4), Aitor Pouseu Blanco (1). [Smith and Turk were local players, from Blacksburg and Radford, respectively.]

Individually, Rimstad racked up several honors in the postseason. In addition to collecting Radford's second consecutive Big South Defense Player of the Year award, Rimstad earned National Soccer Coaches Association of America (NSCAA) All-South Region first team. **The all-region honor was Rimstad's first step to becoming Radford's second NSCAA *All-America* in program history during the NCAA**

Division I era (3rd overall) as Rimstad joined Olympian Dante Washington as the only two Highlanders to hold the honor. Adding to his NSCAA *All-America* third honor award, Rimstad was named to the NSCAA's Scholar *All-America* First Team.

Jo Vetle Rimstad

RU's third All-America selection, and

First RU player drafted into Major League Soccer

Rimstad capped off his already impressive postseason with hearing his named called in the 2017 Major League Soccer SuperDraft. The D.C. United selected Rimstad with the 43rd overall pick in the draft. The five-time Big South Defensive Player of the Week honoree aided Radford to 31 shutouts in his career.

Fraser Colmer became the sixth Big South Men's Soccer Scholar-Athlete of the Year recipient in program history, including the second in the last two years. He also earned a nod on the *CoSIDA Academic All-America®* first team, becoming only the third Highlander in program history to be named to the team. Colmer joined Rimstad on the NSCAA All-South Region squad with a third-team placing.

The 2016 season saw the Highlanders receive its highest national ranking in the NSCAA Coaches' Poll with a ranking of 18th. Radford was ranked inside the Top 25 for three consecutive weeks during the season. Reeves' 2016 senior class capped of their careers with a 49-20-11 record over a four-year span, including a 24-4-5 record inside Cupp Stadium. During that span the Highlanders only allowed 72 goals for a 0.90 team goals against average.

Jo Vetle Rimstad

In the Spring of 2017, Jo Vetle Rimstad made history as the first Highlander selected in the Major League Soccer SuperDraft as the D.C. United selected Rimstad with the 43rd overall pick. In addition, Rimstad was named to the NSCAA *All-America* Third Team, becoming Radford's second *All-America* in NCAA Division I history and third overall. Rimstad also earned NSCAA Scholar *All-America* and All-South First Team honors. Rimstad season-by-season summary:

2016 Season - Selected by the D.C. United with the 43rd overall pick in the 2017 Major League Soccer SuperDraft… NSCAA *All-America* Third Team… NSCAA Scholar *All-America* First Team... NSCAA All-South Region First Team… Big South Defensive Player of the Year… All-Big South First Team… Big South All-Tournament Team…Two Big South Defensive Player of the Week honoree (Aug. 29 and Oct. 10)… Started all 20 matches… Helped aid Radford's defense to a school matching record of 10 shutouts. Allowed a league-low 13 goals on the season… League-low 0.63 goals against average, ninth best in country…Took nine shots, three goals… Logged 1,809 minutes on the pitch.

2015 Season - Named to All-Big South First Team…Earned NSCAA All-South Region Second Team honor… Big South Defensive Player of the Week (Nov. 3)… Started all 20 matches… Scored first career goal in a 5-1 victory over UNC Asheville on Sept. 30… Collected an assist in a 5-1 win versus Longwood on Oct. 7.

2014 Season - Big South Defensive Player of the Week (Oct. 6)… Big South Defensive Player of the Week (Sept. 15)... Named to High Point Plaza Classic all-tournament team.

2013 Season - Appeared in 19 games making 18 starts as a freshman... Became one of the top defenders in the Big South in helping lead the back line to 5 shutouts during the season... Recorded 10 shots with 3 on goal.

First Highlander Drafted in Major League Soccer
BY JORDAN CHILDRESS

Jo Vetle Rimstad '17 made Radford University men's soccer history as the Harestua, Norway, native was selected by the D.C. United with the 43rd overall pick in the 2017 Major League Soccer SuperDraft. Rimstad becomes the first Highlander drafted into Major League Soccer (MLS) in program history and will join Dante Washington as the only two Highlanders to don an MLS jersey.

"I just couldn't be happier right now. D.C. United is the perfect club for me, as I have a lot of friends in the area," Rimstad noted. "It seemed that most Radford students were United fans, so I now have the chance to represent them when I put on the black and red."

Rimstad was named a National Soccer Coaches Association of America (NSCAA) *All-America* and Scholar *All-America*. Rimstad became the second Highlander in program history to be named an NSCAA *All-America* during the Division I era and third overall. In addition to his *All-America* honors, Rimstad earned the fourth NSCAA All-South Region First Team honor in program history. The accolade was the third of Rimstad's career from the NSCAA — he earned second-team honors in 2014 and 2015.

"Our University, alumni, and soccer program are incredibly proud of Jo Vetle. He had an outstanding four years at Radford, both on and off the field," said former head coach Marc Reeves. "He now gets the chance to represent Radford positively and bring great exposure to the school. He is a fantastic person who is fully deserving of this opportunity." Rimstad finished his career as one of the best center backs in Radford University and Big South history. In 2016, Rimstad became the second Highlander in program history to be named Big South Defensive Player of the Year. Rimstad earned All-Big South honors in each of his four collegiate years, earning first-team honors three times.

"Reevo sent me a text message to tell me I was going to be drafted, I just couldn't believe it," Rimstad added. "This is what I have been working for. I never imagined being put in this situation, because I have been enjoying playing soccer for the longest time. I have been working hard for a very long time, and it has finally paid off."

The five-time Big South Defensive Player of the Week honoree aided Radford University to 31 shutouts in his career, including 18 in the last two years. Radford University matched a program-record 10 shutouts during the 2016 season. Rimstad did nothing but win since he arrived on campus in 2013. The Highlanders compiled a

49-20-11 record over the span, including a 24-4-5 record inside Cupp Stadium. Radford won three Big South regular-season championships, one Big South Tournament championship and made two NCAA Tournament appearances during the span.

"Jo Vetle understands that it requires continued true hard work to pursue the goal of being a professional, and he has certainly earned the right to be drafted," Reeves added. "We are thankful for D.C. United for believing in him and wish Jo Vetle the very best." Rimstad will join former Highlander Ryan Taylor in the D.C. United organization. Taylor is a member of the Richmond Kickers, the United's affiliate in the United Soccer League.

Marc Reeves served as head coach of the Highlanders men's soccer program for seven seasons, achieving the highest levels of post-season play ever. In his seven years at Radford, "Reevo" led the Highlanders to an overall record of 75-43-20 (.616) including a 42-15-6 (.682) mark against conference opponents. He led Radford to back-to-back appearances in the NCAA Tournament in 2015 and 2016 and to three straight Big South Conference regular season titles.

Marc Reeves – 2016

One of the more unique occurrences during Reevo's tenure was a decision made by Virginia Tech. Well-respected and long-time Tech coach Jerry Cheynet, who had embraced and promoted the Radford-Tech rivalry, had been replaced in 2002. Cheynet's replacement had been successful but was then dismissed due to alleged violations of NCAA rules. Upon his dismissal, the existing assistant coach at Tech then took over as head coach in 2009. Having lost to Radford in both 2009 and 2011, <u>Virginia Tech refused to schedule Radford from 2013 to 2021</u>.

Unfortunately for Radford, Elon University made Reevo a very substantial contract offer, one that so benefitted his family, he couldn't refuse taking it. Upon hearing of this, an effort was led by **Will Iandolo** and other RU soccer alumni to try to create a fund to supplement Reevo's compensation. It just couldn't compete with the Elon proposal. In true Reevo fashion, he apologized to the administration and to the team. "Saying goodbye to this team was one of the hardest things I have ever had to do. The players and our alumni know that I will always be available to them no matter what or where I am." Reeves added, "I wish nothing but the best and true success in the future for all of Radford's athletic programs." After apologizing, he left after the 2016 season, having taken the program to its highest positions ever.

RADFORD Media Release, 02/22/17: "Radford men's soccer head coach Marc Reeves has resigned from his position to take on the same role for Elon University, Radford Director of Athletics Robert Lineburg announced. A national search for Reeves' replacement will begin immediately.

"We are so appreciative of the job Reevo has done at Radford. He has led this program to tremendous heights on and off the field. We hate to see him leave," Lineburg said. "However, this is an excellent job and we will have tremendous interest. We have a wonderful group of student-athletes and we will find an outstanding coach that is a great fit for Radford Soccer."

Reeves served at the helm of the Highlanders for seven seasons, compiling a 75-43-20 overall record and a 42-15-6 clip in Big South play. Radford posted a winning record in six of Reeve's seven seasons. Under Reeves' tutelage, Radford won three Big South Regular Season Championships (2014, 2015, 2016) and one Big South Tournament Championship (2016). The Highlanders only had two NCAA Tournament appearances in program history (1999, 2000) until Reeves guided Radford to 2015 and 2016 tournament appearances.

In his seven seasons, Reeves guided 41 players to All-Big South honors while being named the Big South's Coach of the Year in 2014 and 2016. Radford collected back-to-back Big South Defensive Player of the Year awards in 2015 and 2016. The Highlanders racked up a whopping 14 national and regional academic awards, including two *CoSIDA Academic All-America*® honorees."

Reevo, 03/06/2024: "I am truly fortunate and thankful that Robert Lineburg gave me the opportunity of my first Head Coaching position at Radford in 2010. We did not know much about the school, area or, being honest, the soccer program. We just knew that we wanted to move out of NY, and have a go at being a Head Coach, and RU seemed like a great place to start.

What we found was an incredible institute, amazing athletic department and a very special place for our family to grow (literally, Jackson was born in Blacksburg and our dog Blitz came from St. Francis service dog training center). We truly found a home at the Highlanders, meeting so many special people along the way and in our seven years there creating some amazing friendships and memories.

I learned a great deal in the first few years as a Head Coach and will always be thankful to those players who very early on bought into the process of creating a culture of high standards and commitment to excel in all aspects. We had some great teams and were able to make history with a three-peat Regular Season titles, we added another Big South Tournament Championship, and a program first of an at-large bid to the NCAA tournament.

With this came many individual accolades earned through the teams'/programs' success on the field. We had some incredibly talented players but more importantly we had young men who believed in being a good teammate on and off the field and were appreciative of the opportunity Radford was giving them. The brotherhood of those groups really was something amazing that gave our teams an edge in being successful on the field. One of my most favorite coaching memories was of us winning the 2016 Big South Championship at Cupp Stadium with the drone footage of our team and fans all rushing onto the field at the final whistle to celebrate together.

Our academic performance was equally impressive with a consistent, high, Team GPA and some outstanding individuals earning Big South Scholar Athlete and Academic *All-America* Awards. I am truly proud of how successful our former players have been in excelling in their own careers and families.

Radford athletics always instilled a commitment to community, and our program was able to impact in many ways. Probably the most prevalent being the close connection we made with Virgina Special Olympics, where we were able to assist in several events like track and basketball, but the most memorable (in all ways) was the Polar Plunge. This was a true team bonding experience that raised funds and awareness to such an amazing organization, and gave our group a sense of pride in being a Highlander.

Our successful and enjoyable time at Radford was hugely aided by a supportive administration, incredibly invested Alumni, and having the good fortune to be surrounded by great staff in so many areas. Everyone played a part (plus went above and beyond) to maximize the student athlete experience. We knew what we had to work with and rolled our sleeves up with a collective attitude of "Find A Way - Make it Work - Solutions not Problems".

I am a big believer in your path/journey takes you to places where you are supposed to be at that specific time. Radford gave our family so much that we will forever be thankful and always enjoy returning to campus or the area to visit friends.

Go Highlanders!"

After reviewing applications, a search committee recommended **Bryheem Hancock** as Reevo's replacement.

Nick Mayhugh Becomes Radford Soccer's Second Olympian

RADFORD, Va., 7/27/2017 – Very few individuals receive the opportunity to represent their country, while playing the game they love. Radford University men's soccer junior Nick Mayhugh did just that this summer for the United States Paralympic National Team. To be eligible for the US Paralympic National Team, players must be ambulant and have one of the following neurological conditions: have had a stroke; have cerebral palsy, or have suffered a brain injury. There are four levels of classification: FT5 (diplegia), FT6 (quadriplegia), FT7 (hemiplegia) and FT8 (players are minimally affected by one of three).

Nick Mayhugh

Mayhugh falls under the FT8 classification, due to suffering a stroke as a child as a result of being a premature birth. "Throughout my entire childhood, no one understood or believed me when I would say that my norm was different," Mayhugh added. "My doctors and family were unaware of the side effects I was experiencing until we later learned the side effects were a result of a stroke." Growing up with the lack of feeling on the left side of his body was normal to Mayhugh and gave it no thought until November 2010. That fall, Mayhugh had a *grand mal* seizure, which led to hours of tests and scans. Doctors found a dead spot on the right side of the brain, which was diagnosed as a result from a stroke he suffered *in utero*.

"All the dots started to connect from earlier in my childhood. I was finally given an explanation for my norm," Mayhugh noted. "The stroke caused the lack of feeling, motor movement and sensation mainly in my left arm, hand and leg." The adventure started for Mayhugh in early May as he saw an advertisement for Paralympic team tryouts on the US Soccer Instagram page and was urged to apply by his brother. Mayhugh reached out to the coaching staff, explaining his background and was invited to training camp in Chicago. The training camp took place June 1-7. At the end of the training camp, participants would find out if they made the cut to travel to Chile for two international friendlies with the Chile Paralympic National Team.

 "As soon as I got to the hotel, we started training. It was no different than our August training camps at Radford," Mayhugh noted. "It was very professional. They treated us the same way that coach Hancock treats us." Mayhugh had to adjust to the Paralympic soccer style of play, which features seven players on the field instead of 11 and two 30-minute periods. The substitution maximum is five within a max of three opportunities in the match. There is no offside rule. The field dimensions are 70m by 50m, while the goal posts are set at 5m by 2m.

"It was definitely a challenge to adapt to the different formations and style of game that we play in the seven-a-side game, but I received a lot of help from the coaches and veteran players," Mayhugh noted. "In the seven-a-side game, you have to be very flexible in terms of positions that you are willing and able to play because of your team's needs. Depending on what certain formations require, you may need to be able to play more than one position." Part of the adjustment was learning a new position as he found himself playing center midfield. "I found myself running a lot more, because of what the position and the seven-a-side game demands from you mentally and physically," Mayhugh added.

Simply happy to be a part of the experience, Mayhugh didn't ask the coaching staff when final selections would be made. During the final days of training camp, Mayhugh was pulled aside to discover that he had made the roster for the Chile trip. In addition to an already life-changing experience, Mayhugh's life changed even more. While in Chicago, Mayhugh and training camp participants visited the Shirley Ryan AbilityLab, which has served as the best rehabilitation hospital in the country for 26 years.

"We were given the opportunity to speak, inspire and interact with patients and parents who have gone, or are going, through the same things that our team has gone through. I can humbly say it was an unforgettable experience that inspired me to change the way I look at my disabilities and how I value those who supported me throughout my medical speed bumps," Mayhugh added. "Since being home, I have been in contact with a few local hospitals to set up times to visit and interact with patients. I would love to continue inspiring patients like those who inspired me in Chicago."

The experiences continued for Mayhugh as he traveled outside the United States for the first time in his life. Once arriving in Chile, the national team trained two times a day in preparation for their matches. Mayhugh played the final 25 minutes of the first match, but does not remember coming onto the pitch due to an overwhelming amount of emotion. "Walking into the locker room, seeing my name on the locker and that jersey inside it was surreal. That is when I realized that all this was actually real and I was representing our country," Mayhugh said. "It was like just any other game as soon as I put the uniform on and the whistle blew."

The first match resulted in a 6-0 victory, in which Mayhugh assisted on two goals. In the second match against Chile, Mayhugh tallied two goals and two assists in 50 minutes of action of a 10-0 victory. On an off day, Mayhugh and his teammates explored the city of Santiago. The group took a train up into the mountains that overlooked the city and at the Andes Mountains. Having teammates from different countries at Radford helped Mayhugh adjust to going to another country. "My international teammates at Radford helped me adjust to this trip. I was surrounded by people who didn't speak my language and were new to us," Mayhugh added. "That is very similar to preseason at Radford, when the new guys come in. We help them adjust to their new surroundings."

After spending time in a soccer-centric country, Mayhugh gained a new respect for the game and how it brings different nationalities together. After returning home for two weeks, the national team traveled to Florida to face the Canadian Paralympic National Team July 21-23. In the first match, Mayhugh scored one goal in a 2-2 draw. For the second time in four games, Mayhugh found the back of the net twice in a 3-1 win to wrap up friendly play. Mayhugh is no stranger to playing in big soccer matches in front of large crowds as he has been a part of two Big South Conference Regular Season Championships and one Big South Tournament Championship, as well as two NCAA Tournaments. "Playing in those big matches and that environment helped make everything calm for me," Mayhugh noted. "The American Outlaws came out to our matches in Florida. They were playing drums and chanting. It was similar to the 2016 Big South Championship match."

Joining former Olympian Dante Washington as the only two Highlanders to represent the United States in international play adds to the memorable experience for Mayhugh. "Dante set a standard for Radford soccer," Mayhugh added. "We strive to leave our mark like he did." The next step for Mayhugh will be to find out if he has earned a spot of the national team's roster for the IFCPF World Championships, hosted in San Luis, Argentina. The championships will run from September 4-24, which will consist of the top teams in the world in a World Cup format. "This is an actual dream come true. I grew up dreaming and wishing to play for the US National Team. I was given the chance to represent our country, while playing the game that I love is something that I can't really describe," Mayhugh said. "Putting on that jersey with the patch, standing in

the starting lineup while the national anthem plays just chokes me up thinking about it. There is nothing better."

Bryheem Hancock Era (2017 – 2019)

3 Seasons

Overall Record: 22-24-6 (.481) - Big South: 13-9-2 (.583)

- 2017 10-4-4; Big South: 5-1-2
    Big South Tournament Semifinals

- 2018 7-9-0; Big South: 5-3-0
    Big South Tournament Semifinals

- 2019 5-11-2; Big South: 3-5-0
    Big South Tournament Quarterfinals

Coach Bryheem Hancock

Assistant Coaches: Riley Butler, Brian Cronin, Scott Bennett

Bryheem Hancock was named the eighth head coach in Radford University men's soccer-program history, as announced by Director of Athletics *Robert Lineburg*. Hancock came to Radford after spending eight seasons as an assistant at South Florida. In Hancock's eight seasons as an assistant, USF finished with double-digit wins in five seasons, advancing to the NCAA Tournament seven times. The Bulls won the 2013 American Athletic Conference Tournament championship and 2011 Big East Red Division Regular Season Championship. USF's 2015 recruiting class headed by Hancock was named No. 3 in the country by College Soccer News.

"I would first like to thank *Robert Lineburg*, *Stephanie Ballein* and President Brian Hemphill. They have given me this opportunity, which I am blessed to have. I am obviously very excited to become a leader here at Radford," Hancock stated. "Just from seeing the campus, meeting the staff and athletic department, I can tell that it is definitely a family and that is something that I obviously want to be a part of." "I felt like this fit was perfect for me. It was not just about the school's success on the field, but how involved the program was in the community and their academic success," Hancock noted. "To me, my three things are: to win in the classroom, to win on the field, and to win in the community. I think that Radford provides all three of those things."

After finishing his professional playing career, Hancock began his collegiate coaching career at South Florida in 2009. Under Hancock's watchful eye, USF goalkeeper Jeff Attinella was named the Big East Goalkeeper of the Year and was also named a first team National Soccer Coaches Association of America *All-America* in his first season. That same year, Attinella posted a 14-4-3 record with seven shutouts and a 0.83-goals against-average.

Hancock spent his collegiate career at UConn (1998-2001), guiding the Huskies to NCAA Tournament appearances all four years, two final four appearances and the 2000 NCAA Division I National Championship. The Middletown, Del., native was named to the NCAA College Cup All-Tournament Team in 2000. Hancock was named Big East Goalkeeper of the Year in 2001 as well as earning NSCAA *All-America* status. In his senior season, he was honored with the 2001 Leadership Student-Athlete Award.

He finished his career at UConn boasting 44 wins, 29 shutouts, 25 goals allowed and a 0.70 goals-against average. Hancock graduated with a Bachelor's of Science degree in Communications in 2001. In addition to his success at UConn, Hancock was part of the U-17 National Team, where he was named captain in 1997 and 1998, and was the starting goalkeeper in the 1997 FIFA U-17 World Championships in Egypt.

After setting the UConn collegiate shutout record at 15 in one season, Hancock played professional soccer in the United States for three years, including stints with the L.A. Galaxy (2001-02), Atlanta Silverbacks (2002-03) and Toronto Lynx (2004) of Major League Soccer (MLS). In 2001, Hancock was the first goalkeeper selected in the 2001 MLS Draft by the L.A. Galaxy. In 2003, Hancock was named the Atlanta Silverbacks MVP while recording the team record for most saves in a season and most saves in a single game. He accumulated additional honors in 2004 with the Toronto Lynx as the team defensive MVP. In his year with the Lynx, he held the team record for most saves in a season.

In his first season at Radford in **2017**, Hancock guided the Highlanders to a 10-4-4 mark, including a 5-1-2 record in Big South play, finishing second in the standings. In the postseason, Radford made its sixth consecutive appearance in the Big South Tournament semifinals. Hancock brought a high-potent offense to the New River Valley as the Highlanders owned the eighth-best scoring offense in the country with 2.11 goals per match, while ranking 10th with 6.28 points per match. **Kieran Roberts**

finished the season with 15 goals, which ranked fourth in the country. **Sivert Daehlie** followed with 12 goals to rank 17th in the country. In addition, Roberts led the nation with 5.44 shots per match and 2.83 shots on goal.

The Bryheem Hancock era started in dominating fashion as Radford opened the 2017 season with a 4-0 victory over Wofford. Kieran Roberts tallied two of the Highlander goals, scoring in each half. Radford was unable to overcome two first half goals as a late push in the final minutes fell just short as Kieran Roberts' third goal on the season wiped the clean sheet in the Highlanders 2-1 loss to No. 5 Clemson. Looking for its first win at Davidson in five attempts, Radford fell, 1-0, despite holding a 17-8 shot advantage in the matchup. Radford avenged its NCAA Tournament loss from a season ago with a 2-1 victory over Coastal Carolina, giving the Highlanders their first win over the Chanticleers since 2014.

Radford picked up its first draw of the 2017 season after ETSU found an equalizer midway through the second half as both teams locked in a 1-1 defensive battle the rest of the way on a rainy night in the Volunteer State. Using goals by Sivert Daehlie and Kieran Roberts, Radford's defense did the rest of the work as the Highlanders collected

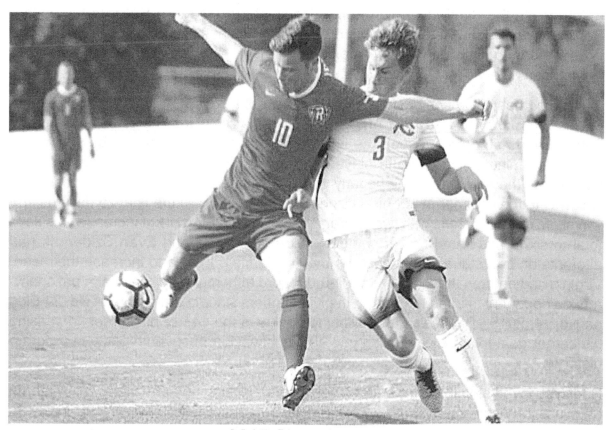

2017 Sivert Daehlie

their second shutout of the season with a 2-0 victory over Howard to move back above .500. After a delayed start time due to lighting in the Radford area, the Highlanders struck early and often, tallying three goals in the first 14 minutes and held off a late second half charge by in-state foe James Madison, 4-3, in their first meeting inside Cupp Stadium in 15 years.

Radford opened Big South play in dominating fashion as five different players tallied goals in a 5-1 victory over Campbell as the Highlanders improved to 9-0-1 in their last 10 Big South openers. The goals were scored by **Kieran Roberts**, **Fraser Colmer**, **Myles Yorke**, **Sivert Daehlie** and **Jakob Strandsäter**. In the last four matches, Radford tallied 15 goals and a major part of that impressive feat was been the play of Kieran Roberts as the redshirt-junior tallied his second career hat trick in the Highlanders' 4-0 Big South home opening win over UNC Asheville.

Radford had its four-match winning streak snapped, but kept its seven-match unbeaten streak intact, on a Sivert Daehlie goal, as the Highlanders earned a 1-1 draw at Presbyterian in the third, double-overtime match between the two Big South foes in their last three meetings. Daehlie extended his scoring streak to eight straight with a late second-half goal as Radford's seven-match unbeaten streak came to an end with a 2-1 loss to Big South rival High Point. Redshirt junior **Kieran Roberts** turned in a Senior Day performance that reminded the Radford men's soccer faithful of the Dante Washington era in the 1990s as Roberts found the back of the net four times in a 5-3 Highlander victory over Gardner-Webb.

The rumor that the number 13 is unlucky was debunked by Radford men's soccer team as the **Highlanders knocked off No. 10 Virginia, 1-0, for the first time, in the 13th meeting all-time between the two Commonwealth foes dating back to 1982**. In the 61st minute, **Victor Valls** played a beautiful ball from 20-yards out to **Sivert Daehlie** on the right side of the penalty box. Daehlie sent the ball past UVa goalie Jeff Caldwell to the near corner for his 11th goal on the season. In the final 25 minutes, the Cavaliers took four shots with two on frame, but **Nicolas Mertzokat** increased his save total to six for his fourth career shutout. **Kieran Roberts** and **Evan Szklennik** had attempts on frame during that span as the Highlanders looked to increase their lead. Virginia had entered the match with a 7-0-0 record at home. The win over a nationally-ranked opponent marked the first by the Highlanders since a 2-0 victory at No. 21 Elon on Nov. 4, 2015. Daehlie's game-winning goal was the 14th of his career, increasing his career goal total to 29, moving into sole possession of seventh place in program history.

Radford moved atop the Big South standings after picking up a 2-0 victory at Winthrop on a pair of Victor Valls goals, as the Highlanders increased their winning streak to three-straight. The season concluded with Big South games against Longwood, tied

1-1, and Liberty, won 4-2. Unfortunately, in the Tournament, Presbyterian tied RU, 0-0, after regulation and triple overtime, and then advanced on penalty kicks, 5-3.

The Highlanders swept the postseason awards as Roberts was named the Big South's Attacking Player of the Year and **Fraser Colmer** earned Co-Defensive Player of the Year. In all, Radford placed four on the Big South First Team (Kieran Roberts, Fraser Colmer, Sivert Daehlie, Victor Valls). **Evan Szklennik** and **Max Edwards** were named to the conference's second team. Edwards joined **Noy Daabul** on the Big South All-Freshman team. Academically, Colmer was named Big South Men's Soccer Scholar-Athlete of the Year for the second straight season, while earning his third straight *CoSIDA Academic All-America*® honor. Colmer also became the first Highlander in program history to be named a *Senior CLASS Award All-America*.

In the Fall of 2017, the Radford University Athletics Fund installed the **"Circle of Champions"** <u>**top donors recognition**</u> emblem and named the **Men's Soccer Locker Room Suite** for donors Will Iandolo, Lynn Iandolo, and John Harves.

Will Iandolo Class of 1982
Greg "Stitch" McCarthy Class of 1985
John Harves Coach '77 – '79
Sean Peay Class of 1991
Anoput Phimmasone Class of 1987
Dr. Jamal Haddad Class of 1980
Willie Shepherd Class of 1988
Michael Ginsburg Class of 1999
Steve Arkon Class of 1991
Tom Lillard Class of 1979
Drs. Jamal & Julia Haddad Class of 1980
Don Staley Coach '85 – '93
Mike Von Essen Class of 2003
Dante Washington Class of 1992

2017 Men's Locker Room Dedication Plaque

At the start of 2018, the NCAA authorized Spring soccer competitions in association with the United States Soccer Federation. Spring soccer is not captured in this treatment.

Radford University and Big South Hall of Fame member **Dante Washington was inducted into the Maryland Soccer Hall of Fame**, May 11, 2018.

2018

In **2018**, his second season, Hancock led the Highlanders to a 5-3 conference record for second place in the Big South. Radford reached the conference semifinals and racked up nine postseason conference awards. An unlucky start to the season saw Radford drop five straight to ODU, 1-0, VCU, 3-0, Georgetown, 2-0, Madison, 3-1, and Campbell, 2-0. Fortunes turned at Morgantown when the goals finally started to fall against West Virginia in a 4-1 victory. The Highlanders came out hungry for a win and ready to play from the opening whistle. They earned an early chance in the 4th minute when **Amadou Macky Diop** found **Nick Mayhugh** in the box for a point blank header that was saved. Four minutes later, **Gonzalo Rodriguez** sent a dangerous corner kick just in front of goal, but that too was blocked just in time and sent away.

It was before the clock struck 10 minutes, however, when Radford would find the back of the net. Senior midfielder **Victor Valls** fired one shot that was blocked before he collected the rebound and hit a low, curling strike into the bottom right of the goal to put his team ahead, 1-0. Radford then doubled its lead in the 17th minute. After a forced turnover, Diop turned and played a ball between defenders to senior **Kieran Roberts** who calmly shot up and over the keeper. Another goal in the 36th minute – this time off the foot of Diop – gave the Highlanders a 3-0 lead before halftime. For

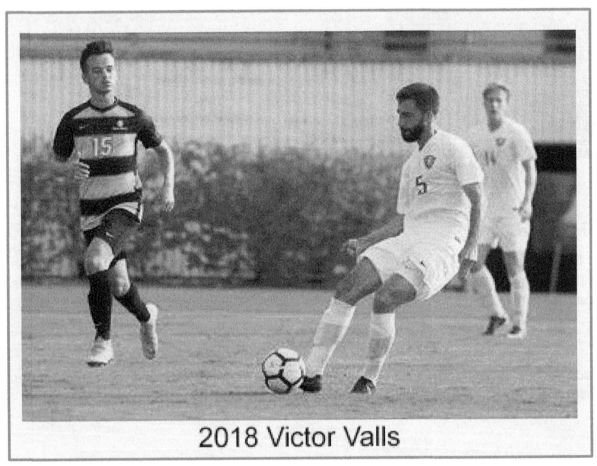

2018 Victor Valls

good measure, Diop scored his second goal of the night in the 56th minute. West Virginia answered soon after in the 57th minute with a header, but it was too little, too late. Freshman goalkeeper **Sam Farrell** made his first collegiate start and he came up big with three saves including a penalty kick save in the 70th minute. He analyzed the Mountaineer PK taker perfectly and dove to his right before getting a hand on the ball and knocking it away. The Highlanders' defense stayed strong and saw the game out from there.

Roberts would score twice in a 4-2 victory at Longwood. Diop had the first score and an own-goal by Longwood would cap the game. With a 2-1 loss in a very physical match with Gardner-Webb sandwiched in-between, Radford defeated Presbyterian, 1-0, on a golden goal scored by Roberts with less than a minute remaining in double overtime. Next, Diop would do the same, with less than three-minutes remaining in double-overtime, to down #16 Charlotte, 2-1. Senior defender **Myles Yorke** collected a loose ball and fired it over the top of the defense to **Max Edwards** who laid it off to Diop.

It was Diop who had opened the scoring in the 47th minute. Junior midfielder **Wyatt Erzen** played a perfect through ball down the middle of the pitch to Diop who calmly dribbled around the goalkeeper and tapped in for the goal. In a third-straight double-overtime match, it was **Dondré Robinson** who had the winner, 2-1, over UNC-Asheville. **Khori Bennett** had the opener after receiving a through-ball from **Gonzalo Rodriguez.**

Radford went stride-for-stride with #6 Virginia, but ultimately fell, 2-1, in Charlottesville. This was followed by a 3-1 victory over Winthrop that extended the Highlanders' Big South winning streak to three games. A 2-1 loss to #12 High Point was disconcerting but a 3-1 win over USC-Upstate earned Radford the Number 2 seed in the Big South Tournament. The 2018 season came to a heartbreaking close as the Radford men's soccer team dropped a 2-0 decision to Presbyterian in the Big South Tournament semifinal.

Freshman phenom **Amadou Macky Diop** was named Big South Freshman of the Year, All-Big South First Team and United Soccer Coaches All-South Region Third Team after scoring nine goals and tallying five assists. **Kieran Roberts** also made the First Team while **Myles Yorke** and **Victor Valls** were placed on the Second Team. **Sam Farrell** and **Thure Ilgner** made the All-Freshman Team and **Benjamin Thiss** earned a spot on the All-Academic Team.

Hancock's third season at the helm, **2019**, saw the Highlanders qualify for the Big South Championships for the 25th consecutive season - the longest such mark of any program in the conference. Radford won only five games overall, going 5-11-2, but three of the wins came in Big South play. The Highlanders season came to an end in the quarterfinals with a loss to Gardner-Webb, 2-1. **Octavio Ocampo**'s fourth goal of the year wasn't enough to continue the season. Five minutes before halftime, Gardner-Webb took a 1-0 lead. The Runnin' Bulldogs doubled their lead in the 6th minute of the second half when a re-directed shot made it past **Joseba Incera**. Ocampo captured a loose ball 10-minutes later. The Highlanders had a golden opportunity to tie the match in the closing stages, as **Dondré Robinson** sent in a cross that **Victor Valls** hit perfectly toward the lower corner, but a Gardner-Webb defender managed to clear the ball off the line just before it went in.

Like the year before, the team lost a one-goal heartbreaker to the University of Virginia, 1-0, in Charlottesville.

Victor Valls and **Octavio Ocampo** each earned Second Team All-Big South honors, while Ocampo and **Mouhameth Thiam** earned a spot on the All-Freshman Team. In addition, **Jacob Wilkinson** became the second Highlander to earn Academic *All-America* honors since Hancock took over at Radford.

2019 Octavio Ocampo

After four scares in a row, being tied in 2016, losing in 2017, and squeaking by with one-goal victories in 2018 and 2019, the University of Virginia stopped scheduling Radford.

In 2018, **Greg McCarthy** was appointed to the Radford University Athletics Foundation Board of Directors. In. 2019, he was named *Radford University Davis College of Business Alumnus of the Year*. Mr. McCarthy has a Bachelor of Science degree in Marketing from Radford University and played on the men's soccer and lacrosse teams during his time at the school. He stated, "I am thrilled and honored to receive the 2019 Alumnus of The Year Award from Dean Bhaduri of Radford University Davis College of Business and Economics! As an alum, I am so impressed by what is offered at the school, the curriculum, collaborative space, research technology, and the securities 'trading room,' make RU's accredited Business School the best value in Virginia." McCarthy and **Will Iandolo** are both members of the Davis College Advisory Board.

Nick Mayhugh was named the *2019 U. S. Soccer Player of the Year with a Disability*, the United States Soccer Federation announced December 16, 2019. Mayhugh, who played for the Highlanders from 2015-2018, had been a fixture in the USPNT squad since 2017 and played a key role for the U.S. Paralympic 7-a-Side National Team that reached its highest-ever ranking in 2019 at No. 4. The midfielder netted 19 goals in 11 games for the Stars and Stripes, including a last-minute winner to down perennial powerhouse Iran. Mayhugh helped the USA secure its first-ever podium finish at the Para Pan-American Games, which included a comeback win over Brazil.

Bryheem Hancock Coaching - 2019

Amid speculation and rumors, Coach Hancock abruptly announced his resignation the very day after the end of the 2019 season to become the head coach at the University of Texas Rio Grande Valley. Assistant men's soccer coach **Chris Barrett** was immediately appointed to take over as interim head coach for the program.

In January, 2020, **Chris Barrett** and **John White**, in keeping with tried-and-true Radford Highlanders, and promoting Radford values, were appointed permanently as Head Coach and Assistant Coach, respectively, to direct the Radford University Men's Soccer program.

Chris Barrett Era (2020 – Present)

4 Seasons

Overall Record: 15-37-6 (.310) - Big South: 10-17-3 (.383)

- 2020 3-5-1; Big South: 2-4-1

- 2021 5-11-0; Big South: 3-5-0

- 2022 4-10-2; Big South: 3-4-1

- 2023 3-11-3; Big South: 2-4-1

- **2024**
    Radford University Men's Varsity Soccer Program 50th Season

Coach Chris Barrett

Assistant Coaches: Andy Cormak, John White, Dorion Dixon, Kevin Nolan, Lucas Mason

Chris Barrett was in his 10th season with the Highlander men's soccer program, and was about to begin his third stint as an assistant coach, when he was named interim head coach in November 2019, with the sudden departure of Bryheem Hancock. He had also spent a decade as an assistant coach for the Radford women's soccer program. Further, Barrett had assistant coaching stops at UNC-Wilmington and West Virginia, as well as ODPs (Olympic Development Programs) in Virginia, West Virginia, South Carolina and Georgia.

In his two previous stints on the men's side (1995-98, 2006-10), Barrett helped lead the Highlanders to 81 wins, including 32 Big South wins, and a Big South regular season title. He had worked primarily with the goalkeepers at Radford in the past, with two earning all-conference honors. Barrett himself was an all-conference goalkeeper for the Highlanders and played four seasons for Radford (1991-94). With the Highlanders, Barrett was also a two-year team captain and a Second Team All-Big South selection in 1994. He finished his career with 207 saves, which is fifth in the program annals of the Big South era. Right after his playing days concluded, Barrett's coaching career began as an assistant to Radford head coach Spencer Smith. Under Smith and Barrett's guidance from 1995-98, the Highlanders won 43 games and claimed their first Big South regular season title. He also volunteered his time as a goalkeeper coach for the Radford women's team.

Barrett has roots with Radford that run deep: not only was he a four-year standout with the Highlanders, his development as a coach began and continued at his alma mater. The 1996 Radford graduate made his return to campus in 2006 and began molding the Highlander goalkeepers. Under his guidance, Zach Roszel earned all-conference honors in 2006 and two seasons later posted the league's top save percentage (.821) and fought through an injury-plagued season to post the Big South's second-best goals against average (0.92).

Before making his return to the New River Valley, Barrett's coaching career included stops at the college, professional, club, and high school levels in locations from Christiansburg, VA, to Georgia. His impact was felt throughout southeastern U.S. soccer, most notably during his four years in Greenville, SC. Barrett was co-director of Greenville FC, as well as the program's director of player development. Barrett also spent time as a coach and director with the Rockdale, GA, Youth Soccer Association and Port City Soccer Club, NC.

Coach Barrett
January Practice in the Snow

2020

In the fall of **2020**, Coach Barrett's reward for accepting the men's soccer position was the Covid-19 (coronavirus) pandemic. This sent all schools, and sports in particular, into a tailspin. Competition was delayed until the following spring and the season shortened. In the modified 2020-2021 spring season, Barrett led the team to a 3-5-1 overall record, 2-4-1 in the Big South. The Highlanders defense held opponents to one or fewer goals in four games that season, picking up wins over Gardner-Webb, VMI,

Chris Barrett with Pape Oumar Gueye on Senior Night - 2020

and Winthrop. Radford opened at Liberty but dropped a 4-0 decision. This was followed by a close, 2-1, loss to USC-Upstate. **Ryan Machado-Jones** then scored the match winner, with Radford's only shot on goal, as the Highlanders gave Barrett his first career victory as a head coach, against Gardner-Webb, 1-0, February 28, 2021.

The win over VMI followed, 4-1, with goals by **Dondré Robinson**, **Pape Oumar Gueye**, **Quincy Etienne**, and **Octavio Ocampo**. **Noah Haddad**, **David Blum**, **Chris Williams**, and **Khalid Poian** made their Highlander debuts in this match. Wins concluded with Winthrop going down by the same score 4-1 score. **Baye Djibril Faye** had two goals and one assist, **Toby Squire** and **Dondre' Robinson** each had a goal, and **Max-Emilio Angelides** had two assists. **Joseba Incera** preserved the win in goal.

A hallmark of the start of the first full season after Covid was Coach Barrett giving an opportunity to the most-ever student-athletes to get out on the field and participate.

2021

Nick Mayhugh was named to the U.S. Paralympic Track and Field Team in June 2021. He would go on to set a world record in the 200-meters.

The **2021** season opened with a bang as Radford downed Concord, 9-0. The Highlanders dominated Concord for the full 90-minutes. The nine goals were the most scored by the men since they tallied seven against Roanoke in 2015. Eight different Highlanders recorded goals, but the scoring was kicked off by **Octavio Ocampo** just two minutes into the game. **Juan Benavides** added the second goal in the 28th minute, while freshman **Yoshiya Okawa** closed out the first half with his first career goal. In the second half, it was pedal to the metal as Radford ran away with the match. **Dorion Dixon** netted two goals, with **Patrick Siczek**, **Ryan Machado-Jones**, **Solomon Clark**, and **Collin Hawes** each adding one of their own. Radford spent a large majority of the match in Concord territory, with the opponent only getting off two shots. Radford led the match with 39 shots, 20 of which were on goal. **Trevor Kallendorf** played all 90-minutes in the net for Radford, completing his clean sheet while only having to make one save. Radford finished the night with 13 corner kicks to Concord's two. Radford's remaining wins came against VMI, 2-0, UNC-Asheville, 2-1 in OT, Presbyterian, 2-1, and Gardner-Webb, 3-2. The Highlanders needed a win or a tie in the finale to make the Big South tournament, but lost 2-1 to Longwood. The lone goal was scored by Ocampo on a penalty kick.

2021 Ryan Machado-Jones

In 2021, freshman **Hansy Velasquez** was selected for the Under-20 Puerto Rico National team for upcoming friendlies and CONCACAF qualifiers.

2022

In the **2022** season, Barrett led Radford to a 3-4-1 Big South record, picking up three consecutive wins over Winthrop, USC-Upstate, and Longwood. It was the Highlanders' first three-game winning streak since 2018. Goalkeeper **Joseba Incera** finished top-10 nationally in saves per game (5.45), posting a 1.82 GAA and .750 save percentage, with three clean sheets. The Highlanders finished the season with an overall record of 4-10-2. In the Longwood win, on the strength of two first-half goals by **Jared Dubose** and **Griffin Gyurci**, along with a stellar performance from goalkeeper Incera, Radford took

2022 Joseba Incera

down the Lancers in a come-from-behind victory, 2-1. Longwood had struck first, in the 5th minute. In the 17th minute, Dubose dribbled the ball into the penalty area along the bi-line from the left and, with a near-zero angle, chipped it past the goalkeeper to even the score. It was Dubose's team-leading fourth goal of the season and his third in the last three matches.

Radford kept up relentless pressure throughout the half and, in a wild sequence in the 36th minute, secured what would be the winning goal. The Highlanders attempted a cross which was kicked away by the Longwood goalie however, the ball went to Gyurci at the top of the box. Gyurci got off a shot and it was deflected by the keeper back to Gyurci who stuck with the play, secured the high rebound through two Longwood defenders, and deposited the ball into the back-left-corner of the net. Midfielder **Patrick Figaro** paced the Highlanders with four shots, while **Samuel Schwarz** had three. In the season finale, Radford lost to UNC-Asheville, 2-1, but 10 players had shots, led by **Samuel Schwarz** with four and Dubose and midfielder **Jan Maldanado** with three apiece. Seniors Incera, **Saber El-Abani**, and **Anthony Giannecchini** were all recognized for their contributions to the program.

In 2022, Coach Barrett carried the largest roster in school history, offering an opportunity to up to 50 student-athletes to showcase their talents.

After a break of nine years, Virginia Tech finally agreed to play Radford again. Upon resuming in 2022, Radford promptly tied Tech, 0-0, and then defeated them, 3-2, in 2023. The reward was that Tech refused to schedule Radford in 2024.

2023 was most unlucky, with a boatload of ties and one-goal losses. The first win didn't come until the middle of October, 2-1, over USC-Upstate. Goals were scored by **Alex Kryazhev** and **Jared Dubose**. A win against Longwood followed, 1-0, on a goal by **Endjick Albert**, but the highlight of the season came against Virginia Tech.

BLACKSBURG, Va., 10/24/2023 – "The Radford men's soccer program took down New River Valley foe Virginia Tech, 3-2, Tuesday night at Thompson Field to finish with a massive win at the end of nonconference play. Tuesday's victory marked the 11th win all-time for men's soccer over the Hokies and the first since 2011. "These guys have shown the resiliency of a Highlander all season" said Head Coach Chris Barrett. "I'm really proud of how these guys reacted after going down two goals early. We played with a lot of heart and guts tonight and hopefully this will continue our momentum into a huge game this Saturday against Gardner-Webb to keep us going for the Big South conference tournament and conference seeding. Again, I couldn't be more proud of a team right now."

Radford trailed early in the first half 1-0, after a pass that cut through the Highlander defense led the Hokies' Marco Vesterholm to go one-on-one with keeper **Alex Eydelman**. The opportunity led to a shot into the bottom left corner to give the Hokies that early advantage. Radford tried to respond but couldn't find the answer early on, having one shot blocked and another go off target. In the 20th minute, Virginia Tech doubled their lead after Eydelman was able to save a shot that lingered in a dangerous area where the Hokies eventually found an opening to secure the 2-0 lead.

However, that would be all Virginia Tech would get in the match. Needing their biggest comeback of the season, Radford responded. The Highlanders were able to strike back with a goal by **Owen Clark** in the 25th minute where he notched a ball into the bottom left corner of the net that would cut the Hokies lead in half. **Jared Dubose** would then go on to quickly even the score against the Hokies after he fired off a shot to the bottom left corner that once more found the back of the net and knotted the match at 2-2.

Mateo Perez Nance, who was credited with the assist for Dubose's goal, was able to snag his first goal of the season in the 37th minute after he fired a shot to the top right corner that would give the Highlanders the 3-2 lead. The Hokies found two opportunities to get the score back level, but a block by the Highlander defense with an Eydelman save kept the scoreline right where it was heading into the halftime break. To open the second half of play, Virginia Tech came out with full force firing two shots on goal in the first three minutes. Eydelman once more preserved the lead with another pair of saves on those shots. After those two early chances, the pace of play slowed as no real opportunities came from either side until twenty minutes later. Virginia Tech once more went on and got off a couple more shots, but the Highlander defense stood strong as they were able to shut down those chances and would ultimately end the match with a 3-2 victory."

2023 Alex Eydelman

The Big South Conference announced the 2023 Conference Award Winners featuring three Highlanders that included **Shady Hammam**, **Alex Kryazhev**, and **Noah Haddad**.

Shady Hammam, a relentless defender, was recognized as second team all-conference having played a total of 15 games for the Highlanders this season. In those games played, Hammam recorded 1,211 minutes of playing time and was also able to rack up 14 shots, averaging almost one per game with five of those shots on goal. In the season finale he was finally able to find the back of the net for his first career goal as a Highlander in the draw against Presbyterian.

Alex Kryazhev was recognized as an honorable mention all-conference. In the 17 games Kryazhev played in the 2023 season, he was able to rack up four goals and two assists for the Highlanders. He also notably was tied for seventh in the conference for shots on goal with 16. Kryazhev was also recognized earlier in the season, having won the Big South offensive player of the week award, the first time a Radford player had won the award since 2019.

Wrapping up the awards was **Noah Haddad**, who not only stood out on the field but also in the classroom to earn the team's all-academic award. Haddad earned an impressive 3.75 GPA. In his career as a Highlander, Haddad was named team captain for his final two years and played in 38 games, accumulating a total of 1,817 minutes of playing time and proved to be a stout defender from the moment he first arrived.

In 2023, Radford men's soccer enjoyed its most television exposure ever, due to the creation of a production trailer for use by ESPN+ for all RU sports. The trailer was made possible because of generous donations from all Radford students, alumni, and former athletes. ESPN+ broadcast 12 games, and the ACCNetwork one game, that year for a total of 13.

RU TV Production Trailer

Spring Commencement 2024: Noah Haddad, College of Nursing

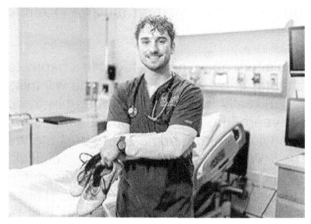

Senior nursing student Noah Haddad comes from a family of healthcare professionals, so he always knew that he wanted to pursue a healthcare career. He was unsure, however, where he would earn his degree and what he would study until he happened to be at a soccer academy showcase in Florida. "I got recruited to play soccer at the showcase by Radford," Haddad says. "But I already had ties to the university. My dad actually played here at Radford, so it was really cool to have the opportunity to follow in his footsteps."

Once he had decided on Radford, the Littleton, CO, native next had to choose what he would study. As he explored his options, nursing quickly rose to the top of his list. "I began looking into the program in regard to how prestigious it was and the super high NCLEX pass rates and it just became obvious that this was the right path for me," Haddad says. "I'm one of those people that if I can do something the hard way, I'm going to do it the hard way. So, I wanted to push myself to be better in all aspects while I was here at Radford."

That determination has paid off for Haddad, whether in the classroom, the lab or on the soccer pitch. This past year, Haddad was named to the Big South Academic All-Conference team. "You know, studying nursing and playing soccer at the same time is not easy," Haddad says. "The nursing program and Radford as a whole has been an important part of my growth and maturity. The right decision is not always a fun decision, but I knew I wanted to succeed. Radford helped me set my priorities straight."

Haddad has worked to integrate the two aspects of his Radford experience by participating in the Student Athlete Advisory Committee (SAAC) for all four of his years on campus. The group is a leadership organization consisting of student-athletes representing all 16 sports at Radford University. SAAC serves as a conduit of communication among student-athletes, coaches and athletic administrators on issues to improve the student-athlete experience and promote growth and education through sports participation.

"I like being the voice for my team," Haddad says. "The athletic community at Radford is super tight knit. We are all really good friends and hang out together. It's like a family and I enjoy being able to advocate for my fellow student-athletes." In addition to his athletic career and extracurricular activities, Haddad is also completing his clinical rotations at Carilion Roanoke Memorial Hospital in the Intensive Care Unit. "As a level one trauma center, the hospital is really fast-paced and that's the type of workflow that I like," Haddad says. "I've been able to meet a lot of people through my clinicals and I've met a lot of super-skilled, intelligent nurses. I've learned so much and made memories with them that I'll never forget."

As he approaches graduation, Haddad says he's torn about how to feel. He's happy to be finishing his degree and starting a new chapter in his life, but he says he will miss Radford and all the university has to offer. "I'm really happy to finally be able to do what I've gone to school for over the last four years," he says, "but at the same time, it's really emotional and kind of sad that I'm moving on from some of the best friends that I've ever had. It's going to be hard to let go." While leaving Radford will be difficult, Haddad says he has only great memories of his time as a Highlander. "Radford is a smaller school and everyone really starts to become like family," he says. "These people that I've met and the memories that I've shared with them are things that I'll hold with me for the rest of my life."

At the Red & White Gala on April 26, 2024, Radford University dedicated the playing surface at Patrick D. Cupp Memorial Stadium as the **TOM LILLARD '79 FIELD**.

Lillard Loves Radford and Radford Loves Him

By Mike Ashley '83

Radford University honored **Tommy Lillard** '79 at our annual Red/White Gala in the Dedmon Center April 26. A record crowd was there for the announcement that the soccer field at Patrick D. Cupp Stadium will be named for founding father Lillard, backed by over $150,000 in donations from people that love him and all he has done for the university.

I think of Tommy and I think of that twinkle in his eye, the one that makes us all smile. He had a hint of tears of happiness Friday at the celebration for a Highlander career well spent.

Coming out of Yorktown High School in 1974, the young army brat had a lot of schools offering him a chance to play soccer, but he chose Radford College, a school that had just started admitting men and didn't even have a varsity team.

"I had come to visit my sister (Susan) and I stayed in a dorm and ate meals in the cafeteria like I was a student," Lillard laughed. "It just felt like home from the first time I was here."

And maybe that feeling was why so many athletes enjoyed playing for Tommy and why he was so good at getting so many people to buy-in on the Highlanders. He garnered a lot of support for his alma mater over 26 years in administration, the last seven as Associate Vice President for University Advancement. More than that, though, Tommy exported untold amounts of goodwill from the New River Valley all the while making others feel at home here, too.

"He has done so much for so many," said RU's first soccer *All-America*, **Billy Gerber** '85. "He took a chance on me and I didn't want to let him down. If not for that man I wouldn't have become the man I am today."

Gerber, who played professionally in the American Soccer League with the Washington Diplomats, is now a Senior Enterprise Account Executive for Siemens. "I was a handful for (Lillard) and (Athletic Director) **Chuck Taylor** and I called **Kathy (Lillard)** every week for advice. I changed my major and had some issues, but they stuck with me and supported me and I know of lot of soccer players that feel that way."

Those players, who Tommy coached on the men's side for six years and on the women's side their inaugural season in 1981, were primary resources in the secret soccer field naming campaign. Many of them were on hand at the gala to see their old coach surprised and honored. You can still make contributions, by the way, by contacting ruadvancement@radford.edu.

147

"He just took a real interest in his players off the field," added Gerber. "He and Kathy, both. He never looked at us as commodities to help the won-loss record. He was a mentor and had a huge heart. He used to call my mom all the time and give her updates when I was here. He just went beyond the norm. He was more like a big brother and Kathy like a big sister watching out for us."

And that care went beyond his players, too. Coach **Don Staley** '91, recruited as an assistant coach to Radford, said he owes his career to Lillard, including his current status as a southeastern sports tourism mogul.

"I was so blessed," said Staley, who had the most wins in RU soccer before leaving to coach at Alabama. "Tommy changed my life. I wouldn't have gotten my degree if he hadn't brought me to Radford. And then he taught me so much. He was a coach of people, too, teaching me how to work with the administration and talking about leadership in all walks of life. I owe him so much."

To say Tommy is a "People Person" is a vast understatement. His genuine care for the folks around him has always made him popular, as does a quick wit, contagious smile and infectious laugh. "What makes Tom special is how much he cares about you as a person," said **Penny Helms White** '85 & '87, the Vice President for Advancement, who worked with Lillard for nearly 30 years at RU and Virginia Tech and then again back at RU. "If you need something, he's the first one there to help. He doesn't ask, he just does it."

Lillard's drive to do such was quickly on display at Radford. He helped form the first soccer club team and then went out and found the right coach for the program after two varsity losing seasons. **John Harves** helped the Highlanders to their first winning record with Lillard in the lineup as a long-haired star on attack in 1977.

"(RU Hall of Fame goalkeeper) **John White** '81, and (former RU player and women's coach) **Will Iandolo** '81 & '82, were playing for me on the Under-18 team in Arlington," said Harves. "John was Tommy's neighbor and Tommy happened by one day and said Radford needed a coach, and that's how it got started."

Radford landed Harves, who had been a grad assistant at Tech, and was considering an offer from Richmond. Both White and Iandolo came, too. When Harves left for a job with the Nuclear Regulatory Commission in 1979, Tommy took over as the program blew up.

Lillard handled the tough challenge of coaching players with whom he had played, going 8-4-3 his first year and claiming an NAIA District title. Then he put together a terrifically talented team, including White in goal, that had a magical run. The 1981 squad claimed a Virginia Intercollegiate Soccer Association win over powerhouse

Averett in the state championship game on Moffett Field. The Highlanders pulled out a 2-1 win in triple overtime and the youthful Lillard was named Coach of the Year.

I remember those teams and Tommy, the young, shaggy blonde coach so approachable for a young sportswriter, and well, for anyone, really. Later, I never really understood how someone who looked so much like they were up to something, could solicit so much money. Tommy could make me laugh with just a look, that twinkle in his eye, and a shake of his head.

One morning I woke up to the sound of hammering outside my Moffett Hall window. It was Tommy – the coach of the soccer team – nailing up signs on the softball backstop in the near corner of the varsity field the Highlanders shared with intramurals.

With a big NAIA playoff game later that day against Rutgers-Camden, Tommy was putting up some pro-RU, anti-Rutgers slogans because he knew none of the student fans were going to get up early and do it. Those are the humble roots our program came from. Tommy was also instrumental in helping us change that over the years as, again, RU showed what it could do. Moving up to Division I, Radford has now won an array of championships and made trips to the NCAA Tournament. Ditto, the women's program, which has been even more successful nationally.

Lillard would stay on to guide Radford into D-I, including a 5-1 Big South record in 1985 when RU fell in the first conference title game. But with he and Kathy eying their young family, Lillard stepped down from his dual position as coach and night manager of the Dedmon Center, soon moving into the alumni office and then advancement, where he advanced quickly.

"It was a hard decision but the family was coming along and you have to support them and have time for them," Lillard said. "So many nights and weekends. (Eldest son) Kevin was on a bus trip with us at six weeks. And Don (Staley) was ready (to take over)."

Tommy was a natural at his true calling – spreading the gospel of Radford to alumni believers and to businesses, corporations and anyone who would listen. And Tommy had a gift for securing gifts, that made him coveted by Virginia Tech and absolutely vital as he returned to Radford.

Staley pointed out, too, that Lillard remained a soccer set piece for the program. "My players knew him and respected him as a coach and he was a mentor for them. Tommy is a Radford guy through and through. The players knew they could go to him as a sounding board. I did, too. He was never heavy-handed but he was always there if we needed him."

Tech advancement recruited Lillard away in 2008, but Radford got him back. New president, Dr. Bret Danilowicz showed a keen understanding of all things RU early on, convincing Tommy to stay on when Lillard first hoped to retire. Ultimately, health concerns forced Lillard to step away. Well, sorta. He's still got a hand in all things plaid, and his health has improved. Getting a field fueled by your own dreams named for you does wonders.

So does a virtual sports equipment travel case of wonderful memories of the home he made at a place he has come to embody – he and Radford are friendly, forward-thinking, and ready to help when folks need it. Over and over again.

Tommy thanked former Radford vice president **Jerry Hutchens** '75 & '76, who helped him move into advancement; former RU president, **Dr. Donald Dedmon**, who signed off on hiring him and really allowed all us guys opportunities at this wonderful place. Athletic Director Chuck Taylor took a chance on a young coach and then his co-workers like Alumni Director **Laura Turk** '87 & '90; Penny White; former alumni director **Jenny Doud** '75 & '80, and former tennis coach and Dedmon Center Director **Ron Downs** '77 & '84, all played important roles alongside Tommy as the university and its athletic program grew. Staley took Tommy's beloved soccer program to new heights.

"It is unique here," said Lillard. "Doing your job becomes your life at a place you love and all the friends along the way make it so much more complete."

Hoping you aren't complete yet, my friend. You make me laugh. You make me want to stay a part of that place I just can't shake. I smiled all weekend at the Gala and at a baseball alumni event I attended. I hate that wording – *attended* – I was there because I really wanted to be because of people there that meant the world to me.

Radford will do that to you. Because of the people. Like Tommy Lillard.

Mike Ashley '83 was a national award-winning writer and columnist ('Sidelines') for the Radford University student newspaper, 'The Tartan,' as an undergrad. He has been a professional journalist since 1983, working at Radford, Virginia Tech and finally, as a freelancer in Fairfax, Va., mostly covering the University of Maryland and mid-major college basketball the last 27 years, including the Highlanders. He witnessed the thrilling 2-1 triple overtime win for the state soccer title in 1981, mostly from a perch atop Moffett Wall, preferred seating back in the day. Ashley writes an occasional column for the Radford website to share his recollections with Highlander fans.

In 2024, Radford University celebrates the 50th Season of the Men's Varsity Soccer Program.

The Radford University Men's Varsity Soccer Program's 50th Season is a cause for long-term celebration! The effort and the institution have passed the test of time. An extended family has been created that is demonstrated annually, not only by attendance at games, but also by local events and participation in Homecoming. New members are added to the family every year and there is great hope now and for the future. The coaches and the team need all the support they can get, both on and off the field, currently and for posterity. *__The Radford University soccer community is called upon to please make significant, ongoing, financial contributions to the program.__*

At a game during the Fall 2024 season, Radford honored the members of the 1975 First Varsity Team with medals and former Coach Tom Lillard for the program's first major title, the 1981 Virginia Intercollegiate Soccer Association (VISA) championship. Lillard was presented with a personal plaque celebrating his State Title. He was also presented with a **Lifetime Achievement Award**.

The engraving on the back of the medal reads:

1975 – First Varsity Men's Soccer Team
Radford University 50th Season – 2024

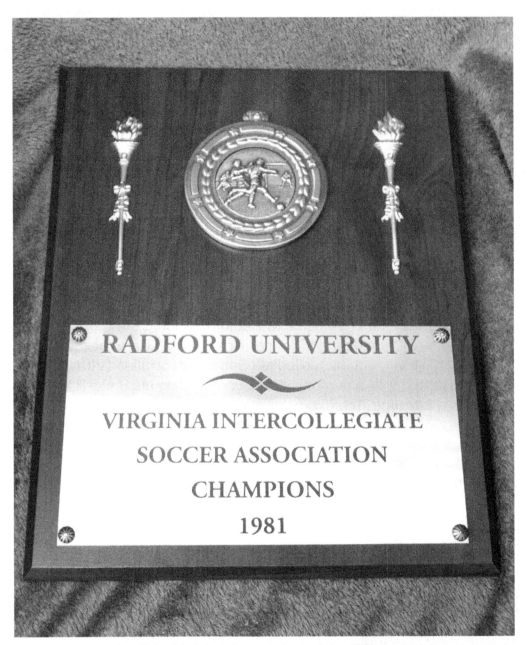

VISA 1981 Championship Plaque
Presented to Tom Lillard

2024 -- Lifetime Achievement Trophy
Presented to Tom Lillard

EPILOGUE

For the participants in the Radford University Men's Varsity Soccer Program, it is more than just the sport, it's part of a community. The players maintained high academic standards and graduated with honors. They have gone on to become doctors, nurses, lawyers, entrepreneurs, business managers, contract managers, government employees (federal, state, and local), educators, program analysts, systems analysts, computer specialists, realtors, social workers, caregivers, volunteers, and members of the armed services.

Others have gone into law enforcement, health care, administration, insurance, and other professions. They have become husbands, fathers and grandfathers. And, yes, many have stayed with the game, either playing for as long as they possibly could or going into soccer coaching, either professionally or volunteering with their own children and grandchildren, and refereeing.

Special recognition is reserved for those former athletes who have maintained lasting relationships with the soccer program, as contributors, and with the University itself in professional roles. This includes Board Members of the Radford University Foundation and the Radford University Athletic Foundation, and visiting professors.

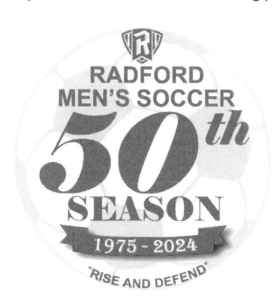

APPENDICES

APPENDICES

Appendix 1

Radford University Men's Soccer
ALL-TIME ROSTER
1975 - 2024

RU Men's Soccer
ALL-TIME ROSTER
1975 – 2024

Aa

Adams, Paul 1980
Adeyemi, Mike 1999-2000
Adolph, Rob 1987-88, 90
Aker, Neal 1975-77
Albiston, Ryan 2013
Allaire, Troy 2012
Allen, Bo 2000-01, 03
Allway, Tallon 2022-23
Amba, Gabriel 2013-16
Amofah, Bismark 2013-16
Anderson, Greg 1999
Anderson, Kadmiel 2023-24
Angelides, Max-Emilios 2017-21
Angelino, Bob 1976
Annetti, Bill 1977
Anson, Josh 1997-98
Aquino, Ian 2007-10
Arboleda, Fabian 1997-98
Arkon, Steven 1987-90
Arzubiaga, Sergio 2012-15
Atwell, Brandon 2014
Avendano, Jose 1994-95
Awosika, Iyiola 2008-11

Bb

Bacharach, Roy 1991
Bailey, Scott 1975-76
Baker, Chris 1984-87
Bangura, Paul 2021
Bankert, Cole 2015-17
Barlow, Timmy 2022
Barnett, Kyle 2016
Barrett, Chris 1991-94
Barrett, James 2022-23
Barry, John 1989-92
Bartman, Adam 2005-06

Bates, Stephen 2001
Baxter, Joe 2008-10
Beach, Kyle...................2011-12
Bell-Cooper, Kameron.................2019
Benavides, Juan 2018-21
Bennett, Khori 2018
Bennett, Matt...................1993
Bentley, Wayne 1979-80
Berger, Mike................ 1976, 78-79
Bergstrom, Nick 1998
Berrang, Matthias.............. 1990-91
Best, Paul...................1978
Best, R. J. 2011
Bishop, Chris...................2008
Bissell, Austin...................2018
Blanchard, Stockton...................2014
Blum, David.............. 2020-22
Bond, Dustin 1999-2000
Borjesson, Rikard.............. 1991-92
Bouker, Pete 1983-86
Bourne, Chris............. 1983-86
Boyar, Kalefa...................2022
Boyd, Michael 1991-93, 95
Boyer, J. P. 1985
Brady, Lee............. 1992-93
Bressler, Rob 1999
Bridi, Ramzi...................2011
Broadbent, Troy 1990-93
Brown, Camden 2007-10
Brown, Jeff............. 1984-85, 87-88
Brown, Jim 1982
Bruce, Brian 1980-82
Brumbaugh, Robert............. 1981-82
Bryan, Mark...................1980
Bryant, Justin 1984-86
Bucey, Eric............. 1995-96
Burke, Joe...................1999
Butcher, Nick............. 1997-98
Butler, Shane 2008
Byrd, Maurice...................1978

Cc

Cadena, Luis 2002-05
Cardozo, Angel 1997-98
Carpenter, Jack...............................1975
Carrabotta, Antonio.......................2013
Carter, Ethan 2017
Carter, Ron 1979-81
Caruso, Paul............................2005-07
Casey, Lance 1985-86
Castillejo, Bill 1996-99
Caton, Ryan........................1998-2001
Cave, Bill 1979
Cazalot, Brian 1995
Chaves, Phil 2001
Chavez, Manuel....................2005-2009
Choi, Tamin................................2023-24
Chomeau, John 1978-80, 82
Cilinski, Brian.................................1983
Clark, Bo..1996
Clark, Chris....................................1991
Clark, Darren 1983
Clark, Owen................................2022-24
Clark, Seth.................................2023-24
Clark, Solomon 2020-22
Clubb, Mark 1990-91
Colas, Patrick 2003-05
Coleman, Dave.........................1975-76
Collantes, Cesar 1977
Colmer, Fraser.........................2014-17
Conlin, Mark 1992
Cooley, Devan 2004-08
Corado, Alex 2018
Cossaboon, David 1988-89, 91
Cox, Dexter....................................1994
Crespin, Jorge 1990
Cross, Guy.....................................2012
Crowder, Mark 1999-2002
Cruz, Christian..........................2021-24
Custer, Keith 1981
Czerlinsky, Brian............................1982

Dd

Daabul, Noy 2017
Dacosta, Demaro 2012
Daehlie, Sivert........................... 2015-17
Dale, Jeff....................................1980
Dalton, Brad 1997-98
D'Amato, Pier 1994
Daniels, Keller........................... 2022-23
Darby, Bryan 2012
Darden, Keith 1989-90
Davies, Felix 2024
De Barros, Fernando 2012-13
Deacy, Liam 2016-19
Delpino, Jeremy 2006-08
Demaio, Jason 1991-92
Dennis, Joey 2009-10
Desarno, Mike............................ 1987-88
Devaldes, John 2010
Dewitt, Jason 1988
Diesel, Bert 1983, 85
Diniz, Lucas 2012
Dixon, Dorion 2018-21
Dopp, Mike.................................. 1983-86
Dougland, Lance 1990
Dramby, Mike 1999-2000
Dridi, Ramzi 2012-14
Drouin, Sacha 1995-98
Dubose, Jared........................... 2022-23
Duffy, Liam 2016
DuPont, Kevin 1979-81
Duran, Alfredo 1977-80
Duran, Edwin 1978-81
Dykstra, Chris 2006

Ee

Eagon, Brian 1986-89
Easton, Billy 1975
Eck, Keith................................. 1990-91
Eckenrode, Jannik 2012
Edwards, Max 2017-18

El-Abani, Saber 2022
Elimbi, Franklin 2006-07
Ellis, Mark 1990-91
Embleton, Ricky 1993
Endijck, Albert 2023
England, Joseph 2021
Ercolano, Rob 1978-79
Erzen, Wyatt 2016-19
Essey, Andrew 2000-03
Etienne, Quincy 2019-21
Evans, Chris 1993
Eydelman, Alex 2021-24

Ff

Farrell, Sam 2018-19
Faye, Baye Djibril.......................2019-20
Figaro, Patrick 2021-22
Finck, Justin................................1990
Findlay, Jody...............................1986
Fisher, Randy 1989-90
Fleming, Kevin...........................2009-11
Fosu, Jon............................1999-2002
Fousse, Baptiste...........................2019
Fox, David 1993
Frias, Jonathan....................1999-2000
Fuentes, Ben 2007-10
Fugate, Hunter............................2008

Gg

Gadelha, Ed...............................1988
Gaffigan, Luke 2019, 21
Gardev, James..........................2022-23
Gavilan, Chris 1990
Gealt, Kevin 1991-95
George, Thomas..........................2009
Gerber, Bill..............................1982-85
Gerstien, Ethan...........................2003
Giannecchini, Anthony 2020-22
Gilmore, Greg 1981
Ginsburg, Mike 1995-98

Gonsalves, Jayden 2019-20
Goyer, J. P. 1984
Grabham, Scott 1989
Grande, Luis 2010-13
Grande, Simon 2019
Grant, Scott 1993
Greco, Mike 1977
Greene, Kevin 1982-83
Grey, Dax 1997-99
Griefer, Jacob 2012
Griggs, Bruce 1987-89
Grinsfelder, Garrett 1997
Grover, Suneel 1995-96
Gunson, Dennis 1978-81
Gursky, Geoff 1996
Gvozdas, Jason 1995-98
Gwanzura, Brian 2009-11
Gyurci, Griffin 2022-23

Hh

Habibelahy, Kevin 2024
Haddad, Jamal 1976-79
Haddad, Noah 2019-23
Hagen, Kyle 2022-23
Hammam, Shady 2023-24
Hance, Scott 1997-2000
Handlin, Mike 2009-10
Hanes, Currie 2015-16
Hanley, Chris 1993-95
Hanson, Matt 1998
Hardman, Yury 2017
Harig, Mike 1985
Harper, Thorsen 2001
Harpula, David 2002-05
Harris, Greg 2021-23
Harris, Ian 1989-90
Hart, Derik 1983
Hasan, Yusuf 1996
Hatcher, Lucas 2008
Hawes, Collin 2021-24
Heling, Jason 2000

Helscher, Cannon 1996-97
Henderson, Che 1992-95
Henry, Fran 1983-86
Hernandez, Andres 2002-05
Hernandez, Geraldo 1999-2002
Hernandez, Roberto 2022
Hill, Andy 1983
Hillegas, Mike 1975-76
Ho Park Kim, Chel 2011-14
Hoare, Jeff 1975
Hooker, Jonathan 2000-02
Hudgens, Stephen 2011-14
Hudson, Ryan 1991
Hughes, Patrick 1993-94
Hurley, John 1981-83
Husadzinovic, Davorin 2005-07
Hutcheon, Michael 2011-14

Ii

Iandolo, Will 1978-79
Ihnainen, Harri 1987-88
Incera, Joseba 2019-22
Inestroza, Jesse 1993
Infante, Kenny 2000

Jj

Janssen, Matt 2011-13
Jefferson, Corey 1999-2001
Jenkins, Taylor 2004-07
Jenks, J. P. 1981-82
Johnson, Koby 2014-17
Johnson, Malcolm 1995
Johnson, Sean 2003-04
Jones, Jonathon 1996
Jones, Myles 2009-12
Jones, Randy 1979-82
Jordan, Charlie 1983
Jordan, Jack 2013
Jordan, James 2009-13
Joseph, Emmanuel 2007-08

Kk

Kallendorf, Trevor...................... 2020-21
Kamara, Mustaph............... 2020-22, 24
Kaneda, Asuka.............................2022
Kauffman, Ryan 1992
Kaufman, Chase 1996
Kee, Willie 1983-86
Keesee, Dustin.............................1998
Keiller, Whitney 1989-92
Kelly, Kevin 1996-97
Kilosho, Sadock 2024
King, Brent 1984
Koren, Ulrik 2016-17
Kouonang, Hivan 2021-22
Kreutzberger, Austin......................2018
Kryazhev, Alex 2022-23
Kuhla, Mike 1987
Kuttner, Christoph 2022
Kyle, Hagen 2024

Ll

Lachance, Troy 1993
Lagunas, Bryan............................2021
Lakatos, Gerald........................ 1991-94
Lambert, John 1982
Lamptey, Cam......................... 2023-24
Langer, Chris........................... 1979-81
Laslie, Charlie 1976-79
Lauler, Mike.........................1977, 80
Lauretano, Vittorio.................... 2010-13
Lea, Greg.............................. 1995-96
Lee, Billy 1995
Lee, Chris............................. 2007-08
Legg, Sam.................................2012
Leigh, Nicholas 2004-06
Leith, James....................... 2007-2010
Leslau, Raphail 2019
Leveski, Tyler.......................... 2004-07
Lewis, Andre 1999-2002

Ligner, Thure.............................2018-19
Lillard, Tom 1975-77
Link, Joe 1976-77
Lisanti, Tony............................1997-98
Lodge, Rick..............................1994-95
Long, Chad 1995-96
Long, Scott 1978
Longsworth, Ted 1980-82
Lopez, Edgar 2007
Lucas, Matt..............................2022-23
Lukerzc, Jim 1996
Lynch, Brian.............................1992-94
Lyngen, Mads 2012

Mm

MacBrien, Trevor 2004-07
Machado-Jones, Ryan...............2019-21
Macias, Aldo 2007-11
Macky Diop, Amadou.................2018-19
Maddox, Jimmy............................2006
Magnusson, John 1988-91
Mahan, Greg.................................1989
Majewski, Doug 1987-90
Majewski, Jeff 1988-91
Malave, Kevin 2022-23
Maldonado, Jan 2021-23
Maldonado, Sebastian 2021
Mann, Tim.................................1977-81
Mapp, Stephen 2004-05
Marcy, Mason 2017
Martensson, Leif 1991
Martin, Taylor 2014-18
Martinez, Tony 2021-22
Martorana, Neil 2014-17
Masudi, Leon 2022-24
Maudire, Romain 2004
Mayer, Joe 2012-13
Mayhugh, Nick...........................2015-18
McAlister, Nick 2000
McCarthy, Greg..........................1981-84
McClaugherty, Don 1987

McClellan, Donovan 2024
McClendon, Mason 2024
McCrary, Josh 2007
McIntire, Jim............................. 1980-83
McIntosh, Kendall 2014-17
McMahon, Pat...............................1987
Mehari, Leul 2021-22
Merrill, Mark 2003
Mertzokat, Nicolas 2014-17
Metzger, Randy........................ 1975-77
Micolucci, Michael..........................2022
Mills, Carter................................2008-11
Mitchelson, Wister..........................1990
Montagne, Joe 1982-85
Moore, Henry 2022-23
Morales, Jeffrey 2021-22
Morton, Lee................................. 1993-96

Nn

Nace, Brian 1975-77
Nalborski, Krzysztof 2014-15
Nall, Travis 2000
Negron, Ramon........................ 2004-06
Nemeth, Corey...............................2015
Neptune, Josh...............................2016
Nguyen, Thai........................1984-85, 88
Nicholas, Andrew 2017
Nicholas, Jeffrey 1999, 2002-03

Oo

Ocampo, Octavio 2019-22
Odum, Jon 1999
Ogburn, Corey 2001-04
O'Grady, Mike 1983
O'Hara, Walter 1984
Okawa, Yoshiya 2021
O'Keefe, Daniel..........................2011-15
Olnhausen, Jeff............................1986
Olsen, Jim.....................................1975
Opoku-Adjei, Abel Prince 2018, 20

Orgetas, Dino 1994-95
Osterberger, Mark.....................1989-92
O'Sullivan, Daniel 2024
Oumar Gueye, Pape..................2018-20
Owens, Chris 1996
Owens, Phil 1984

Pp

Pahl, Adam 2001-05
Pardieck, Matthew 2024
Parish, Kyle 1998
Parvin, Eric 1988
Pasquel, Jorge.............................. 1982
Paterson, Justin............................2002
Patricio, Daryn 2006-09
Pauls, William 2015
Payne, Anthony 2009-11
Peacock, Bryceland 2022-24
Pearson, Nate...........................2000-03
Peay, Sean 1987-90
Pechtimaldjian, Gary.................1975-76
Pendorf, Scott............................. 1980
Perez Nance, Mateo 2022-23
Perez-Costa, Alfredo.................2000-02
Perkovich, Graham 1991-92
Perry, Rick 1975
Pertl, Chris.............................2004-06
Peters, Mitch................................. 1998
Peterson, Justin.......................2001-03
Pettit, Chris 1995-96
Petty, David................................. 1982
Pfeffer, Mike................................. 1986
Pham, Trung 1984-85
Philips, Bret 1976-77
Phimmasone, Anoput.................1983-84
Poian, Khalid 2020-21
Poirier, Greg 1976, 78
Pouseu Blanco, Aitor 2013-16
Price, Ben 2002
Pruett, Miles...............................1982-85
Pulik, Tyler 2022-24

Pyle, Andre.............................. 1990-91

Rr

Ragone, John...............................1982
Ramos, Fernando 2002-05
Ramquist, Magnus 1986-89
Rancel, Mauricio 2014
Rarus, Eric 1995
Rawlins, Spencer 2022-23
Rector, Rick..................................1975
Redding, Landon........................ 2023-24
Redondo, Dario 2011-14
Reid, Erin 1992
Reid, Lennie.................................2006
Rice, Jimmy 1993
Ridgely, Reg............................. 1980-81
Rimstad, Jo Vetle 2013-16
Rivera, Jose 2019-21
Robbins, David.............................1995
Roberts, Kieran 2014-18
Roberts, Stephen 1987
Robinson, Dondre' 2017-21
Robles, Luis 1989
Rodon, Lee 1995
Rodon, Mike.................................1995
Rodriguez, Gonzalo 2018
Rolfing, T. J. 1999-2002
Romero, Armando..................... 2004-05
Rondeau, Frederic 1989-92
Roof, Bryan......................... 1999-2001
Rosen, Chris 1993
Rosenbaum, Neil 1991
Roszel, Zach............................. 2006-08
Rowe, Taylor 2003-06
Rowland, Jamie 1992
Roxio, Dan 1987
Ruano, Eric 1994-97
Ruiz, German................................1975
Rupe, Evan 2023-24
Rusagara, Albert 1994
Ryan, Tim.................................. 1975-76

Ryder, Pete 1990

Ss

Sahagun, Bob 1975-76
Sainz, Leandro 2021
Salop, Mark 2001
Sansbury, Joseph 2004-07
Savopoulos, Savos 1976
Saylor, Billy 1994
Schulte, Steve 1975-78
Schultz, Art 1992
Schultz, Dan 1978, 80
Schwartz, Cole 2017-18
Schwarz, Samuel 2022
Scoffield, Bryan 2018-19
Scott, Ryan 1994
Seyler, Dan 1975-76
Shaffer, Brendan 2007-10
Sheally, Bennie 1992
Shepherd, Richard 1993-96
Shepherd, Willie 1986-87
Sheridan, Fiachra 1992-93
Sherrill, Brian 1976-77
Siczek, Patrick 2017-21
Sigui, Fernando 1994
Sigurdson, Eric 1984-87
Silva, Mark 2021-24
Simmons, John 2022
Simms, Josh 2005-06
Sisson, Brad 1996-97
Slate, Mike 1994
Smetanick, Peter 2007-08
Smith-Sreen, John 1977-80
Smith, Garland 2013-16
Smith, Garnet 1978-80
Smith, Jonathon 2003-06
Smith, Marc 2002-03
Smythe, Austin 2015
Snell, Adrian 2001-03
Sokolik, Erik 2000-03
Soldervilla, John 1987

Somuah, Bright 2020
Sopranzi, Tony 1982
Spooner, Ian.................. 1991-92, 94-95
Springer, Darryl 1990-93
Squire, Toby 2019-22
Stachler, Bill 1984-86
Stannard, David 2004
Steinhauser, Felix 2014-15
Stephens, William 1998
Stevens, Dan 2002-04
Stills, Jambaar 2011-12
Stinnett, Rob 1993-94
Stinnett, Ryan 2009-11
Stoner, Seth 2002-03
Strandsäter, Jakob 2015-18
Summers, Jamie 2012-15
Sweazy, Mike 1996
Szklennik, Evan 2014-17

Tt

Tajtyi, Akos.............................. 2023-24
Tamm, Andrew 2002
Taylor, Kevin........................... 1985-86
Taylor, Noah 1993
Taylor, Ryan 2008-12
Templeton, Troy 1994
Terne, Keven........................... 1996-97
Tettemer, Sean........................ 1993-95
Thiam, Mouhameth 2019
Thiss, Benjamin 2015-18
Thomas, George 2010
Thomé, Edwardo...........................2018
Thompson, Cory 2015
Thoms, Dan 1978-80
Thomsen, Robert 2006-09
Thomsen, Will 2003-07
Thorsen, Harper....................... 2001-02
Tiedemann, Finn 2015
Tierney, Chris...............................1994
Tierney, John........................... 1992-95
Torborg, Tim 1996

Torres, Tommy 1995
Towns, Bubby 2022-23
Trible, Preston 1975-77
Troiano, Kevin 1989
Turk, Zach 2013-16
Turpin, Shawn 1989-90

Uu

Udy, Brian 1982-86
Ulmo, Bernardo 2010-13
Usher, Riley 2023-24

Vv

Vahle, Tom 1980-81
Valencia, Allen 1985-86
Valencia, Nico 2011-14
Valkanos, Dimitrios 2017-18
Valls, Victor 2016-19
Van den Broeck, Andre 1998
Vasquez, Giovanni 2020-21
Veal, Richard 1993-96
Velasquez, Hansy 2021
Von Essen, Mike 1999-2002

Ww

Wadkins, Akire 2022-24
Wales, Patrick 1999-02
Walker, Brett 1990
Walsh, Michael 2014-18
Waltz, Chris 1999-2002
Ward, Travis 1989
Washburn, Scott 1985
Washington, Dante 1988-92
Washington, Troy 1996-98
Weber, Andrew 2021-22
Weidow, Davis 2011
Werner, Chris 2005-08
White, Fred 1982-83
White, John 1978-81
White, Stephen 1983-87

Wilkinson, Jacob 2016-19
Williams, Bruce 1981
Williams, Chris 2020-23
Williams, John...............................1996
Williams, Kevin.......................... 1989-90
Wilson, Craig.................................2007
Wilson, Dane............................2011-13
Wilson, Jay....................................1976
Wilson, Teddy........................... 1987-90
Winstead, Mike 1999-2002
Wissar, Eduardo....................... 1994-95
Wuertz, Christian 2022
Wyzkoski, Joe 1985-86

Yy

Yager, Chris 1994
Yorke, Myles 2015-18
Young, Joe 1995-97
Young, Tommy 1994-95

Zz

Zaccarelli, Pedro 2013
Zamora, Horacio 1996-97
Zeballos, Sammy 2008
Zimmer, Justin.......................... 2006-09
Zimmerman, Derek 1994-97
Zinoveev, Omar........................ 2003-05

APPENDIX 1 – ALL-TIME ROSTER

Appendix 2

Radford University Men's Soccer

TEAM PHOTOS
and ROSTERS

Year-by-Year 1975 - 2024

NOTE: Team rosters are shown in ALPHABETICAL ORDER.

1975

Fall 1975 – The First Radford University Men's Varsity Soccer Team

1st Row: Jack Carpenter, Dave Coleman, Scott Bailey, Jim Olsen, German Ruiz, Mike Hillegas, Jeff Hoare, Randy Metzger, Rick Perry, Gary Pechtimaldjian, Bob Sahagun
2nd Row: Asst. Coach Peter Howes, Dan Seyler, Billy Easton, Preston Trible, Neal Aker, Steve Schulte, Tom Lillard, Tim Ryan, Rick Rector, Mgr. Mary Lee Cline, Brian Nace, Coach John Ravnik

Aker, Neal • Bailey, Scott • Carpenter, Jack • Coleman, Dave • Easton, Billy • Hillegas, Mike • Hoare, Jeff • Lillard, Tom • Metzger, Randy • Nace, Brian • Olsen, Jim • Pechtimaldjian, Gary • Perry, Rick • Rector, Rick • Ruiz, German • Ryan, Tim • Sahagun, Bob • Schulte, Steve • Seyler, Dan • Trible, Preston

1976

First Row (L-R) Joe Link. Dave Coleman. Bob Sahagun. Scott Bailey. Charlie Laslie. Rick Sahagun. Scott Bailey. Charlie Laslie. Gary Pechtimaldi. Ronnie Lonnegan (Mgr). Second Row (L-R) Randy Metzger. Neil Akers. Tommy Lillard. Preston Trible. Dan Seyler. Steve Shutz. Mike Berger. Tim Ryan. Jamal Haddad. Savos Savopoulos. Brian Nace. Missing — Jay Wilson. Brian Sherrill. Brett Philips. Greg Poirier. Bob Angelino.

First Row (L-R) Joe Link. Dave Coleman. Bob Sahagun. Scott Bailey. Charlie Laslie. Gary Pechtimaldjian. Ronnie Lonnegan (Mgr.).

Second Row (L-R) Randy Metzger. Neal Aker. Tommy Lillard. Preston Trible. Dan Seyler. Steve Schulte. Mike Berger. Tim Ryan. Jamal Haddad. Savos Savopoulos. Brian Nace. Missing - Jay Wilson. Brian Sherrill. Bret Philips. Greg Poirier. Bob Angelino

Aker, Neal • Angelino, Bob • Bailey, Scott • Berger, Mike • Coleman, Dave • Haddad, Jamal • Hillegas. Mike • Laslie, Charlie • Lillard, Tom • Link. Joe • Metzger. Randy • Nace. Brian • Pechtimaldjian. Gary • Philips, Bret • Poirier. Greg • Ryan. Tim • Sahagun, Bob • Savopoulos, Savos • Schulte, Steve • Seyler, Dan • Sherrill, Brian • Trible. Preston • Wilson, Jay

1977

1977 RADFORD COLLEGE MEN'S VARSITY SOCCER TEAM
RECORD: 8 – 7

Front: (L-R) Mike Lauler, Bill Annetti, Cesar Collantes, Neal Aker, Randy Metzger, Alfredo Duran, Brian Nace, Charlie Laslie. Back: (L-R) Coach John Harves, Tim Mann, Mike Greco, Steve Schulte, Brian Sherrill, Preston Trible, Tom Lillard, Bret Phillips, John Smith. Not Pictured: Jamal Haddad, Joe Link

Aker, Neal • Annetti, Bill • Collantes, Cesar • Duran, Alfredo • Greco, Mike • Haddad, Jamal • Laslie, Charlie • Lauler, Mike • Lillard, Tom • Link, Joe • Mann, Tim • Metzger, Randy • Nace, Brian • Philips, Bret • Schulte, Steve • Sherrill, Brian • Smith-Sreen, John • Trible, Preston

1978

1978 RADFORD COLLEGE VARSITY SOCCER TEAM
10 - 3 - 3

Front row (left to right): Greg Poirier, Dan Schultz, Dan Thoms, Alfredo Duran, John White, Charlie Laslie, Rob Ercolano, Edwin Duran, John Chomeau, Will Iandolo.
Back row (left to right): Coach John Harves, Dennis Gunson, Tim Mann, John Smith, Maurice Byrd, Scott Long, Garnet Smith, Steve Schulte, Mike Berger, Jamal Haddad, Paul Best, Assistant Coach Tom Lillard.

Berger, Mike ● Best, Paul ● Byrd, Maurice ● Chomeau, John ● Duran, Alfredo ● Duran, Edwin ● Ercolano, Rob ● Gunson, Dennis ● Haddad, Jamal ● Iandolo, Will ● Laslie, Charlie ● Long, Scott ● Mann, Tim ● Poirier, Greg ● Schulte, Steve ● Schultz, Dan ● Smith-Sreen, John ● Smith, Garnet ● Thoms, Dan ● White, John

1979

1979 RADFORD UNIVERSITY VARSITY SOCCER TEAM

11 - 6 - 1
NAIA District 19 Runner-Up

Front Row (left to right): Tim Mann, Dan Thoms, Dennis Gunson, Rob Ercolano, Randy Jones, Chris Langer, Alfredo Duran, Charlie Laslie, John White, Ron Carter, Mike Berger, Will Iandolo.
Back Row (left to right): Coach John Harves, Mgr. Beth Harkins, Edwin Duran, Bill Cave, John Smith, Kevin Dupont, Garnet Smith, John Chomeau, Wayne Bentley, Jamal Haddad, Asst. Coach Tom Lillard, Asst. Coach Reg Ridgely.

Bentley, Wayne • Berger, Mike • Carter, Ron • Cave, Bill • Chomeau, John • DuPont, Kevin • Duran, Alfredo • Duran, Edwin • Ercolano, Rob • Gunson, Dennis • Haddad, Jamal • Iandolo, Will • Jones, Randy • Langer, Chris • Laslie, Charlie • Mann, Tim • Smith-Sreen, John • Smith, Garnet • Thoms, Dan • White, John

1980

Illustration and Publication

Front Row: Dennis Gunson, Randy Jones, Tim Mann, John White, Alfredo Duran, Edwin Duran, Ron Carter, Chris Lange. **Second Row:** Dan Thomas, Jim McIntire, Jeff Dale, Wayne Bently, Brian Bruce, Ted Langsworth, Scott Pendorf, Paul Adams. **Third Row:** Coach Lillard, Mark Bryan, John Chomeau, John Smith, Mike Lawler, Garnet Smith, Kevin Dupont, Tom Vahle, Dan Schultz, Will Iandolo, Assistant Coach, Beth Harkins, Manager

Adams, Paul • Bentley, Wayne • Bruce, Brian • Bryan, Mark • Carter, Ron • Chomeau, John • Dale, Jeff • DuPont, Kevin • Duran, Alfredo • Duran, Edwin • Gunson, Dennis • Jones, Randy • Langer, Chris • Langsworth, Ted • Lauler, Mike • Mann, Tim • McIntire, Jim • Pendorf, Scott • Ridgely, Reg • Schultz, Dan • Smith-Green, John • Smith, Garnet • Thoms, Dan • Vahle, Tom • White, John

1981

1981 MEN'S SOCCER TEAM: (Front Row) Chris Langer, Dennis Gunson, J.P. Jenks, Tom Vuhle, Edwin Duran, John White, Brian Bruce, Tim Mann, Randy Jones, Greg Gilmore, Ted Longsworth, Keith Custer, (Back Row) Assistant Coach Will Iandolo, Ron Carter, John Hurley, Reg Ridgely, Greg McCarthy, Kevin Dupont, Bruce Williams, Robert Brumbaugh, Jim McIntire, Head Coach Tom Lillard.

Information and Publications

Bruce, Brian • Brumbaugh, Robert • Carter, Ron • Custer, Keith • DuPont, Kevin • Duran, Edwin • Gilmore, Greg • Gunson, Dennis • Hurley, John • Jenks, J. P. • Jones, Randy • Langer, Chris • Longsworth, Ted • Mann, Tim • McCarthy, Greg • McIntire, Jim • Ridgely, Reg • Vahle, Tom • White, John • Williams, Bruce

1982

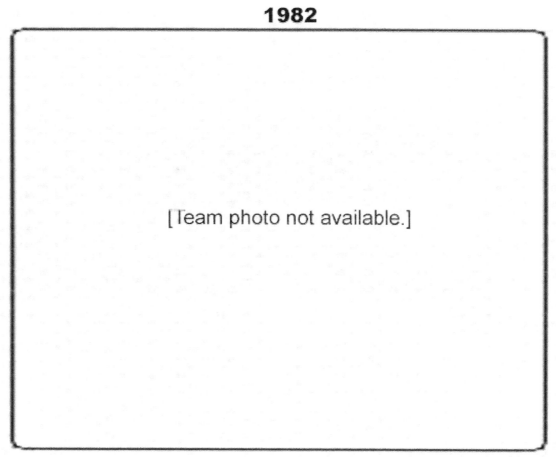

[Team photo not available.]

Brown, Jim • Bruce, Brian • Brumbaugh, Robert • Chomeau, John • Czerlinsky, Brian • Gerber, Bill • Greene, Kevin • Hurley, John • Jenks, J. P. • Jones, Randy • Lambert, John • Longsworth, Ted • McCarthy, Greg • McIntire, Jim • Montagne, Joe • Pasquel, Jorge • Petty, David • Pruett, Miles • Ragone, John • Sopranzi, Tony • Udy, Brian • White, Fred

1983

MEN'S SOCCER: (Front row) Miles Pruitt, John Hurley, Andy Hill, Charlie Jordan, Fred White, Greg McCarthy, Jim McIntire, Brian Udy, Willie Kee, Mike Dopp, Chris Bourne. **(Back row)** Coach Tom Lillard, Pete Bouker, Derik Hart, Bert Diesel, Kevin Greene, Bill Gerber, Darren Clark, Brian Cilinski, Fran Henry, Joe Montane, Mike O'Grady, Steven White, Anoput Phimmasone, Randy Jones (Assistant Coach).

Bouker, Pete • Bourne, Chris • Cilinski, Brian • Clark, Darren • Diesel, Bert • Dopp, Mike • Gerber, Bill • Greene, Kevin • Hart, Derik • Henry, Fran • Hill, Andy • Hurley, John • Jordan, Charlie • Kee, Willie • McCarthy, Greg • McIntire, Jim • Montagne, Joe • O'Grady, Mike • Phimmasone, Anoput • Pruett, Miles • Udy, Brian • White, Fred • White, Stephen

1984

SOCCER: (front row) Captains: Greg McCarthy, Brian Udy, Bill Gerber, **(second row)** Stephen White, Thai Nguyen, Chris Baker, Mike Dopp, Willie Kee, Bill Stachler, Brent King, Chris Bourne, Anoput Phimmasone, Phil Owens, Trung Pham, **(third row)** Coach Tom Lillard, Pete Bouker, Walter O'Hara, Miles Pruett, Joe Montane, Eric Sigurdson, J. P. Goyer, Justin Bryant, Jeff Brown, Fran Henry, Assistant Coach Don Staley.

Baker, Chris • Bouker, Pete • Bourne. Chris • Brown, Jeff • Bryant, Justin • Dopp, Mike • Gerber, Bill • Goyer, J. P. • Henry, Fran • Kee, Willie • King. Brent • McCarthy, Greg • Montagne, Joe • Nguyen, Thai • O'Hara. Walter • Owens, Phil • Pham, Trung • Phimmasone, Anoput • Pruett, Miles • Sigurdson, Eric • Stachler, Bill • Udy, Brian • White, Stephen

1985

Men's Soccer: (front row) Brian Udy, Stephen White, Mike Dopp, Peter Bouker, Jeff Brown, Fran Henry, Justin Bryant, Thai Nguyen, Bill Gerber, Scott Washburn, Willie Kee, Chris Baker. (back row) Assistant Don Staley, Mike Harig, Bert Diesel, Joe Montagne, Lance Casey, Miles Pruett, Joe Wyzkoski, Eric Sigurdson, Trung Pham, J. P. Goyer, Allen Valencia, Kevin Taylor, Bill Stachler, Head Coach Tom Lillard, Trainer Mary Ryman.

Baker, Chris • Bouker, Pete • Bourne, Chris • Boyer, J. P. • Brown, Jeff • Bryant, Justin • Casey, Lance • Diesel, Bert • Dopp, Mike • Gerber, Bill • Harig, Mike • Henry, Fran • Kee, Willie • Montagne, Joe • Nguyen, Thai • Pham, Trung • Pruett, Miles • Sigurdson, Eric • Stachler, Bill • Taylor, Kevin • Udy, Brian • Valencia, Allen • Washburn, Scott • White, Stephen • Wyzkoski, Joe

1986

Baker, Chris ● Bouker, Pete ● Bourne, Chris ● Bryant, Justin ● Casey, Lance ● Dopp, Mike ● Eagon, Brian ● Findlay, Jody ● Henry, Fran ● Kee, Willie ● Olnhausen, Jeff ● Pfeffer, Mike ● Ramquist, Magnus ● Shepherd, Willie ● Sigurdson, Eric ● Stachler, Bill ● Taylor, Kevin ● Udy, Brian ● Valencia, Allen ● White, Stephen ● Wyzkoski, Joe

1987

Adolph, Rob ● Arkon, Steven ● Baker, Chris ● Brown, Jeff ● Desarno, Mike ● Eagon, Brian ●
Griggs, Bruce ● Ihnainen, Harri ● Kuhla, Mike ● Majewski, Doug ● McClaugherty, Don ●
McMahon, Pat ● Peay, Sean ● Ramquist, Magnus ● Roberts, Stephen ● Roxio, Dan ● Shepherd,
Willie ● Sigurdson, Eric ● Soldervilla, John ● White, Stephen ● Wilson, Teddy

1988

Adolph, Rob • Arkon, Steven • Brown, Jeff • Cossaboon, David • Desarno, Mike •
Dewitt, Jason • Eagon, Brian • Gadelha, Ed • Griggs, Bruce • Ihnainen, Harri •
Magnusson, John • Majewski, Doug • Majewski, Jeff • Nguyen, Thai • Parvin, Eric •
Peay, Sean • Ramquist, Magnus • Washington, Dante • Wilson, Teddy

1989

1989 Men's Soccer team: Keiler, Ramquist, Barry, J. Majewski, Cossaboon, Darden, Peay, Osterberger, Magnusson, Eagon, Griggs, D.Majewski, Wilson, Arkon, Fisher, Traiana, Ward, Williams, Robles, Turpin, Washington, Rondeau, Mahan Grabham and coach Don Staley

Adolph, Rob • Arkon, Steven • Brown, Jeff • Cossaboon, David • Desarno, Mike •
Dewitt, Jason • Eagon, Brian • Gadelha, Ed • Griggs, Bruce • Ihnainen, Harri •
Magnusson, John • Majewski, Doug • Majewski, Jeff • Nugyen, Thai • Parvin, Eric •
Peay, Sean • Ramquist, Magnus • Washington, Dante • Wilson, Teddy

1990

Adolph, Rob • Arkon, Steven • Barry, John • Berrang, Matthias • Broadbent, Troy • Clubb, Mark • Crespin, Jorge • Darden, Keith • Dougland, Lance • Eck, Keith • Ellis, Mark • Finck, Justin • Fisher, Randy • Gavilan, Chris • Harris, Ian • Keiller, Whitney • Magnusson, John • Majewski, Doug • Majewski. Jeff • Mitchelson, Wister • Osterberger, Mark • Peay. Sean • Pyle, Andre • Rondeau, Frederic • Ryder, Pete • Springer, Darryl • Turpin, Shawn • Walker, Brett • Washington. Dante • Williams, Kevin • Wilson, Teddy

1991

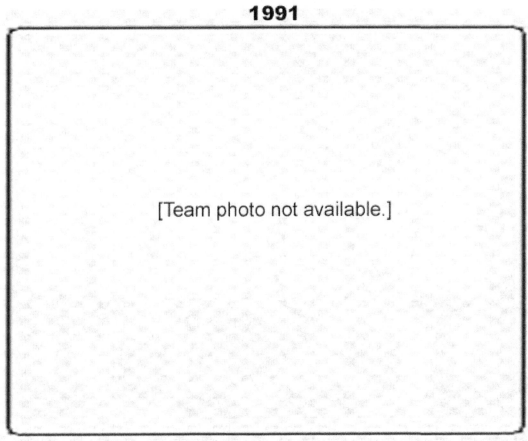

[Team photo not available.]

Bacharach, Roy • Barrett, Chris • Barry, John • Berrang, Matthias • Borjesson, Rikard • Boyd, Michael • Broadbent, Troy • Clark, Chris • Clubb, Mark • Cossaboon, David • Demaio, Jason • Eck, Keith • Ellis, Mark • Gealt, Kevin • Hudson, Ryan • Keiller, Whitney • Lakatos, Gerald • Magnusson, John • Majewski, Jeff • Martensson, Leif • Osterberger, Mark • Perkovich, Graham • Pyle, Andre • Rondeau, Frederic • Rosenbaum, Neil • Spooner, Ian • Springer, Darryl • Washington, Dante

1992

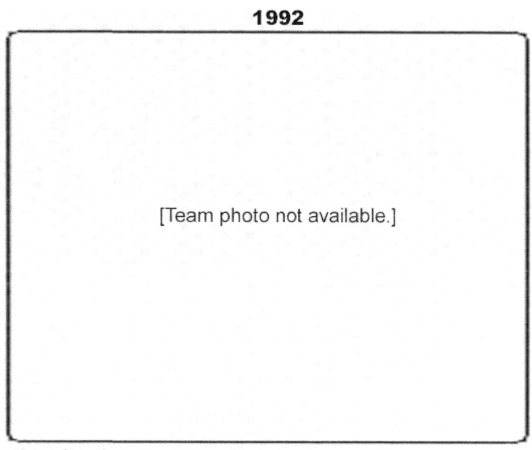

[Team photo not available.]

Barrett, Chris • Barry, John • Borjesson, Rikard • Boyd, Michael • Brady, Lee • Broadbent, Troy • Conlin, Mark • Demaio, Jason • Gealt, Kevin • Henderson, Che • Kauffman, Ryan • Keiller, Whitney • Lakatos, Gerald • Lynch, Brian • Osterberger, Mark • Perkovich, Graham • Reid, Erin • Rondeau, Frederic • Rowland, Jamie • Schultz, Art • Sheally, Bennie • Sheridan, Fiachra • Spooner, Ian • Springer, Darryl • Tierney, John • Washington, Dante

1993

Members of the 1993 Radford University men's soccer team, are, front row, from left: Brian Lynch, Ricky Embleton, Matt Bennett, Darryl Springer, Troy Broadbent, Richard Veal and Jimmy Rice. In the middle row, from left, are: head coach Don Staley, manager Rob Cassels, assistant coach Keith Eck, Scott Grant, Sean Tettemer, Rob Stinnett, Patrick Hughes, Chris Barrett. John Tierney, Noah Taylor, Kevin Gealt and Fiachra Sheridan. In the back row are: Manager Dennis Carwile, David Fox, Chris Evans, Gerald Lakatos, Chris Hanley, Troy LaChance, Chris Rosen, Michael Boyd, Richard Shepherd, Lee Morton, Lee Brady, Che Henderson and Jesse Inestroza.

Barrett, Chris • Bennett. Matt • Boyd, Michael • Brady, Lee • Broadbent, Troy • Embleton, Ricky • Evans, Chris • Fox, David • Gealt, Kevin • Grant, Scott • Hanley, Chris • Henderson, Che • Hughes, Patrick • Inestroza, Jesse • Lachance, Troy • Lakatos, Gerald • Lynch, Brian • Morton, Lee • Rice, Jimmy • Rosen, Chris • Shepherd, Richard • Sheridan, Fiachra • Springer, Darryl • Stinnett, Rob • Taylor, Noah • Tettemer, Sean • Tierney, John • Veal, Richard

1994

The 1994 Radford University Men's Soccer Team. Front row: Edwardo Wissar, Fernando Sigui, Sean Tettemer, Patrick Hughes, Chris Barrett, John Tierney, Che Henderson and Ian Spooner. Second row: Lee Morton, Chris Hanley, Brian Lynch, Jose Avendano, Dino Orgetas, Kevin Gealt, Gerald Lakatos, Richard Veal and Dexter Cox. Third row: Derek Zimmerman, Chris Yager, Ryan Scott, Richard Shepherd, Albert Rusagara, Chris Tierney, Billy Saylor, and Troy Templeton. Fourth row: Coach Spencer Smith, assistant Dustin Fonder, Tommy Young, Mike Slate, Rick Lodge, Pier D'Amato, Eric Ruano, trainer Erin Merica and assistant Keith Eck.

Avendano, Jose • Barrett, Chris • Cox, Dexter • D'Amato, Pier •
Gealt, Kevin • Hanley, Chris • Henderson, Che • Hughes, Patrick •
Lakatos, Gerald • Lodge, Rick • Lynch, Brian • Morton, Lee •
Orgetas, Dino • Ruano, Eric • Rusagara, Albert • Saylor, Billy •
Scott, Ryan • Shepherd, Richard • Sigui, Fernando • Slate, Mike •
Spooner, Ian • Stinnett, Rob • Templeton, Troy • Tettemer, Sean •
Tierney, Chris • Tierney, John • Veal, Richard • Wissar, Eduardo •
Yager, Chris • Young, Tommy • Zimmerman, Derek

1995

1995 Men's Soccer Team: (Front, left to right), Eduardo Wissar, Dino Orgetas, Tommy Torres, Derek Zimmerman, Kevin Fealt, John Tierney, Lee Morton, Richard Veal, Rick Lodge, trainer Gary Scholl. (Second row, left to right), assistant Bill Arthur, Coach Spencer Smith, Sean Tettmer, Tommy Young, Chris Pettit, Chris Hanley, Eric Rarus, Richard Shepherd, Che Henderson, Ian Spooner, Eric Ruano, Jose Avendano, Malcolm Johnson, Greg Lea, assistant coach Keith Eck. (Back row, left to right), Mike Rodon, Lee Rodon, Sacha Drouin, Mike Boyd, Suneel Grover, Brian Cazalot, Billy Lee, Mike Ginsburg, Eric Bucey, Jason Gvozdas, David Robbins, Joe Young, student assistant Chris Barrett.

Avendano, Jose • Boyd, Michael • Bucey, Eric • Cazalot, Brian • Drouin, Sacha • Gealt, Kevin • Ginsburg, Mike • Grover, Suneel • Gvozdas, Jason • Hanley, Chris • Henderson, Che • Johnson, Malcolm • Lea, Greg • Lee, Billy • Lodge, Rick • Long, Chad • Morton, Lee • Orgetas, Dino • Pettit, Chris • Rarus, Eric • Robbins, David • Rodon, Lee • Rodon, Mike • Ruano, Eric • Shepherd, Richard • Spooner, Ian • Tettemer, Sean • Tierney, John • Torres, Tommy • Veal, Richard • Wissar, Eduardo • Young, Joe • Young, Tommy • Zimmerman, Derek

1996

Front Row: Kevin Terne, Chad Long, Derek Zimmerman, Richard Sheherd, Lee Morton, Eric Ruano, Chris Petit, Richard Veal, Troy Washington; **Row 2:** assist. coach Chris Barret, Tim Torborg, John Williams, Bill Castillejo, Jim Lukezic, Greg Lea, Sacha Drouin, Bo Clark, Joe Young, Mike Girsburg, Cannon Helscher, Johnathon Jones, Chase Kaufman, head coach Spencer Smith; **Row 3:** Keith Eck, Horacio Zamora, Suneel Grover, Yusuf Hasan, Chris Owens, Brad Sisson, Kevin Kelly, Eric Burey, Jason Gvozdas, Mike Sweazy.

Bucey, Eric • Castillejo, Bill • Clark, Bo • Drouin, Sacha • Ginsburg, Mike • Grover, Suneel • Gursky, Geoff • Gvozdas, Jason • Hasan, Yusuf • Helscher, Cannon • Jones, Jonathon • Kaufman, Chase • Kelly, Kevin • Lea, Greg • Long, Chad • Lukerzc, Jim • Morton, Lee • Owens, Chris • Pettit, Chris • Ruano, Eric • Shepherd, Richard • Sisson, Brad • Sweazy, Mike • Terne, Keven • Torborg, Tim • Veal, Richard • Washington, Troy • Williams, John • Young, Joe • Zamora, Horacio • Zimmerman, Derek

1997

Sports Information

First Row: Chris Barrett (Assistant Coach), Mike Ginsburg, Derek Zimmerman, Garrett Grinsfelder, Nick Butcher, Angel Cardozo, Eric Ruano, Brad Dalton, Cannon Helscher, Troy Washington, Scott Hance. **Second Row:** Richard Shepherd (Assistant Coach), Brad Sisson, Keven Terre, Kevin Kelly, Bill Castillejo, Josh Anson, Sacha Drouin, Dax Grey, Joe Young, Horacio Zamora, Fabian Arboleda, Tony Lisanti, Jason Gvozdas, Spencer Smith (Head Coach)

Anson, Josh • Arboleda, Fabian • Butcher, Nick • Cardozo, Angel • Castillejo, Bill • Dalton, Brad • Drouin, Sacha • Ginsburg, Mike • Grey, Dax • Grinsfelder, Garrett • Gvozdas, Jason • Hance, Scott • Helscher, Cannon • Kelly, Kevin • Lisanti, Tony • Ruano, Eric • Sisson, Brad • Terne, Keven • Washington, Troy • Young, Joe • Zamora, Horacio • Zimmerman, Derek

1998

Front Row: Angel Cardozo, Ryan Caton, Scott Hance, Andre Van Den Broeck, Josh Anson, Sacha Drouin, Troy Washington, Dustin Keesee, Chris Waltz, Nick Bergstrom.

Back Row: Head Coach Spencer Smith, Rob Bresler, Brad Dalton, Matt Hanson, Mitch Peters, William Stephens, Dax Gray, Bill Castillejo, Jon Odum, Tony Lisanti, Mike Ginsburg, Jason Gvozdas, Trainer Sarah Smith, Assistant Coach Eric Ruano.

Anson, Josh • Arboleda, Fabian • Bergstrom, Nick • Butcher, Nick • Cardozo, Angel • Castillejo, Bill • Caton, Ryan • Dalton, Brad • Drouin, Sacha • Ginsburg, Mike • Grey, Dax • Gvozdas, Jason • Hance, Scott • Hanson, Matt • Keesee, Dustin • Lisanti, Tony • Parish, Kyle • Peters, Mitch • Stephens, William • Van den Broeck, Andre • Washington, Troy

1999

Adeyemi, Mike • Anderson, Greg • Bond, Dustin • Bressler, Rob • Burke, Joe • Castillejo, Bill • Caton, Ryan • Crowder, Mark • Dramby, Mike • Fosu, Jon • Frias, Jonathan • Grey, Dax • Hance, Scott • Hernandez, Geraldo • Jefferson, Corey • Lewis, Andre • Nicholas, Jeffrey • Odum, Jon • Rolfing, T. J. • Roof, Bryan • Von Essen, Mike • Wales, Patrick • Waltz, Chris • Winstead, Mike

2000

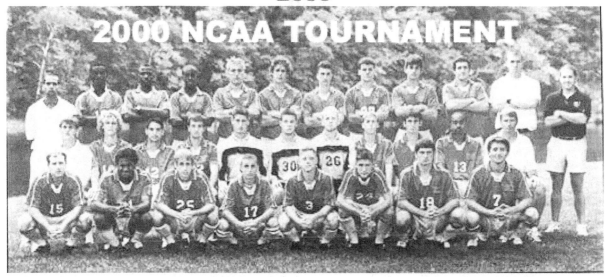

Adeyemi, Mike • Allen, Bo • Bond, Dustin • Caton, Ryan • Crowder, Mark •
Dramby, Mike • Essey, Andrew • Fosu, Jon • Frias, Jonathan • Hance, Scott •
Heling, Jason • Hernandez, Geraldo • Hooker, Jonathan • Infante, Kenny •
Jefferson, Corey • Lewis, Andre • McAlister, Nick • Nall, Travis • Pearson, Nate •
Perez-Costa, Alfredo • Rolfing, T. J. • Roof, Bryan • Sokolik, Erik • Von Essen, Mike
• Wales, Patrick • Waltz, Chris • Winstead, Mike

2001

Allen, Bo • Bates, Stephen • Caton, Ryan • Chaves, Phil • Crowder, Mark • Essey, Andrew • Fosu, Jon • Harper, Thorsen • Hernandez, Geraldo • Hooker, Jonathan • Jefferson, Corey • Lewis, Andre • Ogburn, Corey • Pahl, Adam • Pearson, Nate • Perez-Costa, Alfredo • Peterson, Justin • Rolfing, T. J. • Roof, Bryan • Salop, Mark • Snell, Adrian • Sokolik, Erik • Thorsen, Harper • Von Essen, Mike • Wales, Patrick • Waltz, Chris • Winstead, Mike

2002

Cadena, Luis • Crowder, Mark • Essey, Andrew • Fosu, Jon • Harpula, David • Hernandez, Andres • Hernandez, Geraldo • Hooker, Jonathan • Lewis, Andre • Nicholas, Jeffrey • Ogburn, Corey • Pahl, Adam • Pearson, Nate • Perez-Costa, Alfredo • Peterson, Justin • Price, Ben • Ramos, Fernando • Rolfing, T. J. • Smith, Marc • Snell, Adrian • Sokolik, Erik • Stevens, Dan • Stoner, Seth • Tamm, Andrew • Thorsen, Harper • Von Essen, Mike • Wales, Patrick • Waltz, Chris • Winstead, Mike

2003

Roster 2003 - 2004

B. Allen
L. Cadena
P. Colas
A. Essey
E. Gerstein
D. Harpula
A. Hernandez
S. Johnson
M. Merrill
J. Nicholas
C. Ogburn
A. Pahl
N. Pearson
J. Peterson
F. Ramos
T. Rowe
J. Smith
A. Snell
E. Sokolik
D. Stevens
S. Stoner
W. Thomsen
O. Zinoveev

Allen, Bo • Cadena, Luis • Colas, Patrick • Essey, Andrew • Gerstien, Ethan • Harpula, David • Hernandez, Andres • Johnson, Sean • Merrill, Mark • Nicholas, Jeffrey • Ogburn, Corey • Pahl, Adam • Pearson, Nate • Peterson, Justin • Ramos, Fernando • Rowe, Taylor • Smith, Jonathon • Smith, Marc • Snell, Adrian • Sokolik, Erik • Stevens, Dan • Stoner, Seth • Thomsen, Will • Zinoveev, Omar

2004

Front row, from left: Ramon Negron, David Harpula, Andres Hernandez, Devan Cooley, David Stannard, Tyler Leveski, Armando Romero. Second row, from left: Trevor MacBrien, Patrick Colas, Will Thomsen, Stephen Mapp, Dan Stevens, Omar Zinoveev, Nicholas Leigh, Romain Maudire, Fernando Ramos. Back row, from left: Athletic Trainer Adam Mistr, Student Athletic Trainer Mark Reynolds, Taylor Jenkins, Adam Pahl, Corey Ogburn, Jonathan Smith, Taylor Rowe, Joseph Sansbury, Sean Johnson, Luis Cadena, Chris Pertl, Assistant Coach Jonathan Williamson, Head Coach Spencer Smith.

Cadena, Luis • Colas, Patrick • Cooley, Devan • Harpula, David • Hernandez, Andres • Jenkins, Taylor • Johnson, Sean • Leigh, Nicholas • Leveski, Tyler • MacBrien, Trevor • Mapp, Stephen • Maudire, Romain • Negron, Ramon • Ogburn, Corey • Pahl, Adam • Pertl, Chris • Ramos, Fernando • Romero, Armando • Rowe, Taylor • Sansbury, Joseph • Smith, Jonathon • Stannard, David • Stevens, Dan • Thomsen, Will • Zinoveev, Omar

2005

Bartman, Adam • Cadena, Luis • Caruso, Paul • Chavez, Manuel • Colas, Patrick • Cooley, Devan • Harpula, David • Hernandez, Andres • Husadzinovic, Davorin • Jenkins, Taylor • Leigh, Nicholas • Leveski, Tyler • MacBrien, Trevor • Mapp, Stephen • Negron, Ramon • Pahl, Adam • Pertl, Chris • Ramos, Fernando • Romero, Armando • Rowe, Taylor • Sansbury, Joseph • Simms, Josh • Smith, Jonathon • Thomsen, Will • Werner, Chris • Zinoveev, Omar

2006

Bartman, Adam • Caruso, Paul • Chavez, Manuel • Cooley, Devan • Delpino, Jeremy • Dykstra, Chris • Elimbi, Franklin • Husadzinovic, Davorin • Jenkins, Taylor • Leigh, Nicholas • Leveski, Tyler • MacBrien, Trevor • Maddox, Jimmy • Negron, Ramon • Patricio, Daryn • Pertl, Chris • Reid, Lennie • Roszel, Zach • Rowe, Taylor • Sansbury, Joseph • Simms, Josh • Smith, Jonathon • Thomsen, Robert • Thomsen, Will • Werner, Chris • Zimmer, Justin

2007

Aquino, Ian • Brown, Camden • Caruso, Paul • Chavez, Manuel • Cooley, Devan • Delpino, Jeremy • Elimbi, Franklin • Fuentes, Ben • Husadzinovic, Davorin • Jenkins, Taylor • Joseph, Emmanuel • Lee, Chris • Leith, James • Leveski, Tyler • Lopez, Edgar • MacBrien, Trevor • Macias, Aldo • McCrary, Josh • Patricio, Daryn • Roszel, Zach • Sansbury, Joseph • Shaffer, Brendan • Smetanick, Peter • Thomsen, Robert • Thomsen, Will • Werner, Chris • Wilson, Craig • Zimmer, Justin

2008

Aquino, Ian ● Awosika, Iyiola ● Baxter, Joe ● Bishop, Chris ● Brown, Camden ● Butler, Shane ● Chavez, Manuel ● Cooley, Devan ● Delpino, Jeremy ● Fuentes, Ben ● Fugate, Hunter ● Hatcher, Lucas ● Joseph, Emmanuel ● Lee, Chris ● Leith, James ● Macias, Aldo ● Mills, Carter ● Patricio, Daryn ● Roszel, Zach ● Shaffer, Brendan ● Smetanick, Peter ● Taylor, Ryan ● Thomsen, Robert ● Werner, Chris ● Zeballos, Sammy ● Zimmer, Justin

2009

Aquino, Ian • Awosika, Iyiola • Baxter, Joe • Brown, Camden • Chavez, Manuel • Dennis, Joey • Fleming, Kevin • Fuentes, Ben • George, Thomas • Gwanzura, Brian • Handlin, Mike • Jones, Myles • Jordan, James • Leith, James • Macias, Aldo • Mills, Carter • Patricio, Daryn • Payne, Anthony • Shaffer, Brendan • Stinnett, Ryan • Taylor, Ryan • Thomsen, Robert • Zimmer, Justin

2010

Aquino, Ian • Awosika, Iyiola • Baxter, Joe • Brown, Camden • Dennis, Joey • Devaldes, John • Fleming, Kevin • Fuentes, Ben • Grande, Luis • Gwanzura, Brian • Handlin, Mike • Jones, Myles • Jordan, James • Lauretano, Vittorio • Leith, James • Macias, Aldo • Mills, Carter • Payne, Anthony • Shaffer, Brendan • Stinnett, Ryan • Taylor, Ryan • Thomas, George • Ulmo, Bernardo

2011

Awosika, Iyiola ● Beach, Kyle ● Best, R. J. ● Bridi, Ramzi ● Fleming, Kevin ● Grande, Luis ● Gwanzura, Brian ● Ho Park Kim, Chel ● Hudgens, Stephen ● Hutcheon, Michael ● Janssen, Matt ● Jones, Myles ● Jordan, James ● Lauretano, Vittorio ● Macias, Aldo ● Mills, Carter ● O'Keefe, Daniel ● Payne, Anthony ● Redondo, Dario ● Stills, Jambaar ● Stinnett, Ryan ● Taylor, Ryan ● Ulmo, Bernardo ● Valencia, Nico ● Weidow, Davis ● Wilson, Dane

2012

Allaire, Troy • Arzubiaga, Sergio • Beach, Kyle • Cross, Guy • Dacosta, Demaro • Darby, Bryan • De Barros, Fernando • Diniz, Lucas • Dridi, Ramzi • Eckenrode, Jannik • Grande, Luis • Griefer, Jacob • Ho Park Kim, Chel • Hudgens, Stephen • Hutcheon, Michael • Janssen, Matt • Jones, Myles • Jordan, James • Lauretano, Vittorio • Legg, Sam • Lyngen, Mads • Mayer, Joe • O'Keefe, Daniel • Redondo, Dario • Stills, Jambaar • Summers, Jamie • Taylor, Ryan • Ulmo, Bernardo • Valencia, Nico • Wilson, Dane

2013

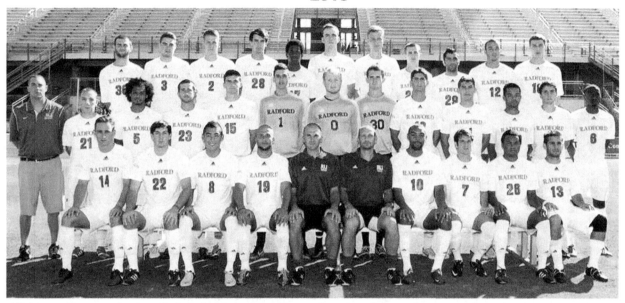

Albiston, Ryan • Amba, Gabriel • Amofah, Bismark • Arzubiaga, Sergio • Carrabotta, Antonio • De Barros, Fernando • Dridi, Ramzi • Grande, Luis • Ho Park Kim, Chel • Hudgens, Stephen • Hutcheon, Michael • Janssen, Matt • Jordan, Jack • Jordan, James • Lauretano, Vittorio • Mayer, Joe • O'Keefe, Daniel • Pouseu Blanco, Aitor • Redondo, Dario • Rimstad, Jo Vetle • Smith, Garland • Summers, Jamie • Turk, Zach • Ulmo, Bernardo • Valencia, Nico • Wilson, Dane • Zaccarelli, Pedro

2014

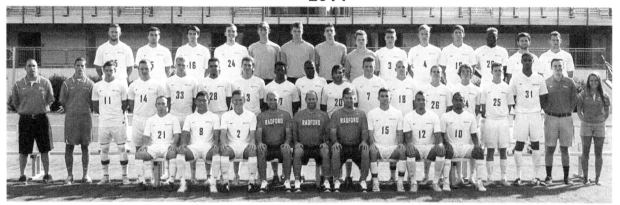

Amba, Gabriel • Amotah, Bismark • Arzubiaga, Sergio • Atwell, Brandon • Blanchard, Stockton • Colmer, Fraser • Dridi, Ramzi • Ho Park Kim, Chel • Hudgens, Stephen • Hutcheon, Michael • Johnson, Koby • Martin, Taylor • Martorana, Neil • McIntosh, Kendall • Mertzokat, Nicolas • Nalborski, Krzysztof • O'Keefe, Daniel • Pouseu Blanco, Aitor • Rancel, Mauricio • Redondo, Dario • Rimstad, Jo Vetle • Roberts, Kieran • Smith, Garland • Steinhauser, Felix • Summers, Jamie • Szklennik, Evan • Turk, Zach • Valencia, Nico • Walsh, Michael

2015

Amba, Gabriel • Amofah, Bismark • Arzubiaga, Sergio • Bankert, Cole • Colmer, Fraser • Daehlie, Sivert • Hanes, Currie • Johnson, Koby • Martin, Taylor • Martorana, Neil • Mayhugh, Nick • McIntosh, Kendall • Mertzokat, Nicolas • Nalborski, Krzysztof • Nemeth, Corey • O'Keefe, Daniel • Pauls, William • Pouseu Blanco, Aitor • Rimstad, Jo Vetle • Roberts, Kieran • Smith, Garland • Smythe, Austin • Steinhauser, Felix • Strandsäter, Jakob • Summers, Jamie • Szklennik, Evan • Thiss, Benjamin • Thompson, Cory • Tiedemann, Finn • Turk, Zach • Walsh, Michael • Yorke, Myles

2016

Amba, Gabriel • Amofah, Bismark • Bankert, Cole • Barnett, Kyle • Colmer, Fraser • Daehlie, Sivert • Deacy, Liam • Duffy, Liam • Erzen, Wyatt • Hanes, Currie • Johnson, Koby • Koren, Ulrik • Martin, Taylor • Martorana, Neil • Mayhugh, Nick • McIntosh, Kendall • Mertzokat, Nicolas • Neptune, Josh • Pouseu Blanco, Aitor • Rimstad, Jo Vetle • Roberts, Kieran • Smith, Garland • Strandsäter, Jakob • Szklennik, Evan • Thiss, Benjamin • Turk, Zach • Valls, Victor • Walsh, Michael • Wilkinson, Jacob • Yorke, Myles

2017

Angelides, Max-Emilios • Bankert, Cole • Carter, Ethan • Colmer, Fraser • Daabul, Noy • Daehlie, Sivert • Deacy, Liam • Edwards, Max • Erzen, Wyatt • Hardman, Yury • Johnson, Koby • Koren, Ulrik • Marcy, Mason • Martin, Taylor • Martorana, Neil • Mayhugh, Nick • McIntosh, Kendall • Mertzokat, Nicolas • Nicholas, Andrew • Roberts, Kieran • Robinson, Dondre' • Schwartz, Cole • Siczek, Patrick • Strandsäter, Jakob • Szklennik, Evan • Thiss, Benjamin • Valkanos, Dimitrios • Valls, Victor • Walsh, Michael • Wilkinson, Jacob • Yorke, Myles

2018

Angelides, Max-Emilios ● Benavides, Juan ● Bennett, Khori ● Bissell, Austin ● Corado, Alex ● Deacy, Liam ● Dixon, Dorion ● Edwards, Max ● Erzen, Wyatt ● Farrell, Sam ● Kreutzberger, Austin ● Ligner, Thure ● Macky Diop, Amadou ● Martin, Taylor ● Mayhugh, Nick ● Opoku-Adjei, Abel Prince ● Oumar Gueye, Pape ● Roberts, Kieran ● Robinson, Dondre' ● Rodriguez, Gonzalo ● Schwartz, Cole ● Scoffield, Bryan ● Siczek, Patrick ● Strandsäter, Jakob ● Thiss, Benjamin ● Thomé, Edwardo ● Valkanos, Dimitrios ● Valls, Victor ● Walsh, Michael ● Wilkinson, Jacob ● Yorke, Myles

2019

Angelides, Max-Emilios • Bell-Cooper, Kameron • Benavides, Juan • Deacy, Liam • Dixon, Dorion • Erzen, Wyatt • Etienne, Quincy • Farrell, Sam • Faye, Baye Djibril • Fousse, Baptiste • Gaffigan, Luke • Gonsalves, Jayden • Grande, Simon • Haddad, Noah • Incera, Joseba • Leslau, Raphail • Ligner, Thure • Machado-Jones, Ryan • Macky Diop, Amadou • Ocampo, Octavio • Oumar Gueye, Pape • Rivera, Jose • Robinson, Dondre' • Scoffield, Bryan • Siczek, Patrick • Squire, Toby • Thiam, Mouhameth • Valls, Victor • Wilkinson, Jacob

2020 Players & Coaches

Angelides, Max-Emilios • Benavides, Juan • Blum, David • Clark, Solomon • Dixon, Dorion • Etienne, Quincy • Faye, Baye Djibril • Giannecchini, Anthony • Gonsalves, Jayden • Haddad, Noah • Incera, Joseba • Kallendorf, Trevor • Kamara, Mustaph • Machado-Jones, Ryan • Ocampo, Octavio • Opoku-Adjei, Abel Prince • Oumar Gueye, Pape • Poian, Khalid • Rivera, Jose • Robinson, Dondre' • Siczek, Patrick • Somuah, Bright • Squire, Toby • Vasquez, Giovanni • Williams, Chris

2021 Players & Coaches

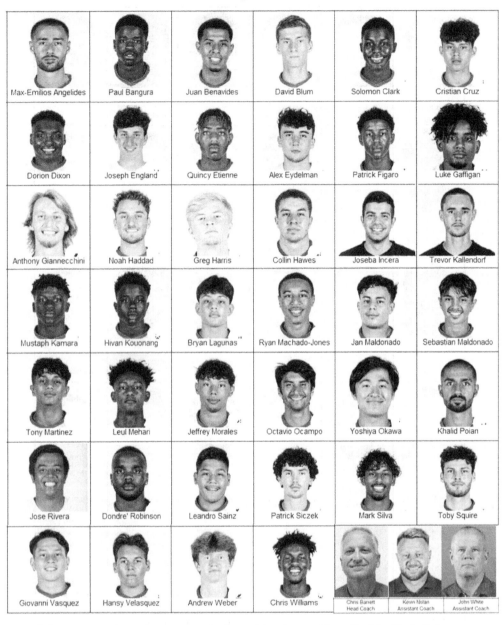

Angelides, Max-Emilios ● Bangura, Paul ● Benavides, Juan ● Blum, David ● Clark, Solomon ● Cruz, Christian ● Dixon, Dorion ● England, Joseph ● Etienne, Quincy ● Eydelman, Alex ● Figaro, Patrick ● Gaffigan, Luke ● Giannecchini, Anthony ● Haddad, Noah ● Harris, Greg ● Hawes, Collin ● Incera, Joseba ● Kallendorf, Trevor ● Kamara, Mustaph ● Kouonang, Hivan ● Lagunas, Bryan ● Machado-Jones, Ryan ● Maldonado, Jan ● Maldonado, Sebastian ● Martinez, Tony ● Mehari, Leul ● Morales, Jeffrey ● Ocampo, Octavio ● Okawa, Yoshiya ● Poian, Khalid ● Rivera, Jose ● Robinson, Dondre' ● Sainz, Leandro ● Siczek, Patrick ● Silva, Mark ● Squire, Toby ● Vasquez, Giovanni ● Velasquez, Hansy ● Weber, Andrew ● Williams, Chris

2022 Players & Coaches

Allway, Tallon ● Barlow, Timmy ● Barrett, James ● Blum, David ● Boyar, Kalefa ● Clark, Owen ● Clark, Solomon ● Cruz, Christian ● Daniels, Keller ● Dubose, Jared ● El-Abani, Saber ● Eydelman, Alex ● Figaro, Patrick ● Gardev, James ● Giannecchini, Anthony ● Gyurci, Griffin ● Haddad, Noah ● Hagen, Kyle ● Harris, Greg ● Hawes, Collin ● Hernandez, Roberto ● Incera, Joseba ● Kamara, Mustaph ● Kaneda, Asuka ● Kouonang, Hivan ● Kryazhev, Alex ● Kuttner, Christoph ● Lucas, Matt ● Malave, Kevin ● Maldonado, Jan ● Martinez, Tony ● Masudi, Leon ● Mehari, Leul ● Micolucci, Michael ● Moore, Henry ● Morales, Jeffrey ● Ocampo, Octavio ● Peacock, Bryceland ● Perez Nance, Mateo ● Pulik, Tyler ● Rawlins, Spencer ● Schwarz, Samuel ● Silva, Mark ● Simmons, John ● Squire, Toby ● Towns, Bubby ● Wadkins, Akire ● Weber, Andrew ● Williams, Chris ● Wuertz, Christian

2023 Players & Coaches

Allway, Tallon • Anderson, Kadmiel • Barrett, James •
Choi, Tamin • Clark, Owen • Clark, Seth • Cruz, Christian
• Daniels, Keller • Dubose, Jared • Endijck, Albert •
Eydelman, Alex • Gardev, James • Gyurci, Griffin •
Haddad, Noah • Hagen, Kyle • Hammam, Shady • Harris,
Greg • Hawes, Collin • Kryazhev, Alex • Lamptey, Cam •
Lucas, Matt • Malave, Kevin • Maldonado, Jan • Masudi,
Leon • Moore, Henry • Peacock, Bryceland • Perez
Nance, Mateo • Pulik, Tyler • Rawlins, Spencer • Redding,
Landon • Rupe, Evan • Silva, Mark • Tajtyi, Akos • Towns,
Bubby • Usher, Riley • Wadkins, Akire • Williams, Chris

2024 Players & Coaches

Anderson, Kadmiel ● Choi, Tamin ● Clark, Owen ● Clark, Seth ● Cruz, Christian ● Davies, Felix ● Eydelman, Alex ● Habibelahy, Kevin ● Hammam, Shady ● Hawes, Collin ● Kamara, Mustaph ● Kilosho, Sadock ● Kyle, Hagen ● Lamptey, Cam ● Masudi, Leon ● McClellan, Donovan ● McClendon, Mason ● O'Sullivan, Daniel ● Pardieck, Matthew ● Peacock, Bryceland ● Pulik, Tyler ● Redding, Landon ● Rupe, Evan ● Silva, Mark ● Tajtyi, Akos ● Usher, Riley ● Wadkins, Akire

APPENDIX 2 – TEAM PHOTOS and ROSTERS

Appendix 3

Radford University Men's Soccer
"THE SCRAPBOOK"
MEMORABILIA, CLIPPINGS & PICTURES
1974 – 2024

1974 Club Practice

1974 Club Game

1974 Club Team

Lillard and Nace-A Winning Combination

The talented duo of Tommy Lillard and Brian Nace are two big reasons the Radford College soccer team has enjoyed success and improvement.

Tommy, a freshman business major, is no stranger to the game of soccer. He played three years in high school and also in several summer leagues. Although he has played mainly halfback and forwards, he is a versatile player, playing all positions.

Tommy believes the team has "really come a long way." He added, "We had some problems in our first few games, but now everyone is really playing together." Though he's had many outstanding games, one of his best was last Tuesday, November 5, against Bluefield College. Tommy led the way with three goals as Radford prevailed 4-3.

Soccer coach, John Ravnik, believes Tommy "has improved very much." Ravnik continued, "The last few games he has been very strong. He's playing a wiser game, and usually he's in a good position. Tommy is more aggressive, but he's doing it intelligently." Summing up, Ravnik said, "Tommy has a strong leg, a good kick, and good height."

His coach is not the only person who has recognized his ability. Teammate Jeff Hoare explained, "Tommy really has helped us. He's brought new ideas, basically organization and

Brian Nace (Photo by R. J. Seyler)

teamwork. Besides that, he's one of the greatest guys I know." One of his teammates another halfback, added, "Tommy without a doubt, is the main stay of our offense. Tommy passes well and has one of the best shots on the team."

Equally talented and experienced is freshman Brian Nace. Brian played four years in high school and has also played in some fall and spring leagues. Playing all positions on the offensive line, Brian has played mostly halfback at Radford.

Brian thinks the team has "improved a great deal." He continued, "If we show as much enthusiasm next year, we'll do really well." Like Tommy, Brian's best game came against Bluefield. But this time it was Homecoming Day as Brian led the team to victory.

Coach Ravnik was also full of praise for Brian. "If there is one crucial position, it is the center halfback which Brian plays," said Ravnik. He continued, "On a number of occasions he has had good form and has spurred the team on. He has a good throw in and an accurate kick."

A teammate commented, "Brian leads the attack. He and Tommy are a working team. Brian brings the ball down and sets up the play."

Brian credited the offensive line to his and the team's success. He added, "That has been our biggest improvement."

Tommy Lillard

1974 -- Lillard and Nace

1975 Game at Moffett

1975 Randy Metzger

1975 Practice Shorts

1975 Game at Moffett

1975 Halftime at Moffett

1976 Extra Opponent

1976 Brian Nace (L)

1976 Game vs. Virginia Tech

1976 Game at Moffett

1976 Tom Lillard (R)

1977 Alfredo Duran vs. Hampden-Sydney

1977 Alfredo Duran

1977 Brian Nace

1977 Brian Nace vs. Hampden-Sydney

1977 Cesar Collantes Scores 1 of 4

1977 Charlie Laslie

New Coach Among The Youngest

Harves Comes To Radford With Experience And Enthusiasm

By Dick Harbin

John Harves, at age 25, must rank among the youngest head coaches on the college scene today. However, as he prepares for his first season as Radford's soccer coach, Harves brings with him a wealth of knowledge, experience, and enthusiasm.

A native of Arlington, Virginia, Harves grew up in an area which has since gained a reputation as a hotbed for soccer talent. He began his own playing career at 14 and began actively coaching 4 years later. His career in soccer continued at Virginia Tech, where he played for four years, until his graduation in 1973.

While coaching the Highlanders, Harves will be enrolled in graduate school at Tech, a fact Harves admits will force him to feel mixed emotions when the two schools meet this fall. "Since I'm now the coach at Radford, I'd like nothing better than to beat Virginia Tech,' said Harves. "Tech is a key game every year for Radford; there is a very natural rivalry involved whenever these two schools play."

Along with Tech, Harves feels that Randolph-Macon and Eastern Mennonite are the key games on this season's schedule. According to Harves, "Both teams are based on good solid programs and never fail to impress. But," he added, "I am cautiously optimistic that we can compete with any team on this year's schedule."

Harves is quick to credit Radford College Athletic Director Chuck Taylor for making his new job a "really enjoyable experience." When he first expressed interest in the coaching position, Harves claims that he was impressed with the ability of Taylor and his staff.

"I've been more than pleased with the cooperation that I've received from the school so far. Coach Taylor has made it very clear that soccer is the major men's fall sport. I am incredibly encouraged," Harves remarked while preparing his squad for the season opener this week against Hampden-Sydney.

With a little more than a week to prepare for the Hampden-Sydney game, Harves is also satisfied with the quick progress that his squad has shown so far. "It's definitely an asset that many of the players have played together for several seasons. That kind of team experience is essential if we are going to win our fair share of games," Harves said.

Harves' approach is dominated by the "total football" concept. "Total football is a very, very difficult concept to achieve," he explained. "Only a few of the best teams in the world have ever been able to master it."

In order to play this "total football" approach with any degree of success, the entire team must be versatile and in excellent physical condition. Veteran players such as Tommie Lillard and Neil Aker form a nucleus of experience and leadership that Harves is relying upon to meet his objective of fielding a highly competitive team each week.

With lack of time being such a crucial factor at this point, Harves is employing what he terms "economical training." His pre-dusk season training program has centered around drills which combine fitness and technique at the same time. "What we are trying to concentrate on are the three essential parts of any good soccer team: tactics, technique and conditioning. If we can accomplish success in these three areas, we will be in good shape."

John Harves is a young man with big plans for the soccer program at Radford College. He is confident that it is just a matter of time before his plans are realized.

1977 Coach Harves

1977 Harves Introduced as New Coach

238

1977 Coach John Harves

Thursday, September 29, 1977, Page 9

1977 Dr. Dedmon at Game

1977 Goal off Corner vs. Hampden-Sydney

1977 Jamal Haddad Congratulates Cesar Collantes on His 4th Goal

1977 Jamal Haddad vs. Hampden-Sydney

1977 (L-R) Collantes, Sherrill, Trible, Phillips vs. Bluefield

1977 Neal Aker Distributes

1977 Mike Lauler

1977 (L-R) Phillips, Sherrill, Laslie vs. Mary Washington

1977 John Smith vs. VMI

1977 Neal Aker vs. Hampden-Sydney

1977 Tom Lillard vs. Virginia Tech

Page 6, Thursday, September 22, 1977, The Grapurchat

Coach Harves Feels 'Soccer Has Arrived'

by Alan Andriek Dick Hoskin

"Soccer has arrived at Radford College", said an enthusiastic John Harves, coach of the Radford squad, after his team scored a 2-1 season-opening victory over Hampden-Sydney Wednesday afternoon at Radford. The win marked a successful coaching debut for Harves.

The Highlanders controlled the tempo of the game from the onset, scoring two first-half goals and displaying a rugged, aggressive defense.

Tommie Lillard scored the initial goal early in the first half. With 11 minutes gone in the game, Jamal Haddad led Lillard with a corner kick from the right side. Lillard met the ball in front of the Hampden-Sydney net and headed it past a bewildered goalie.

"Their goalie kept trying to come out on our corner kicks," explained Harves. "He misjudged two of the kicks, and we burned him both times."

Cesar Collantes capped the Radford scoring with only three seconds left in the first half. From the left corner freshman Tim Mann connected with Collantes who kicked it home, giving the Highlanders a 2-0 halftime lead.

Radford had to withstand a strong second-half rally by Hampden-Sydney. Exploiting their advantage in depth, the Tigers began to move the ball successfully against a tiring Highlander defense. With six minutes remaining in the game, Jay Hundley of Hampden-Sydney scored, pulling the Tigers within one goal, 2-1.

Goalie Neil Aker then was forced to withstand a barrage of last-minute shots by Hampden-Sydney, as the Tigers tried vainly to salvage a tie. Aker, displaying great poise, weathered the attack and assured the win.

"Neil looked real good all game," commented Harves after the match. "His attitude seemed to affect the whole team when we needed it."

Harves was also pleased with the standout performances that he received from fullback Alfredo Ducan and freshmen Tim Mann and John "Smitty" Smith. According to Harves, "These three players have been very pleasant surprises for me so far this season. They played a crucial part in our win over Hampden-Sydney."

Harves also noted that the home crowd for Wednesday's match was very encouraging, and hopes for a similar turnout this Saturday when Radford hosts Washington & Lee at 3:00 p.m.

1977 RU Newspaper September Soccer Article

1977 Schulte (19) Duran (16) vs. Virginia Tech

1977 Neal Aker vs. VMI

1977 Neal Aker vs. Mary Washington

1977 Neal Aker Warmup

1977 Neal Aker vs. VMI

1977 Neal Aker vs. Randolph Macon

1977 Steve Schulte vs. Mary Washington

Soccer Season Over, Team Data Tallied

RADFORD COLLEGE 1977 FINAL SOCCER STATISTICS

September 14	Hampden-Sydney	2-1
September 17	Eastern Mennonite	1-2
September 24	Washington & Lee	0-2
September 28	Averett College	1-0
October 5	Virginia Tech	1-4
October 9	N.C. Wesleyan	1-0
October 12	VMI	1-3
October 15	Liberty Baptist	0-1 (Dbl OT)
October 22	U. of Richmond	3-1
October 23	Randolph-Macon	1-5
October 25	Morris Harvey	3-1
October 29	Mary Washington	6-2
November 2	West Va. Tech	1-3
November 4	Roanoke College	2-1

Season Record: 8-7

Best overall record: 8-7 533

Team season records: Most shots: 265; most assists: 12; most wins: 8; most consecutive wins: 2; most goals: 30; Fewest goals allowed: 28; most shutouts: 2.

Best division record: 2-2, 3rd place in Western Division.

Team game records: Most shots: 47 against Mary Washington College. Most assists: 3 against Bluefield College. Most goals: 7 against Bluefield College.

Individual records: Most goals in one game: 4 by Cesar Collantes vs. Bluefield C. Career scoring mark: 16 by Tommy Lillard (3 yrs.) goalie ave. per season: 1.85 ave. scored against per game Neal Aker (13 games)

Highlander soccer individual scoring as follows:

Alfredo Duran, 7; Jamal Haddad, 6; Cesar Collantes, 5; Tim Mann, 3; Steve Schulte, 3; John Smith, 2; Tom Lillard, 2; Bret Phillips, 1; and Michael Greco, 1. Total, 30.

1977 RU Newspaper Final Soccer Article

1977 Tim Mann up Sideline

1977 Steve Schulte vs. Virginia Tech

1977 Tom Lillard Corner Kick

1977 Tom Lillard

1977 Tom Lillard vs. Virginia Tech

1977 Tom Lillard vs. Mary Washington

1978 Arrow and Soccer Ball Logo

1978 Alfredo Duran PK

1978 Halftime with Coach Harves and Will Iandolo

1978 Dan Thoms

1978 Dennis Gunson vs Virginia Tech

RADFORD COLLEGE
SOCCER ROSTER

No.	Name	Position	Ht.	Class	Hometown
	John White	G	6-0	Fr.	Arlington
	Scott Long	G	6-1	Fr.	Newport News
2	Maurice Byrd	Forward	6-1	Soph.	Alexandria
3	*John Smith	Fullback	5-11	Soph.	Alexandria
4	Edwin Duran	Halfback	5-8	Fr.	Fairfax
5	Dan Thoms	Halfback	5-7	Fr.	Sterling
6	*Timmy Mann	Forward	5-8	Soph.	Fairfax
7	Greg Poirier	Fullback	5-9	Jr.	Fairfax
8	#*Charlie Laslie	Fullback	5-9	Jr.	Springfield
9	Michael Berger	Forward	5-10	Soph.	Springfield
10	Paul Best	Forward	6-0	Soph.	Alexandria
11	Robby Ercolano	Forward	5-7	Fr.	Arlington
12	John Chomeau	Halfback	5-10	Fr.	McLean
13	*Jamal Haddad	Forward	5-10	Jr.	Woodbridge
14	Dan Schultz	Forward	5-8	Fr.	Fairfax
15	Garnet Smith	Fullback	6-4	Fr.	Annandale
16	*Alfredo Duran	Halfback	5-7	Jr.	Fairfax
17	Dennis Gunson	Forward	5-10	Fr.	Williamsburg
18	Will Iandolo	Halfback	5-11	Fr.	Arlington
19	*Steve Schulte	Halfback	6-0	Sr.	Alexandria

*Lettermen
#Captain

Coach: John Harves
Assistant: Tom Lillard
Manager: Beth Harkins

SOCCER SUPPORT TEAM

The Radford College Soccer Support Team manages all record-keeping, time-keeping and sideline duties during the Highlanders' home games. The 1978 members include Linda Convery, Sharon Cross, Nanci Dahlinger, Randi Davis, Donna Dossett, Terri Erdodi, Jill Krehling, Leslie Salvatori, Cathy Salyer and Alexis Sigethy.

1978 RADFORD COLLEGE SOCCER TEAM

Members of the Highlanders' 1978 squad are, front row, from left: Greg Poirier, Dan Schultz, Dan Thoms, Aldredo Duran, John White, Charlie Laslie, Robby Ercolano, Edwin Duran, John Chomeau and Will Iandolo. Back row, from left: coach John Harves, Dennis Gunson, Tim Mann, John Smith, Maurice Byrd, Scott Long, Garnet Smith, Steve Schulte, Mike Berger, Jamal Haddad, Paul Best and assistant Tom Lillard.

JOHN HARVES

John Harves is now in his second year as coach of the Highlanders. In his rookie year last season, Harves guided the Highlanders to a record of eight wins and seven losses—the best record in the team's short history. The 1977 team set new records in every category, including its best Virginia Intercollegiate Soccer Association district finish. Harves is a native of Arlington and is a 1974 graduate of Virginia Tech, where he played college soccer from 1970-73. He also served as an assistant coach at Tech. Before coming to Radford, Harves was a player and manager with the semi-pro Arlington Americans of the Capitol Soccer League. He is a member of the National Soccer Coaches Association of America and has a United States Soccer Federation license. At age 26, Harves has been playing and coaching soccer for 20 years.

1978 Game Program

1978 Garnet Smith vs. Virginia Tech

1978 Jamal Haddad vs. Virginia Tech

1978 John White vs. Virginia Tech

1978 Jamal Haddad vs. Virginia Tech

1978 Mike Berger

1978 News Collage

1978 Jamal Haddad

1978 (L-R) Garnet Smith, Alfredo Duran vs. Virginia Tech

1979 John White

1979 Jamal Haddad

1979 Dennis Gunson

1979 Charlie Laslie

1979 (L-R) John White, Tom Lillard, Coach Harves after loss to Lynchburg

1979 Randy Jones

1979 Dennis Gunson

1979 Tim Mann

1979 Laslie All Star Game

Jamal Haddad -- VISA All-Star Game

=

1979 - Will Iandolo Dribbling

1979 - Will Iandolo Free Kick

1979 - Will Iandolo Header

1979 - Will Iandolo Receiving

VISA ALL - STAR GAME

Sunday, December 2nd at Averett College 1:00pm

EASTERN DIVISION

WESTERN DIVISION

Forwards:
- Greg Simms - R-M
- Dave Bishop - Va. Wes.
- Alan Lindsay - Va. Wes.
- Martin Ferrara - H-S
- Joe Parker - Longwood
- Steve Keller - R-M
- Peter Morris - R-M
- Alvaro Guillem - M. Wash.

Forwards:
- Pekka Kaartinen - Averett
- Tom Emmons - Lynchburg
- Will Iandolo - Radford
- Barry Steel - Lynchburg
- John Vigouroux - Averett
- Jamal Haddad - Radford
- Paul Karch - Roanoke
- Dan Hooley - EMC

Backs:
- Tetsu Kimura - R-M
- Don LaCombe - Va. Wes.
- Stan Taylor - Va. Wes.
- Bill Foster - CNC
- Greg Schwartz - R-M
- Gustavo Leal - Longwood
- Jim Babashak - H-S
- Butch Thomas - R-M

Backs:
- Adil Ismail - Averett
- Tim Kinni - Lynchburg
- Jim Heishman - EMC
- Brian Williams - WSL
- Keith Walklet - Roanoke
- Charlie Lassie - Radford
- John Crismali - Lynchburg
- Jay Cannon - Roanoke

Keepers:
- Greg Seidel - R-M
- Don Staley - Va. Wes.

Keepers:
- Keith Little - Averett
- Ed DelaRosa - Lynchburg

Coach: Helmut Weiner - R-M

Coach: Vesa Hiltunen - Averett

1979 VISA All Star Game Rosters

RON CARTER (3) tries to boot ball downfield while Mike Berger (9) gives support in match against Spring Garden. Photo Courtesy Rick Rogers.

Season Ends For Booters At Hands Of Spring Garden

CHESTNUT HILL, Pa — The Radford University soccer team's 1979 season ended in disappointment Friday as the Highlanders fell short in their bid for a district championship.

The Highlanders lost 2-0 to a fired-up and extremely physical team from Spring Garden College in a match played in Chestnut Hill, Pa. The win gave the Bobcats their second consecutive NAIA District 19 championship.

The Highlanders appeared ready to unseat the defending champions in the early going as they took control in the opening minutes of the match and occasionally pushed the ball toward the Spring Garden goal. But they couldn't connect on a shot and the tide began to turn.

Spring Garden began to put on more and more offensive pressure, and finally, with only two and one half minutes left in the first half, Tom Dennery headed in a shot off a corner kick to give the Bobcats a 1-0 lead. It was the first goal of the season for Dennery.

The Highlanders tried to fight back for the tying score after the intermission, but they were unable to get their offense unhooked. Radford was hurt by the absence of sophomore Will Iandolo, the team's leading point scorer, who missed the match because of an injury. Senior Jamal Haddad, the team's third leading scorer, also was hampered by an injury and saw only limited playing time.

While Radford struggled to get things going, Spring Garden continued to threaten, and midway through the second period, the Bobcats tallied again when Rich Lenta took a pass from Dennery, broke behind the Radford defense and dribbled the ball past sophomore goalie John White and into the net. That proved to be the final score and Spring Garden had the win.

Spring Garden outshot Radford 12-9 in the match. White was credited with seven saves on the day, while backup goalie Chris Langer had three. The Bobcats' Frank Murphy recorded seven saves.

The loss brought Radford's final season record to 11-6-1. Spring Garden, which now goes on to the NAIA's area playoffs, moved to 12-3 with the win.

The loss not only ended the Highlanders' season, it also marked the end of Coach John Harves' coaching career at Radford. Harves, citing "personal and health reasons," had announced before the season that this would be his last job at Radford.

The Arlington native began coaching here in 1977, taking over a team that had compiled a cumulative record of 0-14-1 in its first two years of play as a varsity sport. In his first year, Harves guided the Highlanders to their first winning season at 6-7. Last year, his team went 10-3-1 and this season, the Highlanders set a school record for most wins in a season and earned their first-ever berth in post-season play.

1979 District 19 Tartan Article

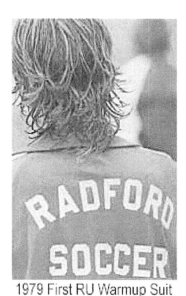

1979 First RU Warmup Suit

1979 Randy Jones Fouled

1979 News Collage

NAIA
District 19
Soccer
Championships

Radford University
vs.
Rutgers University Camden

Friday, Nov. 7, 1980

1980 NAIA Brochure

1981 Randy Jones

THE RADFORD UNIVERSITY STUDENT

Thursday, December 3, 1981

Photo by Neil McNeely

Number One! THE 1981 STATE CHAMPION SOCCER TEAM: (front, from left) Edwin Duran, Ted Longworth, J.D. Jenks, John White, Ron Carter, Joe McIntire, Tim Mann, Brian Bruce, Chris Langer, Greg Gilmore. (standing, from left) Assistant coach Will Fardoto, Keith Custer, Dennis Gunnoe, Robert Brumbaugh, Joan Hurley, Bruce Williams, Kevin Dupont, Tom Vahle, Greg McCarthy, Reg Ridgely, Randy Jones, trainer Tommy Bell, coach Tim Lillard.

1981 Ron Carter

Soccer Team Takes State Championship

By RON BARKER
Sports Co-Editor

a goal heard around the state that gives ed its first-ever men's soccer state ship against Averett College.

...score tied 1-1 in the final seconds of the udden death overtime period, a loose ball d a defender and shots toward sophomore ... He settles it and fires a rising corner ... the Averett goal. The ball hangs just ... goal post with nine seconds left!

... "it's the cocktail hour" as McIntire is ... a huge mass of humanity made up of our ... and squad. Then Radford Coach Tom ... dashes into the pile-up with a tremendous ...

... were right into the middle of the pile ... ball," Lillard said. "It was a swan dive ... the top of them."

McIntire's tremendous shot, the ... had gotten off three shots that hit ... goal post. After the game, assistant coach ... exclaimed, "It was just a matter of ... said told a goal was coming. There were ... in succession that brought us really ...

... added but added that he was expecting ... a mental breakdown after the third

... that hit the post. "If you hit the post three times then you've missed three good chances to score. Usually, it's a little disheartening to hit the post that many times."

But the Highlanders were undefeated at the field of dirt called home and intended to stay that way. Radford entered the state playoffs with an undefeated Western Division record.

Since it was determined earlier that the Western division would play host to the Virginia Intercollegiate Soccer Association Division II playoffs, Radford opened against Lynchburg College. With two early goals by senior Ron Carter, Radford went on to defeat the wild-card team 3-1 and advanced to the state final.

"The state championship was one of our big goals at the beginning of the year," Lillard said. "I knew we were going to do it, this had to be the year."

But the defending state champs were also having a fine year. Averett downed Radford 2-0 during the regular season and won the Central Division. Averett also advanced to the state championship with an easy 5-1 victory over Eastern champion Randolph-Macon College.

This set the stage for the 1981 state championship between Radford 7-2-2 and Averett 15-3-1.

Both teams battled to a scoreless tie at the half.

See Team, p. 16

1981 VISA Champs Tartan Page 1

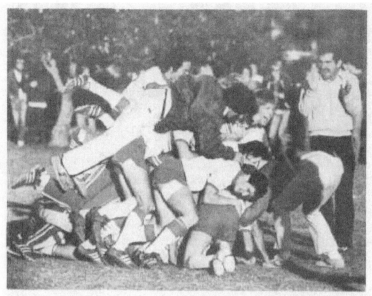

Photo by Neil McNeely

WHERE DID HE GO? Sophomore Jim McIntire is on the bottom of this mass of happy Highlanders. McIntire's long range boot in the third sudden death overtime gave Radford their first stae soccer championship. McIntire, number 9, for the Highlanders, scored the game winner with nine seconds to play in that third and deciding overtime.

Ready For 'Cocktail Hour'

Continued from p. 1

But with 25 minutes remaining in the game, Carter scored his third playoff goal with a fatal us far-post shot from the right side of the goal.

But Averett didn't give up and with 12 minutes left the Cougars' Pekka Kaartinen broke loose and ran toward the right side of Radford's goal. Goalie John White was left with no choice but to tackle the All-American candidate from Helsinki, Finland. Kaartinen was then awarded a penalty kick and he bombed the one-on-one past White.

It seemed as though the momentum might change hands in favor of Averett. But in the final minute of play, White made a terrific diving save to maintain the 1-1 tie and send the game into overtime.

The suspense of a sudden-death championship game was almost unbearable. Just before the second overtime period, Lillard was pacing the sidelines and exclaimed, "This is a hell of a way to make a living."

"I was serious," he added later. "I felt like I was going to go bald before that second overtime period."

To Radford's relief, the Highlanders continued to dominate the overtime period. And after three shots hit Averett's goal post, McIntire blew one by goalie Bob Christian for the championship.

Lillard was particularly pleased with the Highlanders' defense which was successful in shutting down Averett's offense. Fullbacks Kevin Dupont and Edwin Duran gave White plenty of support in containing Kaartinen and John Vigoureux.

Now that the season is over, Lillard is often reminded of the words of his favorite sportscaster Skip Carey of WTBS, who congratulates victors by saying, "You can hear the tinkling of ice cubes in the glass. It's the cocktail hour."

1981 VISA Champs Tartan Page 2

1981 John White

1981 - Coach Tom Lillard at one of the last games at Moffett Field

264

1981 VISA STATE SOCCER CHAMPIONSHIP

RADFORD UNIVERSITY
1981 SOCCER ROSTER

NO	NAME	POS	YR	HOMETOWN
--	Brian Bruce	Goal	So.	Richmond
1	John White	Goal	Sr.	Arlington
2	Ron Carter	For.	Sr.	Alexandria
3	Chris Langer	Mid.	Sr.	Park Ridge, N.J.
4	Edwin Duran	Back	Sr.	Fairfax
5	Reg Ridgely	Back	Sr.	Arlington
6	Tim Mann	Mid.	Sr.	Fairfax
7	Tom Vahle	Back	So.	Arlington
8	Ted Longsworth	For.	So.	College Park, Md.
9	Jim McIntire	Mid.	So.	Falls Church
10	Randy Jones	Mid.	Jr.	Hampton
11	Robert Brumbaugh	Back	Fr.	Hampton
12	Dennis Gunson	For.	Sr.	Williamsburg
14	Kevin Dupont	Back	Jr.	Fairfax
15	Greg Gilmore	For.	So.	Arlington
16	J.P. Jenks	Mid.	Sr.	Fairfax
17	Bruce Williams	For.	Sr.	Fredericksburg
18	John Hurley	Mid.	Fr.	Lynchburg
20	Keith Custer	For.	Sr.	Boones Mill

COACH: Tom Lillard
ASSISTANT: Will Iandolo

RECORD TO DATE: 7-7-2

Radford, the VISA Western Division Champion,
reached the finals by defeating Lynchburg 3-0.

We would like to express our appreciation to the members
of the Radford University Athletic Association for their
generous contributions to our athletic program.

AVERETT COLLEGE
1981 SOCCER ROSTER

NO	NAME	POS	YR	HOMETOWN
--	Joel Butts	Goal	Jr.	Va. Beach
--	Bob Christian	Goal	Fr.	Va. Beach
--	Donnie Jack	Goal	Sr	Greenfield, Ind.
3	Bill Jennsch	For.	Sr.	Neptune City, N.J.
4	Joe O'Leary	Full	Fr.	Central Islip, N.Y
6	David Borinski	Back	Fr.	West Point
8	Bruce Olcott	Back	Jr.	Glen Rock, N.J
10	John Vigouroux	For.	Sr.	Coram, N.Y.
11	Andy Mann	Full	Sr.	Fairfax
12	Matt Grennan	Back	Jr.	Commack, N.J.
13	Jose Cornejo	Back	So.	Coram, N.Y.
14	Jim Martin	Full	Sr.	Danville
15	Neil Nesterak	Full	Sr	Newark, N.J.
17	Timo Mattila	Back	Jr.	Tornio, Finland
19	Jorma Hjelt	Back	Jr.	Kotka, Finland
20	Pekka Kaartinen	For.	Sr.	Helsinki, Finland
21	Jarmo Saloranta	Back	Fr.	Helsinki, Finland
29	Micheal Hartnett	Back	Fr.	Madison, N.Y.

COACH: Vesa Hiltunen
TRAINERS: Mark Castellane, Harold Drunheller

RECORD TO DATE: 15-3-1

Averett, the Central Division Champion, defeated
Randolph-Macon 5-1 in their semifinal match

1981 VISA Championship Game Program

BIG MAC ATTACK — Junior booter Jim McIntire gets Piedmon Center debut against the Univ. of Charleston
a foot in the action as the Highlanders win their 1-0

1982 Randy Jones

1983 - Tom Lillard Presents Bill Gerber's All-America Certificate

1983 Brian Udy

Bill Gerber leaps in the air to head in the winning goal against UDC.

1984 Bill Gerber

Trung Pham gets caught between two UDC players.

1984 Trung Pham

1984 Eric Sigurdson

1984 - Bill Gerber at Dedmon Field

1984 - Bill Gerber Header

Lillard scores win

By LAURA BEITZ
Sports Writer

Coach Tommy Lillard's men's soccer team paved their way into the new Division I status with a 3-2 win over University of Richmond last Saturday.

Freshman Eric Sigurdson, a Sweden native, led the offensive attack at 33:00 minutes, when midfielder Stephen White chipped the ball to him. At 40:00 minutes, Joe Nolan put one in for the Spiders. But, with a mere three seconds remaining in the half, Billy Gerber, taking on the midfield position, brought the Highlanders back on top with a 25-yard kick to the far post.

In the second half at 49:00 minutes, Sigurdson was tripped in the box. RU was awarded a penalty kick, which Gerber took with ease. Eighteen minutes elapsed before U of R was able to penetrate the Highlander defense. The game appeared to be over, but with 1:46 left, the Spiders were given a penalty kick for an RU defensive mistake. U of R's attempt was foiled by goalkeeper, Justin Bryant. The final score RU 3, Spiders 2.

Coach Lillard commented, "We started new people and we're unsure at first. But, they came through; and Justin's save sealed the game."

Radford's emergence into the new competition of play will be enhanced through new talent and old talent in new positions.

Gerber, last year's second team Division II All American sweeper, will be more offensive minded this season in his midfield position. White will also move to the midfield. Lillard will also be looking to forward Joe Montagne, who recorded four goals and two assists last season for scoring production. Defensively, Greg "Stitch" McCarthy will be the background leader.

"We've got quite a few experienced players coming back, but we're still very young," emphasized Lillard. "A lot will depend on how well the new guys respond."

In particular, Lillard will be looking toward Bryant of Tampa Fla. "Justin shores up a big need for us," Lillard said, pointing to five losses by one-goal margins "He can come through in the big games."

Overall, Lillard is confident about the season. "We know we can stay with everyone on our schedule," Lillard said. "We played them all tough last year."

1984 Tartan Article

269

RADFORD UNIVERSITY

NO	NAME	POS	YR	HOMETOWN
--	Justin Bryant	GK	Fr	Cape Canaveral, FLA
--	Jeff Brown	GK	Fr	Tampa, FLA
--	Fran Henry	GK	So	Warrenton, VA
2	Thai Nguyen	MF/F	Fr	Manassas, VA
3	Stephen White	MF	So	Arlington, VA
4	Mike Dopp	FB	So	Alexandria, VA
5	Pete Bouker	MF/FB	So	Warrenton, VA
6	Chris Bourne	FB	So	Alexandria, VA
7	Brian Udy	F	Jr	Woodstown, NJ
8	Billy Gerber	MF	Jr	Annandale, VA
9	Walter O'Hara	MF	Fr	Arlington, VA
11	Chris Baker	F	Fr	Springfield, VA
12	Trung Pham	MF	Fr	Manassas, VA
13	Greg McCarthy	FB	Sr	Timonium, MD
14	Brent King	FB	Fr	Fairfax, VA
15	Joe Montagne	MF/FB	Jr	Reston, VA
16	Bill Stachler	MF/FB	Fr	Randolph, NJ
17	Miles Pruett	FB	Jr	Richmond, VA
18	Anoput Phimmasone	F	So	Chantilly, VA
19	Eric Sigurdson	F	Fr	Eskilstuna, Sweden
20	Phil Owens	FB	Fr	Tampa, FLA
21	J.P. Goyer	FB	Fr	Tampa, FLA

HEAD COACH: Tom Lillard   LOCATION: Radford, VA
ASSISTANT: Don Staley   ENROLLMENT: 6,800
TRAINER: Cammy Conboy   COLORS: Red, Blue & Green
                                NICKNAME: Highlanders

OVERALL RECORD: 9-9-0   CONFERENCE RECORD: 1-1-0

W	3-2	Richmond	W	1-0	Liberty Baptist
L	0-2	James Madison	W	2-1	UDC
W	2-0	Charleston (SC)	W	4-2	Marshall
W	4-1	Baptist	L	0-1	Averett
L	1-2	Campbell	L	1-2	Virginia Tech
L	0-3	George Mason	W	3-2	Longwood
L	1-7	North Carolina	L	0-1	Roanoke
L	0-5	Virginia	W	5-1	VMI
L	1-5	Randolph-Macon	W	3-0	Washington & Lee

1984 Game Program

, 1984 THE TARTAN, Page 11

TARTAN SPORTS

Men's soccer finishes at 10-10

By LAURA BEITZ
Sports Writer

It may have been early, but the Radford University men's soccer team was ready to win. Through the thick clouds and chilly temperatures the Highlanders improved its record to 10-9 last Thursday at 8 a.m. with a 9-0 win over UNC-Asheville.

Sophomore Stephen White led the offense with a goal from the left post at 11:17. Brian Udy followed a minute later with an assist from Chris Baker's dummy play. Trung Pham and Chris Bourne followed with goals to the upper right post.

Baker opened up the second half with a goal at 50:00. Billy Gerber added two more at 58:05 and 65:18. Udy acquired the assist on Gerber's first goal. Pham hit his second goal from mid post with assistance from Joe Montagne. And, Thai Nguyen rounded out the scoring blitz at 80:03.

The Highlanders didn't fare as well in the semifinal round against number one seed Winthrop College.

The Radford booters scored first on a direct kick from Gerber, after a foul was committed inside the circle. Winthrop also placed themselves on the board with a penalty kick.

Although the Highlanders equaled Winthrop's shots on goal, the team couldn't seem to place one in. Winthrop came on strong in the second half and placed two more goals in the cage.

Radford's overall season record ended an even 10-10.

Campbell University captured the first Big South Conference Soccer Tournament championship with a 2-0 upset win over number-one seeded Winthrop College Saturday on the Dedmon Center field.

Winthrop ousted host Radford in the semifinals on Friday in a hard-fought 3-1 match. Junior midfielder Billy Gerber scored Radford's lone goal to give him three in the tournament. The Annandale native had two goals in Radford's 9-0 opening round win over UNC-Asheville.

The Highlanders, who finished their first NCAA Division I season with ...-10 record, were ...... fourth in the eight-team tourn......... field. After the loss to Campbell, Winthrop's record stood at 18-6.

Campbell advanced to the finals with a 6-3 win over Coastal Carolina on Friday. The Camels led by tournament Most Valuable Player David Nisbet of Edinburg, Scotland, finished the season with an 11-6-2 mark.

Radford placed two players on the all-tournament team. Junior midfielder Billy Gerber and sophomore midfielder Stephen White both earned all-tournament honors in the first Big South soccer championships.

WINGMAN TRUNG PHAM and mid-fielder Billy Gerber try to take the ball down field against Winthrop in the Big South Conference. Winthrop won the match 3-1.

1984 End of Season Tartan Article

1985 Bert Diesel

1985 Brian Udy

1985 - Bill Gerber Scores vs. UNCA

1985 - Bill Gerber vs. JMU

1985 Bill Gerber

1985 Joe Montagne

1985 Joe Montagne

WILLIE KEE, a junior striker, and a Ram player, are vying for possession of a loose ball

1985 Willie Kee

RU GOALKEEPER JUSTIN BRYANT recorded his first shutout of the season against JMU last Friday 2-0. The men are now 6-4-3.

1986 Brian Eagon

1986 Lance Casey

1986 Chris Baker

1986 - Tom Lillard and Bill Gerber Receive Their Jerseys

1987 Bruce Griggs

1987 Jeff Brown

1988 Game Ball

1988 - Goalie Jeff Brown

Staff Photo by Jeff Beamer

Dave Cossaboon chases down the ball and takes control during a 2-0 first-round win against UNC-Asheville.

1988 Dave Cossaboon

1988 Bruce Griggs

Staff Photo by Jeff Beamer

Freshman Dante Washington outmaneuvers a Baptist opponent as the Highlanders go on to defeat them to win their first Big South tournament championship in RU soccer history.

1988 Dante Washington End of Season Summary

1988 Magnus Ramquist

1988 Dante Washington

1988 – Teddy Wilson

Men's season ends on high note

By JEFF BLAMER
Sports Editor

The RU men's soccer team racked up a tie and three wins last week to end their season on a high note.

The Highlanders started the four-game week with a meeting against William & Mary. W & M had been ranked 11 in the national polo earlier in the year.

"We had the opportunity to beat them," said coach Don Staley. "We missed a couple of shots that could have given us the win."

The Highlanders tied the Williamsburg school 1-1.

"Everyone gave an all out effort," said Brian Eagen. "We really applied a lot of pressure."

Eagen had the only goal for the Highlanders.

On Saturday, the men began a three-day, three game stretch when they faced UNC-Asheville. The Highlanders did not have too much trouble with them as they took a 4-0 win.

Brian Griggs, Dave Connabeen, Dante Washington and Teddy Wilson scored for the Highlanders.

The men will face UNC-Asheville in the first round of the Big South Tournament this week, so the win really boosted them up.

Lenior Rhyne was the next victim for the Highlanders. RU dropped them 6-1.

The bright spot in the game was national scoring leader Dante Washington. He blasted three in to earn the hat trick on the day.

Another strong point for the Highlanders was the play off the bench.

"The bench really showed some strong play," said Eagen.

RU hosted state rival VMI to round out the week and the regular season. The Highlanders won, 4-1.

Paul Adams found the goal and had twice in the game. Washington and Connabeen added one apiece.

Going into the tournament the Highlanders feel that they are peaking.

"We are playing well. Everyone's attitude is up. We are going to come back with the conference trophy," said Eagen.

Dante Washington rises to take the ball past the goalie in a recent game.

1988 Tartan

1988 Mud Bowl Game

1989 Coach Staley and Team with The New River Rock

1989 Doug Majewski

Rob Adolph challenges the Tech goalie for control of the ball

1989 SOCCER ROSTER

No.	Name	Pos.	Class	Ht.	Wt.	Hometown
	Scott Grabham	G	Fr.	6-0	156	Richmond, VA
	Ian Harris	G	Fr.	6-2	190	Radford, VA
	Greg Mahan	G	Fr.	6-2	205	Richmond, VA
1	Frederic Rondeau	G	Fr.	6-3	190	Quebec, Canada
2	John Barry	M	Fr.	5-9	170	Browns Mills, NJ
3	David Cossaboon	M-B	Sr.	5-11	155	Media, PA
4	Keith Darden	M-S	Fr.	5-6	140	Durham, NC
5	Magnus Ramquist	M-S	Sr.	5-6	150	Eskilstuna, Sweden
6	Jeff Majewski	M	So.	5-9	148	Columbia, MD
7	Teddy Wilson	M	Jr.	5-10	163	Manassas, VA
8	Steve Arkon	B	Jr.	6-0	163	Stone Mt., GA
9	Dante Washington	S	So.	5-11	176	Columbia, MD
10	Brian Eagon	M	Sr.	5-9	158	Richmond, VA
11	Whitney Keiller	S	Fr.	6-0	180	Columbia, MD
12	Bruce Griggs	M	Jr.	6-2	170	Wall, NJ
13	Kevin Williams	M	Fr.	5-11	165	Elmire, NY
14	Sean Peay	B	Jr.	6-0	175	Columbia, MD
15	Doug Majewski	B	Jr.	6-1	169	Columbia, MD
16	Marc Osterberger	B	Fr.	6-2	170	Columbia, MD
17	Randy Fisher	M	Fr.	5-9	145	Cross Lanes, WVA
18	John Magnusson	B	So.	6-2	190	Annandale, VA
19	Luis Robles	S	Fr.	5-10	160	Falls Church, VA
20	Shawn Turpin	M	Fr.	5-9	140	Radford, VA
21	Travis Ward	B	Fr.	6-4	205	Hampton, VA
22	Kevin Troiano	B	Fr.	6-1	170	Va. Beach, VA

HEAD COACH: Don Staley
ASSISTANT COACHES: Joe Wyzkoski, Jerry Bowman

1989 Roster

1989 (L-R) Keith Darden, Brian Eagon, Doug Majewski

1990 Dante Washington

1990 - Steve Arkon

1990 Dante Washington (#9)

1990 Jeff Majewski

1990 Frederic Rondeau

1990 Highlander Pre-Season Roster

NAME	POS	HT	WT	YR	HOMETOWN
Rob Adolph	B	6-0	220	Sr.	Manasquan, N.J.
Steve Arkon	B	6-0	175	Sr.	Randolph, N.J.
John Barry	M	5-10	180	So.	Browns Mills, N.J.
Matthias Berrang	B	6-3	190	Fr.	Durham, N.C.
Troy Broadbent	M	5-8	160	Fr.	York, Pa.
Mark Clubb	M	5-9	145	Fr.	Dallas, Texas
Jorge Crespin	M	5-8	150	Fr.	McLean, Va.
Keith Darden	M	5-8	150	So.	Durham, N.C.
Lance Dougald	M	5-9	150	Fr.	Charlottesville, Va.
Keith Eck	M	5-11	165	Fr.	Springfield, Va.
Mark Ellis	M	5-8	150	Fr.	Port-of-Spain, Trinidad
Justin Finck	M	6-2	175	Fr.	Manassas, Va.
Randy Fisher	B	5-9	160	So.	Cross Lanes, W. Va.
Chris Gavilan	M	6-2	185	Fr.	Richmond, Va.
Ian Harris	G	6-1	190	So.	Radford, Va.
Whitney Keiller	S	6-1	185	So.	Columbia, Md.
John Magnusson	B	6-2	190	Jr.	St. Louis, Mo.
Doug Majewski	M	6-2	185	Sr.	Columbia, Md.
Jeff Majewski	M	5-10	175	Jr.	Columbia, Md.
Wister Mitchelson	S	6-3	200	Fr.	Massies Mill, Va.
Mark Osterberger	B	6-3	195	So.	Columbia, Md.
Sean Peay	M	6-0	180	Sr.	Columbia, Md.
Andre Pyle	M	5-9	160	Fr.	Blacksburg, Va.
Frederic Rondeau	G	6-2	190	So.	Montreal, Canada
Pete Ryder	M	5-8	160	Fr.	Severna Park, Md.
Darryl Springer	B	6-0	165	Fr.	San Fernando, Trinidad
Shawn Turpin	M	5-9	160	So.	Radford, Va.
Brett Walker	M	5-11	165	Fr.	Springfield, Va.
Dante Washington	S	6-0	185	So.	Columbia, Md.
Kevin Williams	S	5-9	165	So.	Elmira, N.Y.
Teddy Wilson	B	6-0	180	Sr.	Manassas, Va.

Head Coach: Don Staley
Assistants: Matt Kinney, Mike Dolinger
Head Trainer: Jackie Clouse
Managers: Luis Robles, Kelly Jones, Jamil Farirdy

1990 Preseason Roster

1990 Win over the University of Maryland

1991 Dante Washington

1991 Dante Washington

1991 - Frederic Rondeau

1991 - Whitney Keiller

1991 Jeff Majewski

1993 Kevin Gealt

1994 Gerald Lakatos

1994 Kevin Gealt and Lee Morton

1995 Che Henderson

1995 Jose Avendano

1995 Lee Morton

1996

Front row: Mike Boyd, Dino Orgetas, Tommy Torres, Kevin Gealt, Che Henderson
Back row: Edwardo Wissar, John Tierney, Ian Spooner, Jose Avendano

1996 Original Highlander
was introduced in 1996.

1997 Nick Butcher (14), Fabian Arboleda (12)

1998 Jason Gvozdas

1997 Nick Butcher

1998 Dustin Keesee

1999 Team With The New River Rock

$1.00

2000 MEN'S SOCCER TOURNAMENT

**November 1-4, 2000
Liberty Soccer Complex
Lynchburg, VA**

2000 Big South Tournament Brochure

2000 Kenny Infante

2000 Mike Adeyemi

2000 Scott Hance

2000 T.J. Rolfing

2001 Ryan Caton

2002 Big South Tournament Cover

2002 Media Guide Cover

Radford University

Roster

No.	Name	Pos.	Ht.	Wt.	Yr.	Hometown (Previous School)
00	Marc Smith	GK	6-2	200	So.	Fredrickburg, VA (Chancellor)
0	Harper Thorsen	GK	6-2	200	So.	Blacksburg, VA (Blacksburg)
1	Andrew Essey	GK	6-2	180	Jr.	Columbia, MD (Hammond)
2	Mike Von Essen	M	5-6	140	Sr.	Bedford, TX (Trinity)
3	Erick Sokolik	M	5-10	150	Jr.	Scottsdale, AZ (Horizon)
4	Johnathan Hooker	M	5-10	160	Jr.	Woodbridge, VA C.D. Hylton)
5	Nate Pearson	D	5-10	150	Jr.	Dumfries, VA (C.D. Hylton)
6	Jeffery Nicholas	D	6-4	170	Jr.	Richmond, VA (J.R. Tucker)
7	Alfredo Perez-Costa	M	5-9	160	Sr.	Lima, Peru (Markham)
8	Chris Waltz	M	6-2	190	Sr.	Manassas, VA (Osbourn)
10	Jon Fosu	D	5-10	165	Sr.	Ghana, W. Africa (Maputo)
11	Adrian Snell	M	6-1	175	Jr.	Hagerstown, MD (Ferrum College)
12	Geraldo Hemandez	M	5-10	165	Sr.	Dale City, VA (C.D. Hylton)
13	Andre Lewis	M	5-11	170	Sr.	Tampa, FL (Hillsborough)
14	Seth Stoner	M	5-11	160	Jr.	Columbia, SC (Spartanburg Meth. JC)
15	Corey Ogburn	D	6-0	170	So.	Jefferson City, TN (Webb School)
16	T.J. Rolfing	F	5-11	170	Sr.	Sioux Falls, SD (O'Gorman)
17	Patrick Wales	D	5-11	165	Jr	Danville, VA (GW Danville)
18	Justin Peterson	M	5-10	160	So.	Edmond, OK. (Edmon Memorial)
19	Adam Pahl	D	6-1	180	So.	Landenberg, PA (Kennett)
20	Mark Crowder	M	6-0	180	Sr.	Woodbridge, VA (Garfield)
22	Mike Winsted	M	5-9	160	Sr.	Birmingham, AL (Hoover)
23	Andres Hernandez	M	5-9	140	Fr.	Arlington, VA (Yorktown)
24	Luis Cadena	M	5-11	155	Fr.	Miami, FL (Columbus)
26	Fernando Ramos	M	5-8	140	Fr.	Stafford, VA (North Stafford)
27	Ben Price	D	5-10	165	Fr.	Blacksburg, VA (Blacksburg)
28	David Harpula	M	5-8	150	Fr.	Kingsport, TN (Dobyns-Bennett)
29	Andrew Tamm	D	5-7	140	Fr.	Phoenix, AZ (Brophy)
30	Dan Stevens	GK	5-11	165	So.	Richmond, VA (J.R. Tucker)

Head Coach: Spencer Smith
Assistant Coaches: Jon Freeman, Greg Anderson

Quick Facts

Location: Radford, VA
Founded: 1910
Enrollment: 9,100
Nickname: Highlanders
School Colors: Red, White & Blue
Stadium/Capacity: Dedmon Center/3,500
President: Dr. Douglas Covington
Athletic Director: Greig Denny
Head Coach: Spencer Smith (Tennessee, '87)
Record at Radford/Years: 81-80-15/ 9 yrs.
Career Record/Years: 115-131-21/ 14 yrs.
Assistant Coaches: Jon Freeman, Greg Anderson
2002 Overall Record: 6-11-1
2002 Big South Record: 3-3-1

Coach Spencer Smith

RU
HIGHLANDERS

2002 Roster

2003 Andrew Essey

2004 Adam Paul

2004 - Cupp Stadium Ground Level

2004 Omar Zinoveev

2006 Paul Caruso

2004 Kike Negron

2006 Chris Pertl

2006 - Paul Caruso

2006 - Jeremy Delpino

2006 - Taylor Jenkins

2006 - Zach Roszel

2007 Davorin Husadzinovic

2007 Joseph Sansbury (14)

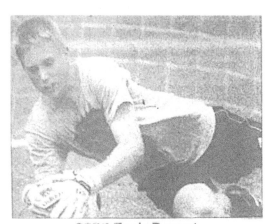

2007 Zach Roszel

2007 Justin Zimmer

2008 Zack Roszel

2009 Brendan Shaffer

2009 Daryn Patricio

2009 Iyiola Awosika

2009 Justin Zimmer

2009 Justin Zimmer

2009 Media Guide Cover

2010 Iyiola Awosika

Former St. John's University and Lafayette assistant Maciej Sliwinski is in his first season on the Radford University men's soccer coaching staff.

At Radford, Sliwinski will assist with all aspects of the Highlander program, with a special emphasis on recruiting and team preparation.

Sliwinski, a former two-year assistant alongside Reeves at St. John's, spent the 2009 season as an assistant at Lafayette.

"Maciej is an enthusiastic young coach who I am excited to welcome as part of our men's soccer staff here at Radford University," Reeves said. "Maciej brings a variety of experiences from varying levels of coaching and has a real desire to impact our program."

Sliwinski worked under Dennis Bohn at Lafayette in 2009, helping the Leopards to a 10-7-2 overall record and a trip to the Patriot League semifinals. While at Lafayette, his duties included goalkeeper training – Sliwinski guided Phillip Nelson to Patriot League Goalie of the Year honors along with a spot on the All-ECAC First Team and the NSCAA Mid-Atlantic Region Second Team.

**MACIEJ SLIWINSKI
ASSISTANT COACH**

Sliwinski spent the two seasons prior to his arrival at Lafayette at St. John's, where he assisted with multiple aspects of the program, including recruiting, team preparation, camps and alumni communications. He worked under head coach Dr. Dave Masur, the 2008 Big East Coach of the Year, and with Reeves, who was named the NSCAA East Regional College Assistant Coach of the Year. In 2008, the Red Storm earned an at-large bid to the NCAA Tournament and advanced to the national semifinals, en route to an overall record of 19-3-3.

A native of Poland, Sliwinski enjoyed a four-year playing career at Iona, where he was a two-year captain and was named to the MAAC All-Academic Team in all four of his seasons. He graduated in 2007 with a degree in finance. During his time at Iona, Sliwinski interned with the New York Red Bulls of MLS, with responsibilities in team operations and game preparation. In 2009, Sliwinski earned his master's degree in sports management from St. John's University.

In January 2009, he was appointed the Director of Coaching with the Brooklyn Italians, in charge of the coaching staff and education programs.

Sliwinski's younger brother is a member of the Philadelphia University men's soccer squad, while his father served as a coach in Poland.

Sliwinski is single and resides in Blacksburg.

2010 Magic Sliwinski

2010 Media Guide Cover

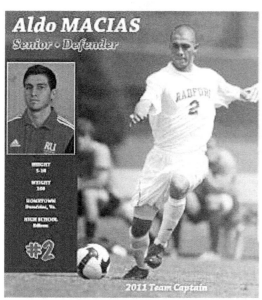

2011 Aldo Macias

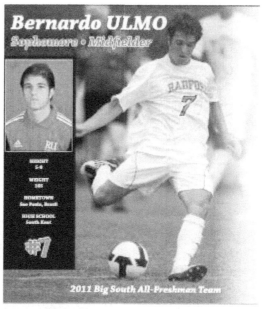

2011 Bernardo Ulmo

2011 End of Game Handshake

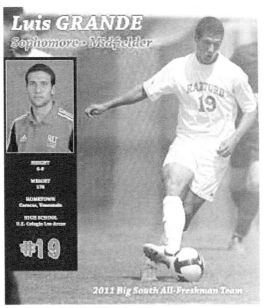

2011 Luis Grande

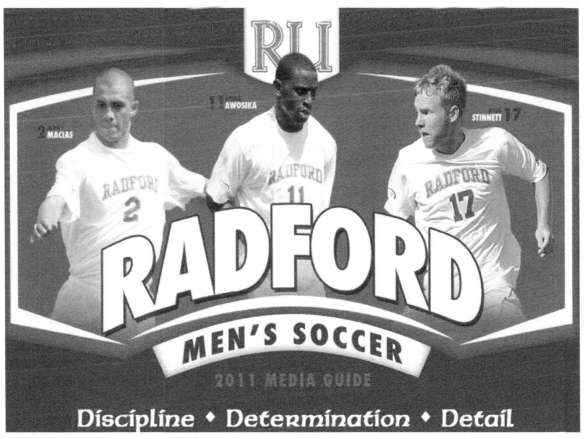

2011 Media Guide Cover

2012 Luis Grande

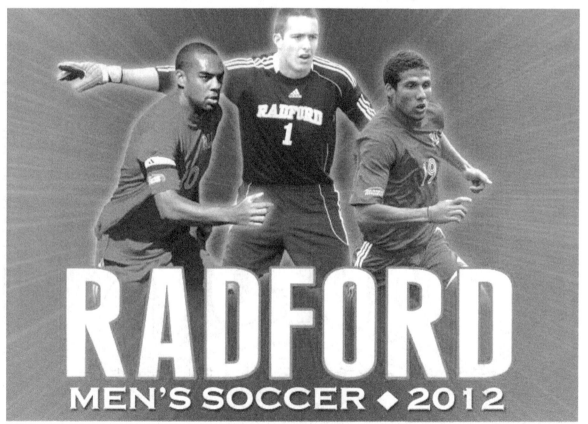

2012 Media Guide Cover

2012 Stephen Hudgens

2012 Team Huddle

2013 Bernardo Ulmo

2013 Garland Smith

2013 Poster

2014 BT's Congratulates Tom Lillard

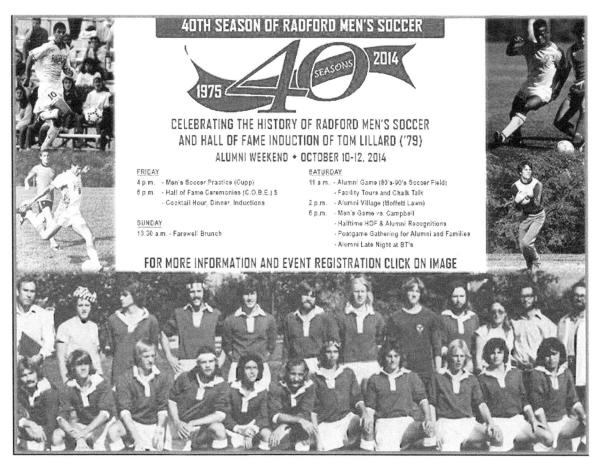

2014 40th Season Notice

2014 Chel Ho Park Kim

2014 Big South Regular Season Champs

2014 Dario Redondo

2014 Fraser Colmer

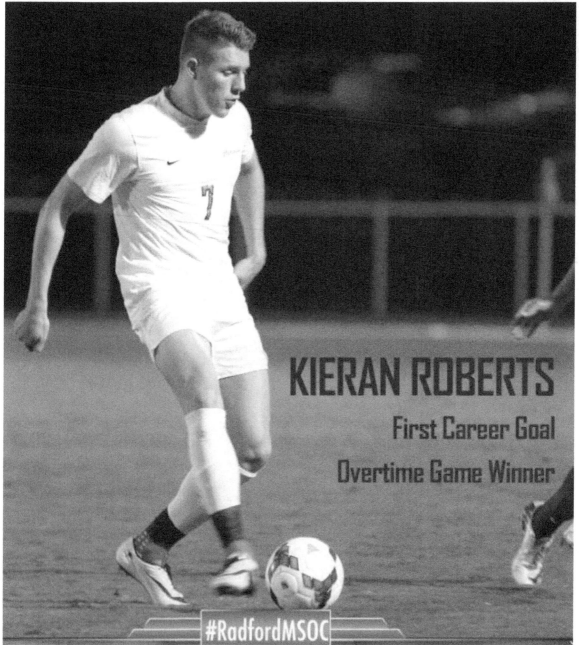

2014 Kieran Roberts

2014 Aitor Pouseu Blanco

 Radford Men's Soccer
February 4, 2014 · 🌐

RUHIGHLANDERS.COM

FORMER STANDOUT KEEPER TAYLOR SIGNS PRO CONTRACT EXTENSION WITH KICKERS

2014 Ryan Taylor Re-Signed

2014 - Lillard Hall of Fame Induction

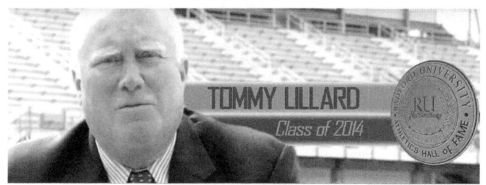

2014 - Lillard Hall of Fame Video

2014 Seniors

2014 Stephen Hudgens

2014 Stephen Hudgens

2014 Winning Streak Recognized

2015 Fraser Colmer

2015 Jo Vetle Rimstad

2015 Youth Camps

2016 Advance to BST Final on PKs

2016 Aitor Pouseu Blanco

2016 Big South Tournament Champions

2016 Big South Tournament Champions

2016 Big South Tournament Champions

2016 Jakob Strandsäter

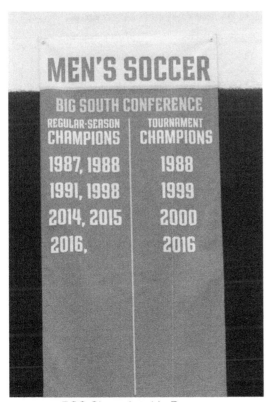

BSC Championship Banner

BSC 2016 Tournament Champion Trophy

2016 Senior Night

2016 Jo Vetle Rimstad

2016 Jo Vetle Rimstad

2016 Selection Show

2017 Fraser Colmer

2017 Jakob Strandsäter

2017 Kieran Roberts

2017 Kieran Roberts

2017 Locker Room Dedication
(L-R) John Harves, Lynn Iandolo, Will Iandolo

2017 Locker Room Dedication Plaque

2017 Neil Martorana

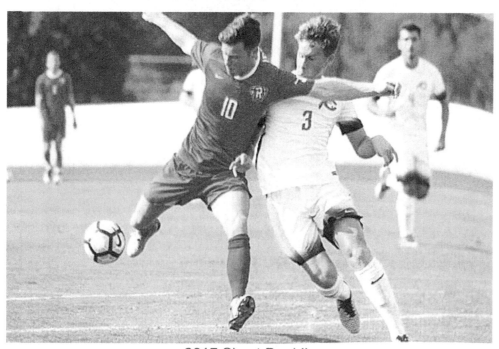

2017 Sivert Daehlie

2017 Victor Valls

2017 Wyatt Erzen

2018 Amadou Macky Diop

2018 Amadou Macky Diop

2018 Kieran Roberts

2018 Michael Walsh

2018 Kieran Roberts

2018 Myles Yorke

2018 Victor Valls

2019 Dondre' Robinson

2019 Octavio Ocampo

2019 Pape Oumar Gueye

2019 Pape Oumar Gueye

2019 Victor Valls

2019 Senior Night

2019 Victor Valls

2020 Ryan Machado-Jones

2020 Solomon Clark

2021 Dorian Dixon

2021 January Snow Practice

2021 Hansy Velasquez

2021 Starting XI

2021 Luke Gaffigan

2021 Senior Night

2021 Yoshiya Okawa

2021 Ryan Machado-Jones

2022 Alex Kryazhev

2022 James Barrett (R)

2022 James Gardev

2022 Joseba Incera

2022 Owen Clark

2022 Samuel Schwarz (L)

2022 Spencer Rawlins

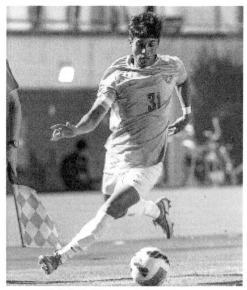

2022 Tony Martinez

2023 Alex Eydelman

2023 Alex Eydelman (42), Mark Silva (7)

RADFORDATHLETICS.COM

Haddad, Kryazhev and Hammam (L-R) recognized as
All-Big South Award Winners - Radford University Athletics

2023 Big South Awardees

2023 - Team Celebrates Win Over Virginia Tech

2023 Hagen Kyle (22), Perez Nance (10)

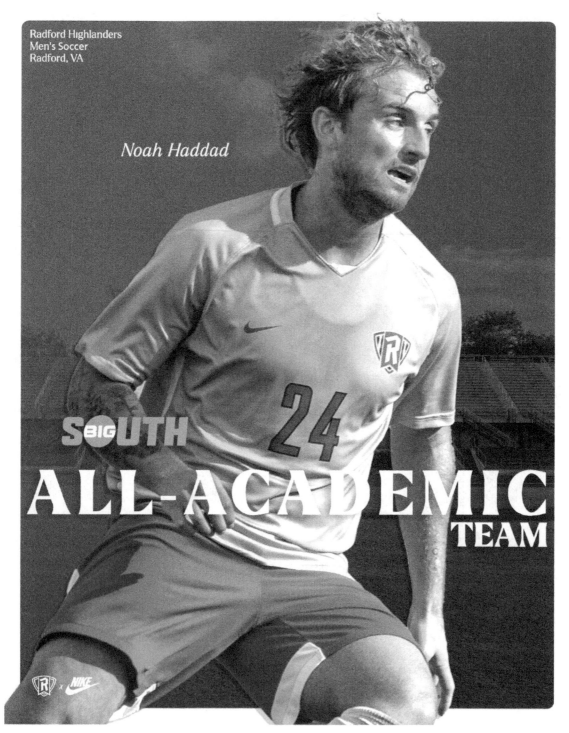

2023 Noah Haddad

2023 Owen Clark

2024 - Cupp Stadium Overhead

2024 - Lillard Field Naming

Appendix 4

DR. DONALD N. DEDMON

DR. DONALD N. DEDMON

Donald N. Dedmon (August 13, 1931 – February 13, 1998)

A member of the Big South Conference Hall of Fame, Dr. Donald Newton Dedmon was named the fourth president of Radford College on March 20, 1972. He was at the forefront of Radford being granted university status, allowing men to be admitted and giving the athletic programs the nickname "Highlanders." During the two decades that Dr. Dedmon served as Radford's president, the university experienced unprecedented growth in campus size, curriculum and student population. As the campus grew, so did the amenities around it.

Located adjacent from the New River, the Dedmon Center, named in honor of Dr. Dedmon, opened in 1981. He was instrumental in the building of the center, which became one of the first buildings in the country designed with an inflated air-supported roof. In 1981, Dr. Dedmon led Radford to NCAA Division II status and then on to a NCAA Division I affiliation in September 1984, thanks to a move to the Big South Conference in 1983. He served as Big South President from May 1986-1992 and his tenure included the conference becoming a full-fledged NCAA Division I member in September 1986. Dr. Dedmon entered the Big South Hall of Fame posthumously.

Wikipedia: "**Donald Newton Dedmon** (August 13, 1931 – February 13, 1998) was an American academic administrator and communications consultant.

Early life and education - Dedmon was born in Wright County, Missouri, and received his undergraduate degree in English and speech from Southwest Missouri State College (now Missouri State University) in 1953, and taught high school before earning a Master of Arts degree in speech in 1956 and a PhD in oral education from the University of Iowa in 1961.

Career - He taught at Saint Cloud State College, in St. Cloud, Minnesota, from 1959 to 1962 and at Southern Illinois University, in Carbondale, Illinois, from 1962 to 1964. He later became chair of the Department of Speech at Colorado State University. From 1966 to 1968, he served as a communications consultant for pharmaceutical company Smith, Kline & French.

Dedmon became the dean of the College of Arts and Sciences at Marshall University in 1968, and was appointed executive vice president the following year, becoming acting president of the University in 1970. In this role, he led the campus through the

November 14, 1970, plane crash in which 37 members of the Marshall University Thundering Herd football team, eight members of the coaching staff, and 25 school boosters were killed. The team was returning home after a 17-14 loss against the East Carolina University Pirates at Ficklen Stadium in Greenville, North Carolina. Dedmon was portrayed by David Strathairn in the movie *We Are Marshall,* which details the aftermath of the crash and its effect on the school community.

Dedmon became president of Radford University on March 20, 1972, and served for more than twenty years, during which time the University experienced rapid growth and a major transition from a small women's college to a co-ed institution, before reaching university status in 1979. The enrollment tripled during his tenure.

Dedmon spent much of the early 1990s away from Radford University on sabbatical in Hawaii and later on medical leave during a lengthy recovery from a ruptured spleen. Due to ill health, Dedmon announced his retirement from Radford University in June 1994, but officially held the presidency while on medical leave until August 1995. His last public appearance at Radford University was in September 1995, when he spoke at the inauguration of his successor, Douglas Covington.

The Dedmon Center at Radford University was named in his honor. The 58,000-square-foot athletic center opened in 1981 and was renovated in 2009. In 2018, Dedmon was posthumously inducted in the Radford University Athletics Hall of Fame.

Personal life - Dedmon married Geraldine Mary Sanders, a native of Canada, in 1957. They had two daughters. After retiring from Radford University, Dedmon moved to South Florida where he spent the remainder of his life. He died in Naples, Florida in 1998 at the age of 66."

Appendix 5

Radford University Men's Soccer
ATHLETIC DIRECTORS

ATHLETIC DIRECTORS

In the first 50 years of the Radford University Men's Soccer program, the institution only had a total of three Athletic Directors. All three proved to be enthusiastic supporters of the soccer program. These Athletic Directors were Chuck Taylor, Greig Denny, and Robert Lineburg.

Dr. Charles (Chuck) Taylor (March 30, 1946 – Sept. 21, 2022)

Chuck Taylor

Radford Athletics is saddened to learn of the passing of Dr. Charles David "Chuck" Taylor on Wednesday, September 21, 2022. The first-ever men's basketball head coach and athletics director in school history, he made an everlasting mark on the history of the Highlanders. Taylor served as athletics director from 1974 -1996, leading Radford on a remarkable journey from a six-sport unaffiliated small college program to Division I. Today, the Highlanders sponsor 16 varsity sports and have proudly played at the Division I level since 1984.

During his tenure, Radford Athletics was nationally recognized as a leader in opportunities for women and minorities, as well as in graduation rates for student-athletes. In competition, seven different programs achieved national rankings in his time guiding the Highlanders. Also serving as men's basketball coach from 1974 - 1978, Taylor compiled a 56-43 record, never suffering a losing season and setting the stage for the program's future success.

The Radford Athletics Hall of Fame inducted Taylor in its third-ever class, enshrining him in 1997. He was also inducted into the Big South Conference Hall of Fame in 2006. "Taylor engineered Radford's rise from a small athletic department with only six sports to a school that joined NCAA Division I in 1984," sportswriter Mark Berman wrote in his profile. "He's a person that saw possibilities and not limitations," former colleague John Montgomery stated. "He was a champion for the women's side," noted Tom Lillard, who previously coached Radford men's and women's soccer teams. "He cared about all the sports."

Greig Denny

Greig Denny

Greig Denny served as Radford's second athletic director from 1996 to 2007.

Having been Chuck Taylor's assistant for 13 years prior to his appointment, Denny played a key role in the continuation of Radford's nationally-recognized success of RU athletics, on the courts and fields, in the classroom, and beyond. He implemented an innovative drug and alcohol program and athletes and administrators alike were familiar with his hands-on style. He also was the University's first baseball coach.

Roanoke Times: "When introduced, Greig Denny arrived for the biggest day of his professional life with a black eye. The fading shiner may serve as an indication to those who love Radford University that its new athletic director isn't afraid of some rough stuff. The black eye was looking better than it had a few days before, Denny said. That was convenient because television cameras were whirring as the new boss of the Radford athletic department was introduced to a crowded roomful of university administrators, faculty and alumni, and various reporters."

"Ran into a moving elbow last Thursday," said Denny, explaining how his regular game of pickup basketball at the Dedmon Center had interfered with the camera-readiness of his visage. Denny is still mixing it up, just as he did as a football player for his alma mater, Cortland (N.Y.) State, back in his college days. A guy who likes to get after it is just the kind of guy that Radford needs."

A native of Adams, NY, Denny received a degree in health education from the New York State University at Cortland, where he played two years of varsity football. He earned his master's degree in sports administration from Virginia Tech in 1983. Denny and his wife still live in Radford.

Robert Lineburg

Since being introduced as Radford University's Director of Athletics in the fall of 2007, Robert Lineburg has served as a steady guide for Highlander athletics, evidenced by Radford's continual success in athletic competition, academic excellence, departmental growth, and community involvement. A staple of Lineburg's success as Director of Athletics has been his ability to hire coaches and administrators who are perfect fits in the New River Valley. Radford's coaches have earned Big South Coach of the Year honors in their respective sports on more than 25 different occasions under Lineburg, including a school single-season record five times during the 2014-15 academic year.

Robert Lineburg

As the leader of Radford Athletics, the Radford, Virginia, native has overseen more than 23 Big South Regular Season Championships, 20 Big South Tournament Championships, and 21 NCAA Tournament Appearances across Radford's 16 varsity sports. In 2014, Lineburg and Radford Athletics took a step forward in its strategic plan initiative of enhancing the overall athletic brand through creating one unified identity. That same year, Radford Athletics inked a deal with Nike through BSN Sports to provide all 16 athletic programs with exclusive apparel and equipment. The new Radford Athletics logo was unveiled on October 14, 2016, which included one primary mark, three secondary marks and an exclusive Radford font. In addition to the athletic logos, Radford launched a new online team shop.

Implemented in April 2017 as a cornerstone fundraising event to take place each year, the inaugural Highlander Pride Weekend consisted of three parts: the Red & White Gala, the Highlander Open golf tournament, and the Highlander Half Marathon/5K race. The first-ever weekend raised $82,000 for the Radford Athletics Student-Athlete Scholarship Fund. Over 600 individuals participated in the event, which consisted of Radford alumni, the New River Valley community, Radford faculty and staff, student-athletes and members of the athletics department.

Academic success has been a major emphasis for Radford University Athletics as well. To this point in Lineburg's tenure, Radford has garnered more than sixteen Big South Scholar Athletes of the Year, more than nine CoSIDA Academic *All-America*s, at least three Big South Women of the Year, and three Christianberry Award winners. The department's Academic Progress Rates (APR) have consistently been higher than the national average and graduation rates remain near 100% year-in and year-out.

A nod to his prominent position in the collegiate athletics landscape, Lineburg was appointed as a member of the NCAA Men's Basketball Rules Committee, effective September 1, 2018. During his four-year term on the committee, Lineburg helped shape the game of basketball on the collegiate level alongside several distinguished coaches and administrators such as Rick Barnes (Head Coach, Tennessee), Bob Huggins (Head Coach, West Virginia), Tad Boyle (Head Coach, University of Colorado, Boulder), Richard Johnson (AD, Wofford) and Stu Jackson (Sr. Associate Commissioner, Big East Conference).

Lineburg has delivered on improvements to facilities across the Radford Athletics complex time and time again. Beginning in the spring of 2008, the Dedmon Center underwent transformations to the basketball/volleyball arena, including a new steel-supported roof, a new basketball playing floor, renovated athletics offices, a new-look natatorium, and improved athletic locker rooms, training rooms, and medical facilities. Along with the initial upgrades to the Dedmon Center, an improved strength and conditioning room, new ticket office and Learning Enhancement Center (LEC), which houses student-athlete academic support, were added in 2009. As a result of a move by the sports performance facility, Radford's most recent athletic facility upgrade has been to the VCOM Center for Sports Medicine as a part of Radford's new student-athlete experience campaign. The department transformed the former sports performance location into a state-of-the-art 4,300 square foot sports medicine facility. This new facility includes separate areas for treatment, taping, rehabilitation, hydrotherapy, and staff offices.

Prior to becoming Radford's third Director of Athletics, Lineburg's corporate knowledge was gained as a marketing associate with Peloton Real Estate Partners in Dallas, Texas. Along with his business experience, Lineburg spent 15 seasons as a college basketball coach, including time as Southern Methodist University's interim head coach. Prior to serving as the Mustangs interim head coach, Lineburg spent eight years as an assistant coach at SMU. Following his interim tenure, he served two more seasons as an assistant coach at Southern Methodist. Lineburg's coaching resume also includes assistant coaching positions with the men's basketball programs at James Madison University and Emory & Henry College, as well as with the Dallas Mavericks summer league team. His coaching experience also took him through the Big South, as he spent time on the sideline at UNC-Greensboro.

A 1991 graduate of Roanoke College, Lineburg started his collegiate basketball career as a Radford Highlander, where he was a two-year letterman before transferring to nearby Roanoke College to play his final two years. He earned his bachelor's degree in political science with a minor in history. In 1995, he received a master's degree in education from Virginia Tech, where he was also a graduate assistant on the men's basketball staff.

Appendix 6

MEN'S SOCCER IN THE RADFORD UNIVERSITY ATHLETICS
HALL OF FAME

1975 – 2024

Each of the following RU Men's Soccer players have been officially inducted into the RADFORD UNIVERSITY ATHLETICS **HALL OF FAME**. (The year of selection is shown in parentheses.)

RADFORD UNIVERSITY ATHLETICS
HALL OF FAME
BILL GERBER (1996)

Gerber was Radford's first men's soccer All America selection, earning the honor in 1983. A four-year starter on defense and as a midfielder, he went on to play professionally with the Washington Diplomats of the American Soccer League. Gerber had 16 goals and 14 assists for the Highlanders from 1982-85, while playing primarily on defense. A second team Division II All America in 1983, the Annandale, Va., native earned a selection on the Division I All-Region team in 1984, and was named to the first Big South All-Conference squad in 1985.

RADFORD UNIVERSITY ATHLETICS
HALL OF FAME
DANTE WASHINGTON (1997)

Washington led the nation in scoring in collegiate soccer in 1988 and 1990, and finished his career at RU in 1992 as the second leading scorer in NCAA history. He tallied 82 goals and an NCAA record 66 assists. He had RU record totals of 27 goals and 22 assists in 1988, leading RU to its first Big South soccer title. A two-time All America, he also earned Academic All America honors in 1992. Washington would go on to compete on the 1992 U.S. Olympic Team, and for the U.S. National squad. He then played for the Dallas Burn of Major League Soccer. A Columbia, Md., native, Washington earned a double major in history and political science.

RADFORD UNIVERSITY ATHLETICS
HALL OF FAME
JOHN WHITE (2000)

One of the most decorated athletes in the early years of men's athletics at RU, White still holds numerous records as a soccer goalkeeper. He was a four-year starter and a three-time Virginia Intercollegiate Soccer Association all-star from 1978-81, and he still holds records for saves in a season (138 in 1979) and saves in a career (475). His four shutouts and 1.19 goals against average (GAA) in 1981 paced the Highlanders to the Division II and III State Championship. In 1979, the Arlington native posted a record six shutouts, including four in a row, on his way to a 0.941 GAA and NAIA All-District honors. His career 1.23 GAA still ranks among Radford University's best ever. White graduated in 1981.

RADFORD UNIVERSITY ATHLETICS
HALL OF FAME
IAN SPOONER (2012)

One of the most accomplished men's soccer players in Radford and Big South history, Ian Spooner ('98) is the only two-time Big South Player of the Year in program history. A native of Oxford, England, Spooner ranks second to Hall of Famer Dante Washington on Radford's all-time list in career points (140), points per game (1.89), goals (58), shot attempts (286) and shots per game (3.86), while sitting third in assists with 24. In addition to his career accomplishments, the two-time all-conference performer ranks among Radford's single-season leaders in total points (3rd / 9th), points per game (3rd / 10th) and goals (3rd / T-5th). Spooner is also among the conference's career leaders in goals (4th) and total points (5th), while sitting 10th in single-season goals and total points. As a freshman, Spooner led the Highlanders to the Big South Regular Season title before earning all-tournament honors. Spooner enjoyed a six-year professional (1995-2000) career in the United Soccer League (USL). In 1999, he was instrumental in the start of Bridgewater College's women's soccer program when he was named the Eagles' first-ever head coach. Following his two-year stint, he returned to his alma mater as an assistant coach of the Highlanders' women's soccer team, which won a Big South championship in 2002.

RADFORD UNIVERSITY ATHLETICS
HALL OF FAME
TOM LILLARD (2014)

From his start as a student-athlete to serving as an administrator, Tom Lillard ('79) made numerous outstanding contributions to RU Athletics. A member of the inaugural men's varsity soccer team in 1975, he served as assistant and then head coach for six seasons (1980-85). Instrumental in the men's program's transition to NCAA Division I, he was also pivotal in the formation of women's soccer in 1981, serving as its first head coach. With the men, Lillard guided RU to an NAIA district title in 1980 and a Virginia Intercollegiate Soccer Association (VISA) title in 1981, earning VISA Coach of the Year. In his final season, he guided RU to a 5-1 Big South finish and its first title game appearance. Lillard also served RU Athletics in various administrative roles until 2008, returning in 2018.

RADFORD UNIVERSITY ATHLETICS
HALL OF FAME
DON STALEY (2017)

Staley ('89) helped build both of Radford's soccer programs and capped off his Radford career with a combined 182 wins. He had 97 wins as the women's coach and 85 as the men's. Altogether, Staley compiled 323 collegiate soccer wins during his career. As the men's leader, he won three Big South regular season championships and one Big South Tournament Championship. With the women, Staley went 14-7-1 in his first year and led the team to an NCAA Tournament appearance. During his tenure at Radford, he coached two All Americas, a men's U.S. Olympic Team member and a women's Hermann Trophy finalist. Staley is the only Hall of Fame member to be named Big South Coach of the Year in two different sports. He won the first with the men in 1991 and then with the women in 1993, during his final stint as a Highlander.

RADFORD UNIVERSITY ATHLETICS
HALL OF FAME
JEFF MAJEWSKI (2019)

Distinguished by four years in a Highlander uniform and four years as a First Team Big South All-Conference member, Jeff Majewski ('92) is one of 23 players in the Big South to earn all-conference accolades four times in a career, earning the distinction each season from 1988-91. Majewski also earned All-Big South Tournament honors three times in his career (1988, 1990, 1991) and was the conference's player of the week on multiple occasions. Throughout his stint as a Highlander, Majewski brought home two Big South Regular Season Championships (1988 & 1991) and one Big South Tournament Championship (1988). Majewski tallied 35 goals and 23 assists in his time at Radford, which added up to 93 points – all ranking inside the top five at Radford. The midfielder was also named to the 1990-99 Big South All-Decade Team, which recognized the top players in the conference during the 1990s.

APPENDIX 6 – THE RU ATHLETICS HALL OF FAME

Appendix 7

THE

DANTE WASHINGTON

FILE

Big South Conference Summary

#9 DANTE WASHINGTON

The most decorated player in Radford and Big South men's soccer history, Dante Washington (1988-92) turned in a Radford career unlike any other player before or since. The Big South highlighted his achievements in its countdown of the conference's top 25 moments, teams and people in celebration of its 25th anniversary.

• As a freshman in 1988, Washington led the Highlanders to the Big South Tournament championship with a school-record 27 goals scored and 22 assists for a Big South single-season record 76 points – a Conference record that still stands today.

• The all-conference selection also led the nation in scoring in 1988.

• Washington missed the 1989 season due to a broken ankle, but came back in 1990 and picked up where he left off as he tallied 23 goals and 18 assists for 64 total points to again lead all of NCAA Division I in scoring..

• In 1991, Washington led the Highlanders to a school-best 15-4-2 overall record and the regular season Big South championship. He was voted Big South Player of the Year after leading the league in scoring for the third time, and his 16 goals and 14 assists for 46 points made him the Big South's all-time leading goal scorer and point scorer during that season.

• He became Radford's first Division I consensus First-Team All-American in 1991 and was also Virginia's Player of the Year.

• Washington also participated on the U.S. U-23 team in 1991 and became the first African-American to score a goal for the U.S. National Team.

• In the summer of 1992 he played for the U.S. Olympic Men's Soccer Team at the Barcelona Olympic Games, where he led the team with six goals in qualifying action.

• Washington concluded his collegiate career later that fall with 13 goals and 11 assists in his senior season to finish his brilliant career with 82 goals scored, 66 assists and 230 total points – all Radford and Big South Conference records. His 82 goals scored still rank second all-time in NCAA history.

• Following his Radford career he spent eight seasons in Major League Soccer with the Columbus Crew (1996, 2000-05), FC Dallas (1996-99) and Real Salt Lake (2005) scoring 52 goals and dishing out 30 assists in 170 games.

• A two-time MLS all-star (1997, 2000), Washington is fifth all-time on the Crew's goal scoring list.

Dante Washington Scores for Radford University

1990 Columbia (Md.) Flier

By Mike Easmeil

Radford's Dante Washington Fulfills All Expectations With 'Columbia Magic'

What was once one of the best kept secrets in collegiate soccer turned Radford University soccer into a feared giant-killer.

Dante Washington burst onto the collegiate soccer scene just two years ago at a once "up and coming program" at Radford University. Washington dazzled everyone, leading the nation in scoring (27 goals and 22 assists) in only his freshman season. He also led the Highlanders to their first Big South Conference Championship while rewriting school and conference record books.

Highlander soccer coach Don Staley, who also coaches the women's soccer team at Radford, won the recruiting battle for the highly touted Washington over several other top programs.

"I knew right away he'd fit into our program. We're a lot like the Los Angeles Lakers of collegiate soccer, and he fit right in." said Staley.

If Staley likens the Highlanders' style of play to the Lakers, Washington can only be compared to a Magic Johnson in a pair of cleats. In his rookie season with the Highlanders, Washington accomplished enough for a career for most players. He was a Big South all-conference and all-tournament selection. The freshman sensation also made the third team all-South Atlantic and was selected for the East Team in the United States Olympic Sports Festival held in Norman, Oklahoma last summer.

"He's one of the top strikers in the country," said Keith Tucker of Howard University.

situations," said Washington. "There are lots of times when I make a move and I couldn't duplicate it if someone asked me to."

This past season Washington was sidelined because of a broken leg suffered in the second match of the year. After a spectacular showing at the U.S. Olympic Sports Festival, he had already picked up three goals and two assists in the first two matches of the season.

Washington came back in this past indoor season to notch a phenomenal 19 goals in three tournaments.

At the Atlantic Ten Challenge Cup, in Williamsburg, Va., Washington showed everyone he was definitely back.

"Dante erupted," said Staley. "You could tell he's back. I think he's better than he was before. He's matured and stronger. I think he gained from the injury, he didn't lose anything."

Washington scored five goals as the Highlanders finished up the tournament 2-2-1, with the lone tie coming against 18th ranked William & Mary.

Virginia Tech, in Blacksburg, Va. was the site of another tourney that saw the sophomore explode, this time for eleven goals and four assists. Washington led the Highlanders to defeats of 16th ranked JMU and Marshall University among others to finish the two day even with a 6-3 mark. Marshall coach John Gibson got his first glimpse of Washington at the Hokies' tournament.

"He's the best striker I've seen," said Gibson. "He can certainly play anywhere in the country. He's got excessive quickness and incredible skill and, along with

his great throw-in, that's a frightening combination. If he applies himself all the time, I don't see what he shouldn't play on the national team some day."

Chances are he will be on the national team, if Gibson's standards hold true. Washington is his own worst critic and he's never satisfied with his performance.

"I'm kind of a perfectionist," said Washington. "If you become satisfied you've lost the battle.

"In my situation where I don't have much time for recruiting, I have to depend on guys like [Washington's former coach] Don Shey," said Staley. "He really sold me on Dante."

The Radford coach is also appreciative of the help he gets from Bill Stara and Rudy Storch, two other Columbia, Md. coaches that aid Staley in recruiting. They helped bring the duo of Doug and Jeff Majewski to Radford.

Staley divides his time between three part-time jobs. He is the men's soccer coach, the women's coach, and the night manager for the university's athletic complex the Dedmon Center. Radford, a school of roughly 9,000 students, can't fund a full-time coach, so Staley works overtime to build national class soccer teams.

The 30-year old coach, entering his fifth year at Radford, consistently takes on top twenty teams including a match-up with the University of Virginia, the national champions.

Tucker is not looking forward to playing the Highlanders this year.

"I think this is Radford's year," said Tucker. "They have some great juniors and seniors."

July 26, 1990 Columbia Flier

Dante's still a soccer success

Scott Huelskamp

Dante Washington got the call shortly after returning home from the Olympic Sports Festival last month in Minneapolis, Minnesota.

"We would like you to be a member of the under-23 national soccer team," said the voice on the other end of the line.

Washington, an all-state striker at Oakland Mills High School in 1987 who now attends Radford University on a soccer scholarship, gladly accepted.

SOCCER

"I was really surprised, but I was happy," said the 21 year-old Washington, who is back in Minneapolis, where the practice sessions are in full swing. "I know they need offense."

If Washington hadn't had such an impressive couple of weeks at the Sports Festival, the phone probably would not have rung. He had a goal and two assists in four matches for the bronze medal-winning East team.

"He has some qualities that we need," said under-23 team assistant coach Colin Lindores, who is also the head soccer coach at California State University-Hayward. "He's got strength, power and great acceleration."

Mixed in with his other talents like great ball control and an amazing 40-yard throw-in and Washington is, for the moment, in the door. All he has to do is keep that door from closing in his face.

It won't be that easy. Of the 23 members currently on the team, 18 were at the Sports Festival. The level of competition and talent "is not that much different — it's tough," Washington said.

For the last two weeks, Washington's schedule has been strictly soccer (two practices a day), eat, then sleep. "Then get up and do it again," said Washington. There's time for relaxing but not sightseeing or staying up late.

Somehow, though, Washington has not tired of the routine.

It's a small sacrifice and a big step towards being selected for 1990 Olympic team, which will carry between 18 and 22 mem-

Photo courtesy of Radford U.

Dante Washington is training with the under-23 national soccer team.

bers. Although players can be picked from throughout the United States, the practice and experience of being on the under-23 team puts Washington and his teammates a kick ahead of the competition.

"It is a continuous process and we are constantly bringing new people in and letting others go," said Lindores. "We hope that the individuals we bring in stay with us for awhile and stick it out. We have to find the right mix of players."

These 23 players will stay together at least long enough to play three more games against quality competition before the

Olympic qualifying rounds next April. The team played the Arizona Condors of the professional Western Soccer League last Friday.

Washington, a forward on a squad that Lindores says lacks real front runners in terms of strikers, didn't start against the Condors but played in the second half. Lindores said he will get the chance to start in upcoming games with the Canadian Olympic team or in an exhibition in Atlanta.

"He'll get a lot of exposure and he'll have every chance to show us what he's got," Lindores said.

Washington plans to capitalize on every opportunity.

"I know I'll have to score. That's what I've done my whole life and it's what I'll have to do here."

Judging from his past accomplishments, putting the ball in the net shouldn't be a problem. As a freshman at Radford University, Washington led the nation in scoring with 27 goals and 22 assists to lead the Highlanders to the Big South Conference championship.

Washington's hopes of defending that title where shattered when he broke his leg in the second game of his

sophomore season. He still used that time on the bench to improve.

"It gave me the chance to look at the game from a different perspective for a year, to take it all in from another point of view," he said. "Of course, I always wanted to be out on the field. But now I don't see myself as losing any ground.

"I have a goal that I want to accomplish (here)," Washington adds. "I want to start and play well. Actually, if I just play well then that's OK. And if that warrants starting, then I'll be twice as happy."

July 26, 1991 USA Today

USA TODAY, PAGE 10C   JULY 26, 1991, FRIDAY

Top U.S. under-23 scorer says school top priority

By Roscoe Nance
USA TODAY

Forward Dante Washington, the No. 1 scorer for the U.S. under-23 team in Olympic qualifying and a junior at Radford University, says he's in no hurry to turn pro.

"I don't think I'm ready to go," said Washington, who led the USA in scoring as a freshman and sophomore. "I want to get done with school. That's a big concern."

A history and political science major, Washington says he needs three semesters to graduate.

"I'd get a lot better playing with better players and getting good coaching," he said. "But I don't want to make soccer so much a part of my life that everything depends on it."

August 14, 1991 USA Today

USA TODAY. August 14. 1991

By Eduardo DiBaia, AP

GOLDEN GLOW: USA's Dante Washington is hoisted by teammate after team's 2-1 gold-medal victory against Mexico in Pan Am soccer final Tuesday night.

USA tops Mexico for soccer gold 2-1

By Juan J. Walte
USA TODAY

HAVANA — The U.S. soccer team scored a significant international victory Tuesday night, defeating Mexico 2-1 in overtime to win the gold medal in the Pan Am Games.

The win was marred by an altercation as the game ended. As the U.S. players — most of whom will represent the USA at next summer's Olympics — gathered and hugged at midfield, U.S. forward Dante Washington, who had been battered all game by the Mexican defense, was pushed.

"I saw one of our players being pushed around and I went to help him," said U.S. reserve goalie Kasey Keller, who was knocked flat. "I got knocked on the ground, I got up to see it, and No. 6 on their team (Agostin Valdez), caught me with one."

Midfielder Joe-Max Moore, from Irvine, Calif., scored the winning goal in the fourth minute of the overtime after the two teams played to a 1-1 tie during regulation.

Moore, 20, scored with a free kick from just outside the goal area that went into the left-hand corner of the Mexican goal.

"This is a very big accomplishment for the U.S.," Moore said. "We haven't done very well in soccer in the Pan Am Games. This shows a few people we've come along a little."

U.S. coach Lothar Osiander echoed those comments.

"This is wonderful," he said. "I thought the players did an admirable job, especially in the second half.

"They battled and fought, and that's our style. These are great players for us to try to win with in the qualification

and maybe we can gain some more in the Olympics."

Earlier, Cuba won the bronze medal with a 1-0 decision against Honduras.

After Moore's goal, goalie Brad Friedel of Bay Village, Ohio, made three spectacular saves to protect the lead.

"I'm not the only one who did it. My teammates blocked a lot," Friedel said. "The toughest one, the one that surprised me the most, was the one I hit over the bar. It came in at an odd angle. He put some knuckle-spin on the ball and it caught me by surprise."

Friedel said the U.S. team had a game plan for the overtime.

"We wanted to pack it in and form a wall and not let them get through," he said.

1991 Radford University Men's Soccer Media Guide

#9   Dante Washington
6-0, 185, Junior, Striker
Columbia, Md.

Year	GP-S	Shots	Goals	Asst	Pts
1988	24-24	120	27	22	76
1989	2-2	13	3	1	7
1990	23-23	133	23	18	64
Tot.	49-49	266	53	41	147

Dante Washington has led the nation in scoring in each of his two full seasons of collegiate play. Now internationally reknowned as one of the great players in the United States, Washington had a stint with the U.S. World Cup team last March and spent all of this past summer traveling with the Under-23 National Team. Washington has an inside track to be a member of the 1992 Olympic Team. He will be a marked man this season as he aims to add to his Radford scoring records, earn Big South All-Conference honors for a third time and become Radford's first Division I soccer All-America selection. His 76 points in 1988 was a school record and tied a Big South mark. He needs just one assist this season to take sole possession of the Radford career assists record. He was Big South All-Tournament after assisting both Radford scores in overtime of the 1988 conference championship game. Named to Soccer America's Freshman All-America Squad, Washington also starred that summer at the U.S. Olympic Sports Festival. He broke his ankle in Radford's second match of 1989 and was redshirted. Last year, he returned to again lead the nation in scoring and he has twice, during his career, scored a Radford-record six goals in a match. Washington also has excelled in the classroom as a pre-law major. He has been a fixture on the Big South Conference President's Honor Roll since his freshman year.

February 26, 1991 Radford News Journal

SPORTS

6-RADFORD, TUESDAY, FEBRUARY 26, 1991

(Not) Everybody's All-American

Dante's inferno rages toward Olympic goal

By RALPH BERRIER
News Journal Sports Editor

Dante Washington is a lot of things — star collegiate soccer player, all-around athlete, possible future Olympian, model student and lawyer-to-be.

The muscular, good-looking softspoken junior is just about everything an all-American boy should be.

The one thing Dante Washington isn't, is an All-American.

Washington, a redshirt sophomore last fall for head coach Don Staley's record-setting Radford University men's soccer team, led the Highlanders to a best-ever 15-8 record and in the process led the nation in scoring for the the second time in his two-year career.

Despite his flashy stats and his phenomenal athletic ability, Washington has yet to crack the lineup of postseason All-America squads. While his absence from such teams miffs some folks at Radford, it doesn't appear to be diminishing his chances of making the 1992 United States Olympic Soccer Team.

Besides, there's no question which title — All-American or Olympian — Washing-

ton prefers.

"The Olympic spot is more important," Washington said not long ago, "by far."

Washington is spending a portion of his spring semester crisscrossing the Western Hemisphere, traveling with the U.S. 23-and-Under National Team. His most recent trip with head coach Lothar Osiander's squad ended a little over a week ago, when the National Team completed workouts in Pomona, Cal. Escapades to Guadalajara, Mexico, and Sheffield, England, loom in the not-too-distant future.

While in California, Washington scored the only goal in a 2-1 loss to a Swiss team In January, he scored two goals in 22 minutes of action to lead the Americans to a 3-1 win over Volendam, a team from Holland ("Volendam Struck by Dante's Inferno," the cover of Soccer America read).

"As a team, we didn't play well in a big game," Washington said of the California trip. "The only bright spot for me was that I scored when we played the team from Switzerland."

Dante Washington's future is full of

See DANTE, page 7

Ruth Babylon Photo

When it comes to scoring proficiency, Dante Washington leaves the opposition behind.

April 28, 1992 Roanoke Times & World News

ROANOKE TIMES & WORLD NEWS, PAGE B4   APRIL 28, 1992, TUESDAY

Washington on U.S. team

Radford soccer star bound for Summer Olympics in Spain

Staff report

RADFORD — Radford University soccer standout Dante Washington will be on the team that represents the United States in the Summer Olympic Games in Barcelona, Spain, the university announced Monday.

The U.S. team qualified for the Olympics with a 3-0 victory Sunday over Mexico.

Washington, from Columbia, Md., was unavailable for comment Monday.

Washington became Radford's first Division I All-America selection this season, leading the High-landers to a 15-4-2 record. He scored 16 goals, had 14 assists and was voted Big South Conference and Virginia player of the year.

He saw limited action Sunday

■ U.S. team schedule in Score-board. B6

---

against Mexico because of an injury. He scored the game-winning goal in a 4-3 victory over Honduras on April 5.

Washington holds Radford career records for goals (69) and assists (55).

A political science and history major, Washington has been a fixture on the Big South Conference Presidential Honor Roll. He has one season of college eligibility remaining and is due to graduate in December.

Also on the U.S. team are University of Virginia players Mike Huwiler, Erik Imler and Claudio Reyna.

The U.S. team has pre-Olympic matches against Canada on May 10 in Bloomington, Ind., and on May 17 in St. John's, Newfoundland.

April 29, 1992 Roanoke Times & World News

ROANOKE TIMES & WORLD NEWS, PAGE B5   APRIL 29, 1992, WEDNESDAY

A world of success

RADFORD'S *Dante Washington once was an unknown star at an obscure soccer school. First came NCAA scoring titles, then All-America honors. Now on the U.S. National team, Washington's next proving ground is the 1992 Summer Olympics in Barcelona, Spain.*

By JOHN SMALLWOOD
SPORTSWRITER

RADFORD — Since he started hanging out with the United States National soccer team two years ago, Radford University star Dante Washington has built up a lot of frequent-flyer points.

This weekend, Washington earned his biggest bonus trip when the U.S. team defeated Mexico 3-0 in Bethlehem, Pa., and qualified for the 1992 Summer Olympics in Barcelona, Spain.

It's a trip that even Washington, who has no great love for long periods of international travel, is looking forward to.

"This is the pinnacle of my success so far," said Washington, an All-America striker who is Radford's career leader in goals (69) and assists (55). "I can't believe it. I know it's going to be even more of a shock when I actually get to Barcelona.

"This is the Olympics, and I'm expecting the world."

Washington's trip to Barcelona concludes a two-year journey from a collegiate unknown whose two NCAA scoring titles were viewed with skepticism to one of the rising stars in the national team program.

On a team manned almost exclusively by players from traditional collegiate powers — including three from 1991 NCAA champion Virginia (Claudio Reyna, Mike Huwiler and Erik Imler) and former Cavalier Curt Onalfo, who plays professionally in France — it's not hard to pick out Washington and Radford as the oddballs on the roster.

"When I came out of high school, I wasn't highly recruited," said Washington, a 21-year-old senior from Columbia, Md. "This says a lot for the lesser-known colleges. It shows that you can make it, but it takes a lot of effort. You have to be persistent and determined."

Washington first gained national prominence in 1990 when he was the leading scorer for the gold medal-winning East team in the Olympic Festival. In his first international match, he scored a goal against Mexico, becoming the first black American to score for the national team.

He was a member of U.S. team that won the gold medal at the 1991 Pan American Games in Havana, Cuba. In less than a year, Washington has 11 goals for the Olympic team.

From trips to Cuba to France to Haiti and across the continental United States, Washington has became a national star without interrupting his education or harming his 3.17 grade-point average. He is 15 credits from a double-major degree in political science and history, and he is scheduled to graduate in December.

Unlike some of the other players, Washington did not take a release from classes to compete with the U.S. team this spring.

"I thought long and hard about leaving school for a while," he said, "but I'm so close. I want to get it done. I weighed the advantages and disadvantages, and I felt like staying in school was best for me."

He traveled to competitions on weekends. Those times when he had to miss class, he arranged to have his assignments faxed to his professors.

"My professors have been a great help in that they trusted me to do my work and not try to take advantage of them," Washington said. "It's taken a lot of discipline, and luckily my mom instilled that in me at a very early age.

"Right now, I'm pretty much on cruise control. I've been living this style of life for two years now, and I've gotten used to it. It's like riding a bicycle, except I can't fall off."

Washington soon may have to decide between school and soccer.

April 29, 1992 Radford News Journal

NEWS JOURNAL, PAGE 5   APRIL 29, 1992   WEDNESDAY

Washington scores big for Olympians

By RALPH BERRIER
News Journal Sports Editor

RADFORD — After two years of criss-crossing the globe with the United States National Soccer Team, Radford University soccer standout Dante Washington has finally reached his goal.

He will be an Olympian.

It comes as no great shock. For nearly two years now, Washington and his U.S.A. teammates have been expected to qualify for the Olympics. A gold-medal showing in last summer's Pan American Games solidified that notion.

It also caused the pressure to mount. No other American soccer team has had so much expected of it.

"It's a big relief," said Washington, who has returned to Radford to take his final exams this week. "I've had this big thing hanging over my head for two years. I've had to explain to people what team I'm playing on, telling them it's the Under-22 National team.

"Now I can just say it's the 1992 Olympic team."

The United States qualified for the upcoming

Ralph Berrier Photo

Radford University soccer star Dante Washington led the U.S. to wins in Olympic qualifying matches.

Summer Games in Barcelona by beating Mexico 3-0 in last weekend's qualifying round.

Washington saw limited action in that game because of a groin pull, but he had helped place his team in good position by scoring the game-winning goal in a 4-3 win over Honduras two weeks earlier.

The U.S.A. team still has to play two qualifying matches against Canada, but the hardest work is over for now, meaning Washington can turn his attention toward his exams.

Even though he has returned to Radford for the first time in weeks, Washington never really left school. His professors faxed and phoned lessons to him as he skipped across the world.

1992 Roanoke Tribune

Radford's Washington Headed to Olympics

BETHLEHEM, PA—The United States Under-23 men's soccer squad downed Mexico 3-0 last Sunday to qualify for the 1992 Olympic Games in Barcelona, Spain. Radford University's Dante Washington is a striker for the U.S. Team.

Washington's action Sunday was limited because of a groin injury but the United States team remained undefeated through four matches in the fourth round of Olympic qualifying, clinching a berth to the 1992 Summer Games. Washington scored the game-winning goal with just over three minutes to play in the United States' 4-3 win over Honduras April 5 in St. Louis, Mo.

A native of Columbia, Md., Washington became Radford's first Division I All-American when he earned that honor this past season. Washington, also the Big South Conference and the State of Virginia Player of the Year, led the Highlanders to a 15-4-2 record, scoring 16 goals and tallying

DANTE WASHINGTON

14 assists.

He owns school career records for goals (69) and assists (55). A political science and history double major at

Radford, Washington plans to return to school in the fall following the Olympics. He will graduate in December.

Washington has been a fixture on the Big South Conference Presidential Honor Roll and was one of 66 Radford student-athletes recently honored at a banquet for academic achievement. He has one season of collegiate eligibility remaining.

Washington has returned to Radford this week for final exams for the spring semester. He did not take a release from classes to compete with the U.S. Team this spring but did travel to competitions on the weekends and missed as few classes as possible.

The U.S. Team has qualifying round matches May 12 against Canada in Bloomington, ID and May 17 against Canada in St. John's, Newfoundland.

Also among the 19-member U.S. Team are current University of Virginia players Mike Huwiler, Erik Imler and Claudio Reyna.

July 23, 1992 Baltimore Sun

U.S. soccer team hopes opposites attract goals

Washington, Snow turn on offense

By Bill Glauber
Staff Writer

BARCELONA, Spain — One is a college dropout who plays for cash in Belgium and jogs around a soccer pitch like some sort of Lenny Dykstra in shorts — snarling, brooding, demanding to be heard and seen.

The other is a college star who talks of politics and teamwork, and then turns a waltz of a sport into a 90-minute sprint.

Steve Snow and Dante Washington are opposites thrown together on the forward line of the U.S. Olympic soccer team.

WASHINGTON

They may take different routes on the field, but their objective remains the same: scoring goals and lifting the United States from soccer's Third World to its first.

Tomorrow night, as the Olympic torch arrives in Barcelona, the United States will have an idea of how far it may advance in the Olympic tournament. Before the first dance of the opening ceremonies, before a caldron is ignited, the United States will meet gold-medal favorite Italy.

And, for the first time, the United States will be bringing home-grown scoring stars to an international match.

There is Snow, the 20-year-old from Schaumburg, Ill., who earns his living with Standard Liege, a first-division Belgian team, but who made his reputation in America with 19 goals in his past 18 international matches. And there is Washington, 21, of Columbia, Md., one semester shy of receiving a political science degree from Radford University, a part-time player with a world-class shot.

Together, they give the Americans a chance to break from a defensive shell and score goals.

"We're always the underdog, but we feel we can pull off an upset," Washington said.

As usual, the Americans bring a patchwork team into an international match. Their coach, Lothar Osiander, works as a host in a San Francisco restaurant. Five UCLA players form the core of the defense and midfield.

In the Olympics, an under-23 tournament, young Americans may be able to fend off young Italians. They may even be able to advance from a qualifying group that includes Kuwait and Poland to reach the quarterfinals.

But win the gold? Unlikely.

"The players read like a who's who in Italian soccer in the younger age group," Osiander said. "If you look at the front-runners, you have to be impressed. If you look at the midfielders, you have to be scared. And if you look at the defense and goalkeeper, you realize you won't score much. Hopefully, they'll be friendly with us. Hopefully, they'll remember Christopher Columbus discovered America, and we are discovering Italian soccer. So I hope they let us discover it without crucifying us."

Snow doesn't plan on backing down to anyone. Not the Italians. Not even his teammates. Once described as a "cocky little twerp" by Osiander, Snow has learned to modulate his on-field arm-waving and finger-pointing. Still, he demands the ball.

"My only role on this team is to score," said Snow, recovering from strained left knee ligaments. "If I play terrible for 89 minutes and score in the last minute, then I've had a good game."

The Europeans have noticed. Signed in Belgium two years ago after a spectacular appearance at the Under-20 World Cup in Saudi Arabia, Snow has fought tenaciously to break out of a reserve role.

"There is a lot I miss being overseas," he said. "I miss home. Pizza. My family. My girlfriend. Speaking English. But when you're a soccer player in America, that's what you have to do to get good. You have to play in Europe."

Washington doesn't anticipate playing abroad. With the 1994 World Cup in America on the horizon, Washington, like the rest of his teammates, is hoping to parlay a starring Olympic performance into a slot on the U.S. National team.

"For all of us, this is the best opportunity we've ever had to prove ourselves," Washington said.

Washington nearly missed his Olympics debut after straining a groin muscle on a game-winning, goal-scoring play against Honduras March 21. Slowed for months, he just moved back into the starting lineup last week, and scored a goal against a French second-division team, Rodez.

"I'm feeling better and better," Washington said. "I haven't had any trouble getting in the proper mood for this. I'm excited."

He calls tomorrow night's game the biggest of his career.

"Everyone has been commenting on how far American soccer has come within the last 10 years," Washington said. "Maybe, years ago, teams would go in, and they would know they would be in for a large margin of victory against the U.S. Now, teams know there is a good possibility that we could beat them. We could win a medal. It could even be a gold."

390

July 28, 1992 USA Today

USA TODAY, PAGE 3E   JULY 28, 1992, TUESDAY

With 3-1 victory, U.S. team poised to go beyond first round

By Roscoe Nance
USA TODAY

SOCCER

ZARAGOZA — The USA is positioned to advance beyond the first round of the Olympics for the first time after rallying to beat Kuwait 3-1 Monday.

The Olympic soccer victory is the first since 1984 for the USA, which scored all its goals in the second half and matched its highest Olympic total.

Dario Brose, Manny Lagos and Steve Snow scored the U.S. goals.

The USA earned two points and is tied for second in Group A with tournament favorite Italy, a 3-0 loser to Poland Monday. Poland is first with four points. The top two teams from each of four groups advance.

The USA will advance as the first-place team if it defeats Poland Wednesday by six or more goals. It will advance as the second-place team if:

▶ The USA beats Poland, and Italy loses to Kuwait; or it ties and Italy loses.

▶ The USA and Italy win and the USA has a greater goal difference than Italy.

▶ The USA and Italy tie and it has a greater goal difference.

"Advancing would show we're on the track toward becoming a soccer nation," coach Lothar Osiander says. "It would also be a great reward for these college players for their sacrifices, and very gratifying for me as a coach.

"We're playing well. I can't complain. We're playing against professionals. We've reached a level that is surprising to everyone."

Says midfielder Yari Allnut: "I think we'll do well. We just have to play. Everybody needs to have a decent game, and we'll advance."

Kuwait coach Valmir Louruz agrees.

"The U.S. is stronger in the attack and has better athletes," he says. "The U.S. is superior to the Polish team."

The teams played to a 1-1 draw last summer in the Toulon (France) Hopes Tournament, the only time they have faced off at the under-23 age level.

"It will be a big game for Poland," Osiander says. "It's a toss-up."

The USA had the better of play for most of the game with Kuwait. But midway through the match, it appeared all it would get for its effort was its second loss of the tournament.

The USA failed to convert four dangerous scoring opportunities in the first eight minutes. Kuwait goalkeeper Falah Al-Majidi deflected Joe-Max Moore's shot from inside the penalty area.

Snow's shot from inside the penalty area hit the crossbar. Claudio Reyna missed a header, and Cobi Jones, looking at an open goal, pulled a shot wide left.

"We played good the first 20 minutes and the last 20 minutes. In between, we looked like crap," Osiander says. "We went into (the game) with the intent of playing more (aggressively). We had all good technical players."

Osiander, looking for more offense after the USA's 2-1 opening loss to Italy, juggled the lineup. He started Snow at forward and midfielders Brose and Moore.

Kuwait withstood that opening volley and then scored on Ali Al-Hadiyah's goal in the 30th minute to lead at the half.

"I was never in doubt we'd win," Osiander says. "We're a second-half team."

The USA, which came from behind in three of its five victories in the final round of qualifying for the Games, proved Osiander correct.

Brose scored on a free kick in the 57th minute to tie the score, and Lagos' goal in the 78th minute put the USA ahead. Snow got an insurance goal in the 80th minute.

1992 Radford University Men's Soccer Media Guide

#9 Dante Washington
6-0, 185, Senior, Striker
Columbia, Md.

Year	GP-S	Shots	Goals	Asst	Pts
1988	24-24	120	27	22	76
1989	2-2	13	3	1	7
1990	23-23	133	23	18	64
1991	21-21	108	16	14	46
Tot.	70-70	374	69	55	193

Dante Washington became Radford's first NCAA Division I first team All-America selection last season after finishing sixth in the nation in scoring with 46 points. Washington attained an even higher honor, competing in the Olympics in Barcelona this summer as a member of the United States Olympic Team. Already Radford's all-time leader in every major offensive category, Washington became the Big South Conference's all-time scorer this past fall and earned conference Player of the Year honors to go along with first team All-South honors and a selection as Player of the Year in Virginia. Washington has 15 multiple goal games in his career, including two school-record, six-goal performances. Last year, he registered a goal or an assist in 18 of RU's 21 matches and the three times he didn't manage any points, Radford was shut out. Washington led the nation in scoring as a freshman in 1988, equaling a Big South record with 76 points that season, including assists on Radford goals in overtime of the conference title match. He was named to Soccer America's Fresh-

Dante has twice led the nation in scoring, despite facing defenses set up to stop him.

man All-America Squad and also starred that summer at the U.S. Olympic Sports Festival. He missed all but two matches the following season with a broken leg but returned in 1990 to again lead the country with 64 points and earn a stint with the U.S. World Cup team and a regular spot on the Under-23 National Team. A three-time all-conference selection, Washington is also a fixture on the Conference President's Honor Roll as a history and political science double major at Radford. A finalist for the prestigious Missouri Athletic Club Player of the Year Award, he was the only member of the U.S. Olympic squad to stay enrolled in school as the team geared for the games last spring.

Appendix 8

CAMPUS MAP

and the

RU STUDENT SPORTS COMPLEX

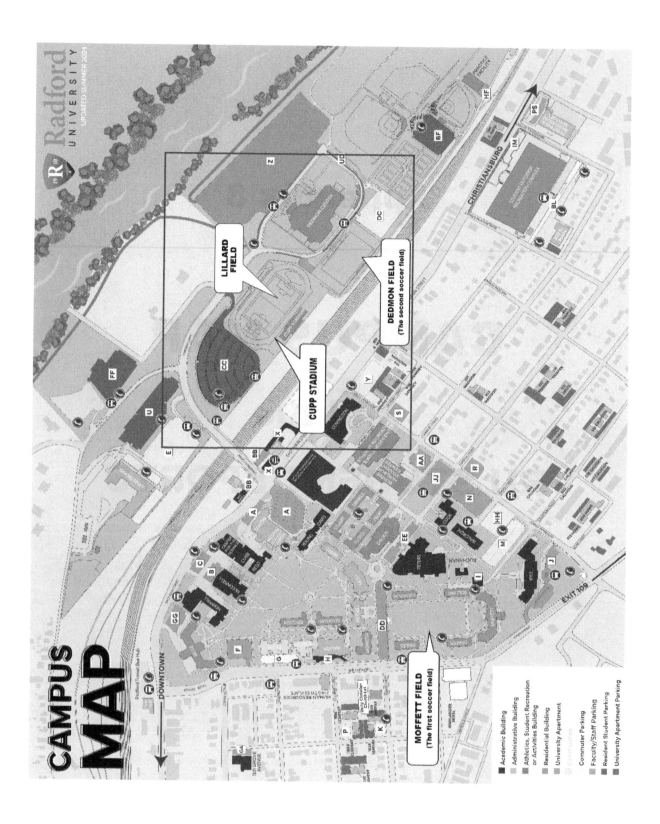

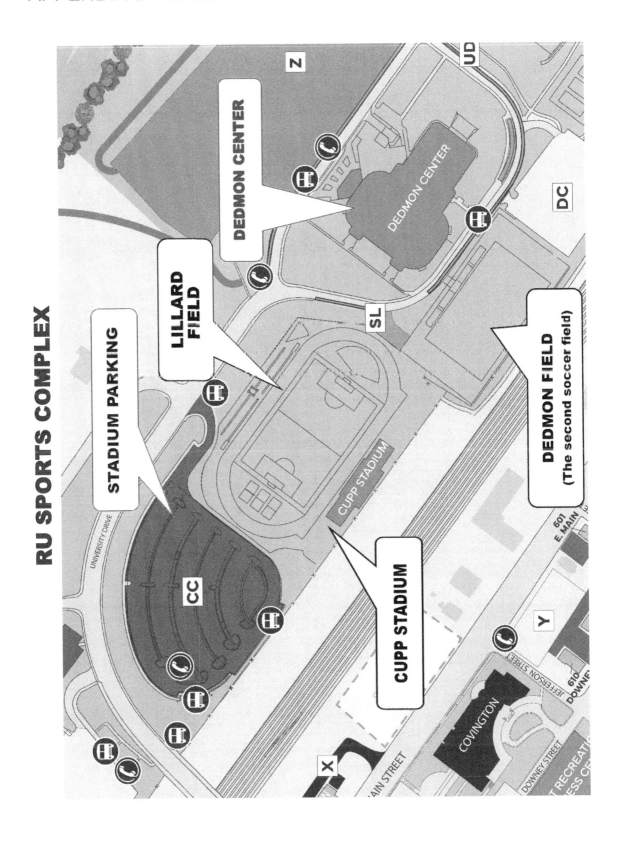

Appendix 9

SOURCES

SOURCES

Wikipedia

Big South Conference Media Releases

Radford University Yearbooks – The Beehive

Radford University Student Newspaper –The Tartan (formerly, The Grapurchat)

Radford Athletics

Radford Alumni Magazine and other Publications

Radford University Sports Information and Publications

Radford University McConnell Library Special Collections

Interviews and Personal Submissions

The Roanoke Times

Facebook.com – I Played Soccer at Radford University

Official Radford Men's Soccer page, www.facebook.com/RadfordMSOC/

(Corrections are welcome and may be emailed to: CoachingAmericanSoccer@gmail.com.)

Appendix 10

THE

JOHN HARVES RADFORD UNIVERSITY MEN'S SOCCER FUND

Established by Will Iandolo in 2009

GIVE A GIFT THAT KEEPS ON GIVING:

PLEASE SUPPORT THE RADFORD MEN'S SOCCER PROGRAM

by making a generous donation to the

JOHN HARVES RADFORD UNIVERSITY MEN'S SOCCER FUND

Credit card contributions may be made on-line:
Visit **https://connect.radford.edu/together-give**
Using the "Other (please specify)" selection, designate your
gift to the "John Harves Soccer Fund"

Fund: Other (please specify)

Other (please specify): John Harves Soccer Fund

To donate by check, please mail your check to:
Radford University Foundation, Inc.
PO Box 6893
Radford, VA 24142

1001

Your name
Street address
City, State ZIP

Date: _____

PAY TO THE ORDER OF _Radford University Foundation, Inc._____

_____ DOLLARS

MEMO _John Harves Soccer Fund_____

123456

EDITOR'S NOTE: This permanent endowment fund was established by Will Iandolo in 2009, in honor of John Harves' groundbreaking, tireless, and enthusiastic contributions to RU's soccer program. The initial funding came from Iandolo and other former teammates who had played for Harves. Every donation goes into the endowment's capital fund. (Of course, neither Will nor John receive a penny from these funds.) To ensure the ongoing viability of the fund, only the *earnings* are available for use in the men's soccer program. RU Men's Soccer and *especially the students/players* appreciate your financial support!

Editor's P.S.: This book is another of the countless significant examples of John's substantial and indefatigable contributions to RU soccer and to the many people who have been a part of this program. You could not imagine -- or maybe you can! -- the many months and the many, many hundreds of hours he has tirelessly worked to bring this project to completion. To truly give a gift that keeps on giving, please consider making a generous contribution to this fund, to help change the lives of dozens of these student-athletes each year for many years to come. If you can, make it an annual event!

401

RADFORD UNIVERSITY MEN'S SOCCER

The First 50 Years: 1975 – 2024

INDEX

RADFORD UNIVERSITY MEN'S SOCCER
The First 50 Years: 1975 – 2024

"Nine months from conception to birth, this book isn't just a history of men's soccer at Radford University, it's a labor of love that captures the essence of collegiate sports."

"This book is all about people, not just the coaches and the players, but everyone who has helped their favorite soccer program to flourish."

"This book is absolutely amazing because it captures hundreds of memories, stories, and photos about Radford University men's soccer in a way that has never been compiled in one place before."

"Anyone interested in playing soccer at Radford, anyone with a student at Radford, anyone who ever played sports at Radford, anyone who ever attended Radford, parents of current players, parents of future players, parents and students who may attend Radford, *all will enjoy owning and reading this amazing book*!"

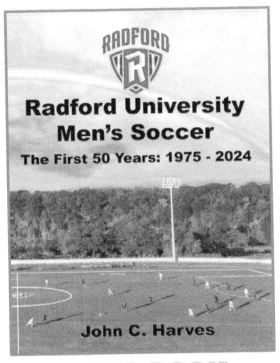

Available at

"This is the definitive history of the first 50 years of the overachieving soccer Highlanders of Radford University. It's a story of great people, including *All-America* players and legendary coaches, on an amazing journey from a 1970's sports start-up to a Division I dynamo. In the bucolic and beloved Blue Ridge Mountains of Virginia, the big wins, tough heartbreaks, and marvelous moments are all still part of the Radford University men's soccer championship DNA."

– Michael Ashley

Mike Ashley is a national award-winning writer and columnist ('Sidelines') who wrote for 'The Tartan' – the Radford University student newspaper.

The Ultimate SOCCER DICTONARY of American Terms

The Ultimate SOCCER DICTIONARY of American Terms is the largest and most complete soccer dictionary ever published in the United States. Now with definitions for more than 5,000 terms, the Second Edition of *The Ultimate SOCCER DICTIONARY of American* Terms remains the vital resource to help coaches, players, parents, fans, administrators, and journalists better understand American soccer terminology and jargon and to further appreciate the sport.

Available at Amazon.com

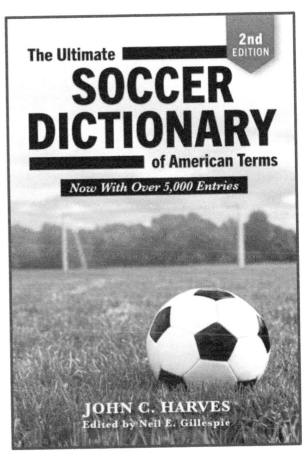

"I am astounded by the amount of detail that has gone into this book. Every coach and fan should own one. It will give them insights into the nuances of the game and raise their soccer I.Q."

– **Jim Bruno**, United Soccer Coaches National Private School Girls **Coach of the Year**